Making History

University of Pennsylvania Press
MIDDLE AGES SERIES
Edited by
Edward Peters
Henry Charles Lea Professor
of Medieval History
University of Pennsylvania

A listing of the books in the series appears at the back
of this volume

Making History

The Normans and Their Historians in Eleventh-Century Italy

Kenneth Baxter Wolf

University of Pennsylvania Press

Philadelphia

Copyright © 1995 by the University of Pennsylvania Press
All rights reserved
Printed in the United States of America

Library of Congress Cataloging-in-Publication Data

Wolf, Kenneth Baxter, 1957-
  Making History : the Normans and their historians in eleventh-century Italy /
Kenneth Baxter Wolf.
      p.   cm. — Middle Ages series)
  Includes bibliographical references and index.
  ISBN 0-8122-3298-4
    1. Normans—Italy—History. 2. Normans—Italy—Sicily—History.
3. Mediterranean Region—History. 4. Italy, Southern—History—535-1268. I. Title.
II. Series.
DG847.14.W65 1995
945'.03—dc20   94-44633
                                                                        CIP

To my children,
Owen and Ellie,
and the histories they will make

Contents

Acknowledgments

This book is the principal product of a two-year membership at the Institute for Advanced Study that I enjoyed from 1989 to 1991. Not surprisingly, then, the people who have exercised the most influence over its shape and contents are those whose stints at the Institute overlapped my own. Jim Muldoon, Jim Powell, Margaret Gibson, Alan Bernstein, Pat Geary, John Freed, Ben Arnold, David and Kathy Ringrose, and, of course, Giles Constable each contributed information and encouragement in some form or another. I particularly benefited from the advice of Dwayne Carpenter, who served as a sounding board and gentle critic when the project was first coming into focus. Later I had the good sense to share my thoughts with Sylvia Schafer, who appreciated my subject despite its distance from nineteenth-century France and helped me begin to see it through the eyes of a cultural historian.

I would be remiss if I did not gratefully acknowledge the support of the Institute itself, and all of the kind and conscientious employees who made my time there so productive and memorable. Finally I would also like to thank Pomona College for allowing me to interrupt my assistant professorship to pursue this project as well as for its help in deferring some of the publication costs of this volume.

Abbreviations

AASS
> *Acta Sanctorum quotquot toto orbe coluntur*, ed. Bollandists (Antwerp, 1643-).

Adhemar
> Adhemar of Chabannes, *Cronicon*, ed. J. Chavanon [Collection de textes pour servir à l'étude et à l'enseignement de l'histoire, 20] (Paris, 1897).

Alexiad
> Anna Comnena, *Alexiad*, tr. E.R.A. Sewter (London, 1969).

Amari
> Amari, Michele, *Biblioteca arabo-sicula*, 3 vols. (Turin, 1880–89).

Amatus
> Amatus of Montecassino, *L'Estoire de li Normant* [*Historia Normannorum*], ed. Vincenzo de Bartholomaeis, *Storia de' Normanni di Amato di Montecassino* [Fonti per la storia d'Italia] (Rome, 1935).

Ann. Barenses
> *Annales Barenses*, ed. G. H. Pertz, MGH SS 5:52–56.

Ann. Beneventani
> *Annales Beneventani*, ed. G. H. Pertz, MGH SS 3:173–85.

Ann. Cas.
> *Annales Casinenses*, ed. G. Schmidt, MGH SS 30 (pt. 2): 1385–1449; continuation: ed. G. H. Pertz, MGH SS 19:305–7.

Ann. Cav.
> *Annales Cavenses*, ed. G. H. Pertz, MGH SS 3:185–91.

Ann. Rom.
> *Annales Romani*, ed. L. Duchesne, in LP 2:331–37.

Ausgew Quell
> *Ausgewählte Quellen zur deutschen Geschichte des Mittelalters.*

Benzo
> Benzo of Alba, *Ad Heinricum IV imperatorem libri VII*, ed. G. H. Pertz, MGH SS 11: 597–681.

Bernold
> Bernold, *Chronicon*, ed. G. Waitz, MGH SS 5:385–467.

Bonizo
> Bonizo of Sutri, *Liber ad amicum*, ed. E. Dümmler, MGH *Libelli de lite* 1:571–620.

Bruno
> Bruno of Segni, *Libellus de Symoniacis*, ed. E. Sackur, MGH *Libelli de lite* 2:543–62.

CBN
> *Chronicon Breve Nortmannorum*, PL 149:1083–88.

Chr. S. Petri. Vivi
> *Chronicon Sancti Petri Vivi Senonensis*, ed. and tr. R.H. Bautier and M. Gilles (Paris, 1979).

CMCas
> Leo Marsicanus and Peter the Deacon, *Chronica Monasterii Casinensis*, ed. H. Hoffman, MGH SS 34 (Hanover, 1980).

Desiderius
> Desiderius of Montecassino, *Dialogi de miraculis sancti Benedicti*, ed. G. Schwartz and A. Hofmeister, MGH SS 30 (pt. 2): 1111–51.

Geoffrey
> Geoffrey Malaterra, *De rebus gestis Rogerii Calabriae et Siciliae Comitis et Roberti Guiscardi ducis fratris eius* [*Historia Sicula*], ed. Ernesto Pontieri [Rerum Italicarum Scriptores, 2nd ed., v. 5, pt. 1] (Bologna, 1925–28).

Glaber
> Raoul Glaber, *The Five Books of the Histories*, ed. and tr. John France, in *Rodulfus Glaber Opera*, ed. John France, Neithard Bulst, and Paul Reynolds [Oxford Medieval Texts] (Oxford, 1989).

Gregory VII, *Register*.
> *Das Register Gregors VII*, ed. Erich Caspar, MGH Epistolae Selectae 2 (Berlin, 1920).

Henry, *Epistola*
> Henry, *Epistola* 16, *Ausgew Quel* 12.

Hermann
> Hermann of Reichenau, *Chronicon*, ed. K. Nobbe and R. Buchner, *Quellen des 9. und 11. Jahrhunderts der Hambürgischen Kirche und des Reichs*, ed. W. Trillman and R. Buchner, *Ausgew Quell* 11: 628–717.

Jaffé
> P. Jaffé, ed. *Regesta Pontificum Romanorum*, 2nd. ed., rev. S. Loewen-feld, F. Kaltenbrunner, and P. Ewald (Leipzig, 1885).

LP
> *Liber Pontificalis*, ed. L. Duchesne, 2 vols. (Paris, 1955).

Lupus Proto.
> Lupus Protospatarius, *Chronicon*, ed. G. H. Pertz, MGH SS 5:52–63.

MGH
> *Monumenta Germaniae Historica*.

MGH SRG
> *Monumenta Germaniae Historica, Scriptores rerum Germanicarum ad usum scholarum*.

MGH SS
> *Monumenta Germaniae Historica, Scriptores*.

Ord. Vit.
> Orderic Vitalis, *Historia ecclesiastica*, ed. and tr. Marjorie Chibnall, *The Ecclesiastical History of Orderic Vitalis*, 6 vol. [Oxford Medieval Texts] (Oxford, 1969–80).

PL
> *Patrologiae cursus completus, series Latina*, ed. J. P. Migne, 221 vols. (Paris, 1844–64).

PRV
> *Pontificum Romanorum Vitae*, vol. 1: *Pontificum Romanorum qui fuerunt inde ab exeunte s. IX usque ad finem s. XIII*, ed. I. M. Watterich (Leipzig, 1860).

Romuald
> Romuald, *Annales*, ed. G. H. Pertz, MGH SS 19:398–412.

William
> William of Apulia, *De rebus gestis Roberti Wiscardi*, ed. and tr. Marguerite Mathieu, *Le Geste de Robert Guiscard* [Istituto Siciliano di studi Bizantini e neoellenici, testi e monumenti, 4] (Palermo, 1961).

Wipo
> Wipo, *Gesta Chuonradi II Imperatoris*, ed. H. Bresslau, MGH SRG 41 (Hanover, 1915), pp. 1–62.

Introduction

The narrative histories that are the focus of this study can be made to yield information about the past in two fundamentally different ways. On the one hand, we can take them at face value as descriptions of the events they recount. With the judicious application of critical reading techniques, we can correct for the biases of their authors and be left with a reasonable approximation of the order and contours of the events themselves. To speak in more historiographical terms, we can, to some degree, distill a "chronicle" of events from the contemporary narratives by carefully stripping them of their more fictive literary trappings.[1] On the other hand, the same histories can be used to tell us how the people who wrote them conceived of the events occurring in the world around them. In this case the biases laid bare by source criticism are not weeded out but are appreciated in their own right for what they can tell us about the conceptual categories that the authors employed to make sense out of their worlds, past and present. These categories—reflected in the author's choice of material as well as the way in which that material has been fashioned into a story to be shared with an audience—are as worthy a subject of historical study as the events that they seek to comprehend, for they help us to appreciate the ways in which people living in a particular time and place construed their world and located themselves within it. Again in the language of the profession, this approach treats the narrative histories as textual artifacts that must necessarily reveal something about the mental processes of both the artisans who produced them and the audiences who appreciated them.[2]

As distinct as these two basic approaches are, they cannot be considered in complete isolation from one another, for both rely on the same tools of source criticism. Each must make use of the same basic critical techniques to separate "what really happened" from "how it was described" before being able to privilege one category of data over the other. In so far as both approaches assent (at least tacitly) to the possibility of effecting this separation, each must see its chosen data in something of a dialectical relationship with the other. Thus for historians opting for the first approach it is necessary to appreciate the narrative setting within which the events are presented and adjust for it. Conversely, historians choosing the second approach must have some sense of "what really happened" in order to appreciate the ways in which the events might have been narrativized.

The contemporary histories of the Norman conquest of Italy and Sicily have been the subject of repeated studies of the first type. The aim of their authors has been simply to reconstruct a plausible account of the events that made up the conquest. The best example of this approach is still the magisterial *Histoire de la domination Normande en Italie et en Sicile* of Ferdinand Chalandon (1907). But a number of others have appeared in the meantime, three of the more recent being Wolfgang Jahn's *Untersuchungen zur normannischen Herrshaft in Suditalien* (1989), Pierre Aubé's *Les empires normands d'Orient, XIe–XIIIe siècle* (1983), and H. E. J. Cowdrey's *The Age of Abbot Desiderius: Montecassino, the Papacy, and the Normans in the Eleventh and Early Twelfth Centuries* (1983).

Attempts to use these same texts to recreate the interpretative structures imposed by their authors are less common. The Italian scholars who were the first to edit and study these sources traditionally offered assessments of their *valore storico* that included identifying the archaic elements of eleventh-century historical writing that distinguished it from the more "scientific" approach to which they themselves subscribed.[3] But this kind of approach lent itself to a dismissive and/or apologetic attitude about the patterns and constructs that characterized historical thought in the past, an attitude that precluded any real appreciation of them in their own right. In her address to the medievalists gathered at Spoleto in 1968, Laetitia Boehm called attention to the absence of more sympathetic and synthetic treatments, observing that "a history of Norman historical writings that focuses on their underlying themes has yet to be written."[4] Ovidio Capitani reiterated her point at the Lincei lectures in 1974, noting that "despite everything, we seem only recently to have convinced ourselves not to judge the Norman chronicles solely as a reservoir of factual information but to view them as an expression of the cultural and political interests of their age as well."[5] But while each offered some interesting observations and suggested future lines of inquiry, neither Capitani nor Boehm took on the task of initiating a full-blown study of the Norman histories. To date Vincenzo d'Alessandro stands out as the one who has done the most to fill this gap, thanks to his close reading of the earliest of the Italo-Norman histories, but so far he has not produced any broader comparative study.[6] The tantalizingly-titled "Mentalità ed evoluzione della storiografia normanna fra l'XI e XII secolo in Italia" delivered by Massimo Oldoni at the 1975 conference on Count Roger suffers from precisely the opposite problem: it is far too broad and cursory an overview for a subject of such magnitude.[7]

Another promising—if unintentional—step toward appreciating the structural aspects of the Norman historians was taken by R. H. C. Davis with the publication of *The Normans and Their Myth* in 1976.[8] Davis's point was to challenge the conventional wisdom of his day that regarded the Norman conquerors of England, Italy, and Antioch as "a separate and distinct people" capable of conquering and settling disparate regions far from home while still retaining their identity as Normans. In the process, Davis all but reduced the idea of "pan-Norman" identity to a fiction created by medieval historians like Orderic Vitalis and perpetuated by modern historians like Haskins, Jamison, and Douglas. For our purposes, the most significant part of Davis's approach is the importance that it placed on appreciating contemporary Norman histories, not for their "historical accuracy," but for the "evidence which they supply for the beliefs and aspirations of the Normans at the date at which they were written."[9] But although Davis pointed his readers in this new and exciting direction, he too stopped short of actually leading them down that path. The combination of the breadth of Davis's scope and the brevity of his book simply did not allow for any depth of analysis in this area.[10]

It was with such "false starts" in mind that the present study was conceived. It has been designed to provide an in-depth, comparative analysis of the first generation of narrative histories produced on behalf of the Norman conquerors of Sicily and southern Italy. I have deliberately limited myself to those histories produced in the so-called "conquest period" in an effort to underscore the remarkable creativity of their authors, who managed to fashion ex nihilo full-blown histories of these parvenu invaders and, in the process, made them look like they actually deserved to rule what they had taken largely by force.

In terms of both function and structure, the eleventh-century histories of the Normans in Italy are very similar to the works of the so-called "barbarian historians" that appeared all over Latin Europe in the wake of the dissolution of the western Roman empire. Just as Jordanes, Gregory of Tours, and Isidore of Seville historiographically elevated the Ostrogoths, Franks, and Visigoths to the status of legitimate heirs to the Romans, so Amatus of Montecassino, William of Apulia, and Geoffrey Malaterra transformed the Norman invaders of southern Italy and Sicily into the rightful heirs of the Greeks and Lombards. The consistent task of the "barbarian historians," regardless of when they were writing, was to effect a historiographical "conquest" concomitant with the territorial ones achieved by the barbarian rulers. They did so by appropriating and refashioning the history of the conquered for the benefit of the conqueror. This was a two-part process. It involved, first of all, explaining how it could be that a traditionally indomitable, longstanding power like the Roman or Byzantine empire should come to yield before upstart "barbarian" forces. Second, it required the transformation of the raw military power of these barbarians into something resembling the legitimate political authority once exercised by the powers they displaced. In short, these historians had to recast the barbarians—who had always played peripheral, antagonistic roles in histories dedicated to the Roman empire—as the protagonists of their own historical dramas. Put another way, they had to tell an entirely different story about the past, one which offered an *apologia* for their unanticipated success against the protagonists of a previous generation of historians.[11] In the process, each of these authors effectively made history and bestowed it on a people that did not have one before.

Late Antiquity is the most promising period for studying this process, for it was a time when the political unity of the western Roman empire was giving way to a patchwork of individual kingdoms dominated by non-Roman peoples, many of which came to recognize the value of producing self-justifying historical narratives in the Roman tradition. Pierre Courcelle's pioneering study, *Histoire littéraire des grandes invasions germaniques* (1948),[12] assesses narrative aspects of late antique histories as well as other sources in this period. Walter Goffart's *The Narrators of Barbarian History (A.D. 550–800)* (1988)[13] focuses more closely on the work of four late antique historians—Jordanes, Gregory of Tours, Bede, and Paul the Deacon—showing how each promoted the legitimacy of a barbarian people through historiographical construction. My own *Conquerors and Chroniclers in Early Medieval Spain* (1990)[14] analyzes the histories of John of Biclaro, Isidore of Seville, and two of their Spanish-Christian continuators from the eighth and ninth centuries with many of the same questions in mind.

Later periods in Latin European history, being on the whole more stable in geo-political terms, may not be able to boast the same wide distribution of such histories. On the other hand, those conquests that *did* take place after the millenium often attracted the attention of more than one historian simply because by the eleventh century history as a genre had become much more popular among Latin authors. The Normans who, as Davis wryly observed, never seem to have tired of writing about their achievements,[15] were particularly well represented in the historical writings of this period. And none of the regions that the Normans conquered produced as many histories as quickly as did Italy: in fact, no less than three, full-length narrative accounts of the Norman conquests dating from the last quarter of the eleventh century. Moreover, not one of these three appears to have been written with any direct knowledge of the other two.[16] This means that modern readers are afforded the rare opportunity of seeing how three different historians effected the transformation of the Normans from a "barbarian invader" to a legitimate power in Italy and Sicily. These three independent exercises in historiographical legitimation presumably reflect something of the range of conceptual possibilities open to a late eleventh-century mind for giving an upstart people its own history. It is this range that I hope to illustrate in this study.

The first chapter offers a concise but complete account of the Norman conquests in Italy and Sicily based on the principle sources that have survived. This overview is designed to provide readers not only with a summary of Norman history in this region, but with a basic "chronicle" of events which will allow them to appreciate more fully the various ways in which these same events were construed by the contemporaries who wrote about them. I am sensitive to the epistemological pitfalls inherent in such an exercise. My own overview of Norman history, inasmuch as it will take the form of a narrative account, has no more claim to veracity, philosophically speaking, than the contemporary narratives that are the focus of this study. Each in its own way attempts to tell a story, and stories are not (necessarily)[17] inherent in the subject matter that informs them, ensuing as they do more from the mind of the story-teller than from the events themselves. It is, in other words, more consistent with the spirit of this project to regard the overview chapter as simply another narrative account, subject to the same fundamental liabilities as any other, distinct from its eleventh-century counterparts only in that it was written for a different audience. Whether my readers choose to treat this initial chapter as an account of "what really happened" or as a narrative designed to be convincing to professional historians living in the late twentieth century, they will find the distance between it and the eleventh-century accounts great enough to allow for an appreciation of the peculiar ways in which eleventh-century minds conceived of the past.

The second and third chapters attempt to reconstruct the earliest, antagonistic views of the Normans preserved in papal and Casinese sources. For the most part the papal images fall into the category of letters and apologetic treatises defending the policies of Leo IX and Gregory VII, both of whom expended a great deal of energy trying to dislodge the Normans from southern Italy. Only when Gregory VII is forced to work with Robert Guiscard to protect himself against Henry IV do we begin to see any softening of the rhetoric applied to the Normans. The monastery of Montecassino had its own share of difficulties with the Normans, specifically with those ensconced in the region of Campania, and its monks produced their own negative images of the Normans. These disparaging views of the Normans provide us with something of a "before picture," which allows us to appreciate not only how the Norman conquests were narrativized when the writing of history was in the hands of their enemies, but how far the later, more sympathetic historians had to go in their revisionist efforts to transform the Normans into protagonists.

The fourth chapter considers in detail the pivotal work of the Casinese monk Amatus who, sometime shortly after 1078, completed the very first history dedicated specifically to the Normans in Italy. Sponsored by Abbot Desiderius, who twenty years before had accepted the Norman Richard of Capua as the protector of Montecassino, the *Historia Normannorum* transformed the Normans into a positive force in Italian history. The fifth and sixth chapters treat the other two histories of the Normans in Italy: the *Gesta Roberti Wiscardi*, written by William of Apulia, and Geoffrey Malaterra's *De rebus gestis Rogerii et Roberti*. Both of these accounts were written in the waning years of the eleventh century at the request of Norman leaders: the former sponsored by Roger Borsa, the latter by his uncle, Roger of Sicily. In the case of each of these three full-blown histories, I will begin by reconstructing, as much as the sources will allow, the historical circumstances that led the author in question to record his impressions of the Norman presence in Italy. I will then move on to a detailed consideration of the text itself, in an effort to uncover and appreciate the narrative patterns that its author imposed on the events in his attempt to make the conquests make sense to himself and to his audience.

Notes

1. For an optimistic assessment of the viability of this prospect, see Morton White, *Foundations of Historical Knowledge* (New York: Harper and Row, 1965). Others have been less confident that such a distillation can, in fact, yield truly objective history. Such criticism has not, however, had any discernible impact on the way most historians today write history. For a concise history of the evolution of historical relativism and its (relative lack of) effect on the discipline, see Lionel Gossman, "History and Literature: Reproduction or Signification," in Robert H. Canary and Henry Kozicki, eds., *The Writing of History: Literary Form and Historical Understanding* (Madison: University of Wisconsin Press, 1978), especially pp. 26-39. Gossman observes (p. 32) that "despite decades of demonstrations by philosophers and by historians themselves that history is a construct, the belief that it is an immediate representation of reality, and the historian's own complicity with this belief, have remained remarkably vigorous."

2. I borrow the term "artifact" from Hayden White's "The Historical Text as Literary Artifact," in *Tropics of Discourse: Essays in Cultural Criticism* (Baltimore: Johns Hopkins University Press, 1978), pp. 81–100, but I use it differently. For White, a piece of historical writing can be considered a literary artifact in so far as it partakes of the "fictive" structural elements commonly associated with pieces of literature. Thus his classic treatment of the works of nineteenth-century historians (*Metahistory: The Historical Imagination in Nineteenth-Century Europe* [Baltimore: Johns Hopkins University Press, 1973]) concerns itself with the deep structures of the narratives: whether, for instance, a particular account of the French Revolution is being presented in the mode of irony or that of synecdoche ("Historical Text as Literary Artifact," p. 58), and what precisely it means to "decode" and "recode" such narratives. My own approach uses the artifact idea more broadly, as a way of extracting information about the *mentalité* of the author and his audience by appreciating the specific ways in which the events described in the text are ordered and shaped. Walter Goffart, author of *The Narrators of Barbarian History* (Princeton, NJ: Princeton University Press, 1988), says essentially the same thing, only more elegantly, when he writes: "An author approached as though he were a body of ore is prized mainly for pure metal content. One taken seriously in his own right stands a chance of having *his opinions and literary talent valued as an integral part of the information he conveys; he may just possibly be seen* not only as a reporter of the past, but *as a component of the past that he transmits*" (p. 15; emphasis my own).

3. Ernesto Pontieri's prefatory study of Geoffrey Malaterra's *De rebus gestis Rogerii* (Bologna: Nicola Zanichelli, 1925–28) is typical in this regard. See also Michele Fuiano, "Guglielmo di Puglia," in his *Studi de storiografia medioevale ed umanistica*, 2nd ed. (Naples: Giannini, 1975): 1–103 [first published in 1960].

4. "*Nomen gentis Normannorum*': Der Aufstieg der Normannen im Spiegel der normannischen Historiographie." *I Normanni e la loro espansione in Europa nell'alto medioevo*, Settimane di studio 16 (1968) (Spoleto: Centro italiano de studi sull'alto medioevo, 1969), p. 631. In her words: "eine Geschichte der normannis-

chen Geschichtsschreibung unter Einbeziehung der angedeuteten Themenkreise müsste erst noch geschrieben werden."

5. "Specific Motivations and Continuing Themes in the Norman Chronicles of Southern Italy in the Eleventh and Twelfth Centuries," *The Normans in Sicily and Southern Italy*, Lincei Lectures 1974 (Oxford: Oxford University Press, 1977), p. 4.

6. See in particular his study of Amatus's *Historia Normannorum*, in his *Storiographia e politica nell'Italia normanna* (Naples: Liguori, 1978), pp. 51–98 [first published in 1971]. See also: "Roberto il Guiscardo nella storiografia medievale," in *Roberto il Guiscardo tra Europa, Oriente e Mezzogiorno*, Potenza-Melfi-Venosa, 1985 (Galatina, 1990), pp. 181–96.

7. In *Ruggero il gran conte e l'inizio dello stato normanno*, Bari, 1975 (Rome: Il Centro de ricerca, 1977).

8. *The Normans and Their Myth* (London: Thames and Hudson, 1976).

9. Davis, *The Normans and Their Myth*, p. 50.

10. This is a particular shortcoming of the chapter on the Normans in Italy and Sicily, pp. 71–100. Davis's thesis inspired a number of elaborations and rebuttals, but most of them managed to leave untouched his observations on the constructed nature of Norman history in their efforts to assess the "Normanness" of those areas conquered by the Normans. G. A. Loud's 1981 article, "How 'Norman' was the Norman Conquest of Southern Italy?" *Nottingham Medieval Studies* 25 (1981): 13–34, is a case in point. Loud's concern was to determine whether the dominant role in the conquest and settlement of southern Italy was indeed played by Normans. His relative lack of concern with the historiographical construction of Norman identity is reflected in the type of evidence upon which he built his case: charters, onomastics, and genealogy, rather than the contemporary histories, which, as Loud observed, "must clearly be taken with some care" (p. 20).

11. Boehm, *Nomen gentis normannorum*, p. 641.

12. 3rd ed. (Paris: Etudes augustiniennes, 1964).

13. Princeton, NJ: Princeton University Press, 1988.

14. Liverpool: Liverpool University Press, 1990.

15. Davis, *The Normans and Their Myth*, p. 15.

16. Pontieri, in Geoffrey, pp. xv–xix.

17. David Carr in his *Time, Narrative, and History* (Bloomington: Indiana University Press, 1986) has challenged the notion, subscribed to by narrativist philosophers of history like Hayden White, Paul Ricoeur, and Louis Mink, that past events have no intrinsic storylines, by positing narrative structures inherent in the actions of the individual historical actors themselves.

1. The Norman Conquests in Southern Italy and Sicily: An Historical Overview

The establishment of Norman control over all of southern Italy and Sicily, a process which was completed by the early 1090s, is all the more remarkable when one considers the degree of political fragmentation that characterized the region when the first of the Normans set foot there in the 1010s.[1] At that time the mainland was effectively divided between those areas—essentially Apulia, Calabria, and the Basilicata—that owed their allegiance to Constantinople, and those governed by one of the three Lombard dynasties centered in Benevento, Capua, and Salerno. The principal exceptions to this rule were the western ports of Naples, Amalfi, and Gaeta, which had managed for the most part to retain their independence from empire and Lombards alike. Participation in the struggle for hegemony in southern Italy, however, was not restricted to the powers that actually resided there. The papacy and the German empire each regarded the region as falling within its own sphere of influence and each intervened as frequently as its other interests would allow. Moreover, while the heyday of Muslim attacks had passed a century before, the potential threat of invasion from the emirates of Sicily and Tunisia remained.

I

It was within the context of one of the perennial uprisings against Byzantine rule in Apulia that the Normans first appeared on the scene. The Lombard Melo, who had already been responsible for at least one rebellion in Bari (1009–1011),[2] was soliciting assistance from the Lombard princes to resume his efforts when he came into contact with a group of Norman émigrés, probably in the year 1016. The sources are far from unanimous regarding the circumstances that brought the Normans and Melo together. For his part Amatus of Montecassino recounted how a band of forty Norman pilgrims, returning from Jerusalem "before the year 1000," relieved Salerno from a siege by the Saracens,[3] prompting Salerno's prince Guaimar IV to send to Normandy for more knights of this caliber to serve him. Among those who responded to this invitation were Gilbert Buatère—who was being sought by Count Robert I of Normandy[4] for killing a viscount—and his four brothers Rainulf, Asclettin, Osmond, and Lofuld. They passed through Rome en route to Capua where they met and joined Melo.[5] William of Apulia, on the other hand, placed the initial point of contact at Monte Gargano,[6] where a number of Norman pilgrims chanced upon the rebel Melo and were moved by his plight. Upon their return to Normandy, the pilgrims encouraged their compatriots to make their way to Italy, fight the Greeks, and make their fortunes. These Norman recruits proceeded via Rome to Campania, where they were welcomed and armed by Melo before being led into Apulia.[7]

The problem with the accounts offered by Amatus and William is that they have come down to us embedded in narrative histories that date from sixty to eighty years after the events they pretend to describe.[8] For more contemporary and less narrativized accounts, one has to turn to Raoul Glaber's *Historiarum Libri Quinque* and the *Chronicon* of Adhemar of Chabannes, the latter written in 1028, with the relevent portions of the former probably dating from the late 1030s.[9] Raoul's account has a Norman named Rodulf incurring the wrath of Count Richard II and taking his case before Benedict VIII in Rome. There the pope enlisted the aid of Rodulf and his men to fight against the Greeks on behalf of the princes of Benevento.[10] Adhemar's more concise version says nothing about Rodulf's problems in Normandy but does describe how Benedict sent him from Rome to Apulia to fight the Greeks.[11] Unfortunately although Raoul and Adhemar recorded their versions within a generation of the events they described, they did so from the distant vantage point of France, making them as suspect in their own right as the later Italian accounts.[12] Perhaps the most trustworthy source is the first redaction of Leo Marsicanus's *Chronica monasterii Casinensis*, which, though dating from the early years of the twelfth century (before 1105), presumably relied on earlier sources that are no longer extant. It has the exiled Rodulf and his men simply looking for opportunities for military service in Capua, where they find and join the exiled Melo.[13]

In any case Melo, assisted by the Normans among others, made his way from Campania to Apulia in 1017 where he repeatedly engaged the Greek army until his forces were decisively beaten by the catapan Boioannes at Cannae in October 1018.[14] Melo fled to Germany, where he later died lobbying Henry II for assistance for yet another Apulian campaign.[15] The Normans who had fought under him split up, variously entering the service of Guaimar IV of Salerno (999–1027), [16] Pandulf III of Benevento (1011–59), and Pandulf IV of Capua (1016–49).[17] One contingent reached an agreement with Abbot Atenulf of Montecassino (1011-22), brother of the ruler of Capua, to serve as protectors of the monastery. Even Boioannes used Normans to help garrison the recently fortified town of Troia (1019).[18]

Concerned about the newly bolstered Byzantine presence in Italy, Benedict VIII petitioned Henry II to intervene. The emperor responded by leading an army south in 1022. While Henry concentrated his efforts on a siege of Troia, he sent a separate force to deal with Pandulf IV and his brother Atenulf, both of whom had been quick to side with the catapan in the wake of Melo's defeat. Pandulf IV, who was taken into imperial custody,[19] was replaced by count Pandulf of Teano (Pandulf V)[20] as prince of Capua. Henry also presided over the election of Theobald (1022–36) as abbot of Montecassino in place of Atenulf.[21] Henry then placed two of Melo's nephews in charge of Comino (in the Garigliano valley), and left with them a number of Normans.[22]

Benedict VIII's death in April 1024, followed by that of Henry II three months later, dealt a major blow to this effective anti-Byzantine coalition. Guaimar IV of Salerno petitioned Conrad, the new German king, to release his brother-in-law Pandulf IV[23] from custody. For some unknown reason, Conrad complied.[24] This led to the formation of an alliance of southern Italian powers around the liberated Pandulf, intent on undermining Henry II's efforts in the region. Guaimar, Boioannes, the counts of the Marsi, and the Normans of Salerno and Comino, all participated in a siege of Capua that culminated a year and a half later with the restoration of Pandulf IV (May 1026).[25]

The displaced Pandulf V of Teano escaped with his family to Naples,[26] where his presence provided Pandulf IV with an excuse to take Naples from Sergio IV in early 1028.[27] Though Sergio managed to regain control of Naples a short time later,[28] the ongoing threat that Pandulf IV posed to Sergio's position led the Neapolitan prince, in late 1029 or early 1030, to invest the Norman Rainulf[29] with the town of Aversa and to arrange a marriage between him and Sergio's own recently widowed sister.[30] Thus emerged the first significant Norman lordship in Italy. As the new ruler of Aversa, Rainulf set about to attract other Normans to his service.[31]

Still Pandulf IV continued to extend his hegemony over the region, taking advantage of the fact that after Guaimar IV's death in 1027, Salerno was in the hands of Gaitelgrima, Guaimar's widow (and Pandulf's sister), who acted as regent on behalf of her minor son, Guaimar V. In 1032 Pandulf gained control of Gaeta, which had strengthened its ties to Sergio during his brief exile.[32] Then he turned to Montecassino, replacing Abbot Theobald[33] with Basil, a former minister to the bishop of Capua. According to Leo Marsicanus, Pandulf forced the monks of Montecassino to swear allegiance to him, delegated the fortresses that were under Casinese control to Normans in his service, and began to transfer monastic revenues to his own treasury.[34] Pandulf also took advantage of the death of the Norman Rainulf of Aversa's wife—the sister of Sergio IV—to offer him his own niece[35] in marriage. Rainulf accepted Pandulf's proposition in 1034 despite his former alliance with Naples.[36] Sergio IV responded by abdicating as prince of Naples and entering a monastery.[37]

Pandulf's fortunes finally turned in 1037 when Conrad conducted his own imperial expedition into Italy.[38] The emperor was met in Milan by a delegation from Montecassino asking for assistance against Pandulf. Conrad entered Capua in May 1038 and oversaw the restoration of Montecassino's property as well as the election of a new abbot, the Bavarian Richer (1038–55).[39] He then invested Guaimar V with the city of Capua, forcing Pandulf to flee with his son to Constantinople.[40] Before Conrad returned to Germany, he also recognized Rainulf as the count of Aversa under the feudal lordship of Guaimar V.[41]

Sometime during Conrad's Italian campaign (1037–38), a new group of Normans arrived in Italy led by William and Drogo, the first of many sons of Tancred of Hauteville who would make their way to the region.[42] According to Geoffrey Malaterra, they first offered their services to Pandulf but ultimately found Guaimar's terms more attractive.[43] It was Guaimar who sent them, as part of the Salernitan contingent, to participate in the Byzantine campaign to reconquer Sicily in 1038.[44] The allied imperial army, under the command of George Maniakes, succeeded in occupying Messina in 1038 and by 1040 had taken Syracuse. But further progress was hampered by dissension within the army, part of which involved Harduin, the commander of the Salernitan forces, who felt victimized by what he saw as an unfair distribution of booty. His protests unheeded, Harduin left for Italy, taking with him his partly Norman army.[45]

After returning to Italy in 1040, Harduin was appointed governor of the northern Apulian city of Melfi by the catapan Doukeianos.[46] A year later, as Apulia was beginning to erupt in rebellion, Harduin met with Rainulf of Aversa who provided him with a force under the command of William and Drogo, with the understanding that Harduin would divide any conquered territory with the Normans.[47] The Normans occupied Melfi and proceeded to extend their authority over Venosa, Lavello, and Ascoli.[48] Doukeianos, who seems to have been in Sicily when the insurrection began,[49] returned to Apulia, put down the rebellion in Bari, and proceeded north to deal with the uprising at Melfi. But he was met and defeated by the Norman army in two separate encounters near the Olivento and Ofanto rivers in March and May 1041.[50] The replacement of Doukeianos with Boioannes, the son of the earlier catapan of the same name, did not prevent the Normans from defeating the Greek forces a third time the following September near Montepeloso.[51]

Harduin's fate is unclear. All that we know is that in the midst of these skirmishes, the Normans transferred their allegiance to Atenulf, the brother of Pandulf III of Benevento.[52] Within a year (March 1042) Atenulf was himself replaced by Argyro, the son of Melo, who had returned from exile in Constantinople in 1029. Argyro used the Normans of Melfi to wreak havoc throughout Apulia.[53] But in the midst of a siege on Trani (July 1042), he was brought over to the imperial side by promises of being made catapan himself.[54] Argyro's abrupt volte-face disappointed many who had supported his rebellion. The Normans responded by electing one of their own, William of Hauteville, as their leader in September 1042.[55] Guaimar V came to Apulia, accompanied by Rainulf of Aversa, and, assuming the role of feudal overlord, recognized William as the count of Melfi and arranged for him to marry his niece.[56] William, apparently assisted by Guaimar and Rainulf, proceeded to distribute among the Normans the Apulian towns and fortresses that had been secured thus far.[57] From that point on there were two Norman principalities in southern Italy, one based in Aversa and the other in Melfi, both, at least for the time being, under the feudal lordship of Guaimar V of Salerno. The Normans of Melfi, with the assistance of Salerno and

Aversa, set out to extend their power at the expense of the Greeks in Apulia and Calabria.

The return to Italy of the irrepressible Pandulf IV in 1042—presumably part of a Greek effort to unravel the Salernitan-Norman alliance that threatened their position in Apulia—forced Guaimar to attend to matters closer to home. Thus when Rainulf of Aversa died in June 1045 and his nephew and heir Asclettin[58] followed him to the grave a short time later, Pandulf supported the claims of another of Rainulf's nephews (Rainulf Trincanocte) over and against those of Guaimar's choice, Rodulf Cappello.[59] With Pandulf's help, Rainulf escaped confinement in Salerno and made his way into Aversa, where he managed to garner local support and eject Rodulf in late 1045 or early 1046.[60]

At about the same time, Count William of Apulia died.[61] Guaimar intervened to make certain that William would be succeeded by his brother Drogo and strengthened his ties to the new count by giving Drogo his daughter in marriage.[62] Following the lead of his older brother, Drogo remained loyal to Guaimar, ultimately acting as an intermediary to defuse the Aversa situation: Guaimar finally recognized Rainulf (II) as the legitimate count of Aversa.

Montecassino's proximity to Aquino, which was firmly allied with Pandulf IV, made it vulnerable throughout this period of growing resistance to Guaimar's hegemony. Shortly after his return from exile, Pandulf IV had managed, with the help of Atenulf of Aquino, to restore Abbot Basil—who had returned from exile with Pandulf—at least until a Norman army, dispatched by Guaimar, forced Basil to flee to Aquino.[63] But Aquino was not the only, or even the most immediate, threat to the monastery at this time. The Normans, who from the time of Abbot Atenulf controlled many of the fortresses on the monastery's lands, proved to be less than consistent allies. A group of them ignored the abbot when in 1045 he told them to desist from their unauthorized fortification of the nearby fortress of San Andrea. The leader of these Normans at San Andrea, named Rodulf, came to San Germano in May with a number of his followers and, while attending services in the church, was ambushed by men loyal to Richer.[64] The abbot then summoned the counts of the Marsi, who expelled the garrison from San Andrea and forced the remaining Normans to flee the *terra sancti Benedicti* for Aversa.

Henry III came to Italy for his imperial coronation in the autumn of 1046. At the synod of Sutri he deposed the three rival popes and elevated his own candidate, Clement II, in their place. He then received the imperial crown from the hands of his new pope. Early the following year, Henry and Clement made their way south. After visiting Montecassino, they came to Capua in February 1047. In an apparent effort to reduce the power of Guaimar V in the region, Henry handed Capua back to Pandulf IV and his son (the future Pandulf VI), recognized Atenulf of Aquino as the duke of Gaeta, and confirmed Drogo and Rainulf II as the counts of Apulia and Aversa respectively.[65] Whether this act of investment meant that the Norman counts were free of their ties to Guaimar is not clear.[66]

Sometime in 1046 or 1047, Richard—another of Rainulf I's nephews—arrived in Italy from Normandy. He was not well received by Rainulf II,[67] and turned for support to the sons of Tancred of Hauteville.[68] But Rainulf II died a short time later (in late 1047 or early 1048) and the people of Aversa petitioned Guaimar to allow them to elevate Richard. Guaimar responded by naming him regent on behalf of Rainulf II's young son Herman, but the boy's death shortly thereafter (c. 1050) cleared the way for Richard's formal accession as count of Aversa.[69] Meanwhile Pandulf IV had died in early 1049 and was succeeded by his son Pandulf VI as prince of Capua.[70]

Robert Guiscard, the oldest of Tancred's sons by his second wife, arrived in Italy at approximately the same time as Richard, following in the footsteps of his older half-brothers. Drogo eventually sent him to the fortress of Scribla in Calabria.[71] From there Robert led pillaging expeditions in the surrounding area trying to secure enough provisions and booty to keep his men together. After moving his men to San Marco Argentano,[72] Robert continued his raids, managing on one occasion to capture and ransom Peter, the Greek governor of nearby Bisignano.[73] Robert's first real break came when he was offered the hand of Alberada, the young aunt of Gerard, the Norman lord of Buonalbergo. With her came a dowry of two hundred knights.[74] With the help of his new army, Robert proceeded to secure the capitulation of Bisignano, Cosenza, and Martirano.[75]

II

In early 1049, the Lotharingian bishop Bruno of Toul, a kinsman of Henry III, became the third in a quick succession of imperial appointments to the papacy, assuming the name Leo IX (1049–54). From early in his pontificate, he seemed to pay special attention to Benevento, which turned to Rome for protection from the Normans who were beginning to encroach on Beneventan territory. During one of his tours in the region, Leo took the opportunity to visit Melfi and chastise the Normans for their military forays into the region.[76] Later he specifically charged Drogo and Guaimar V of Salerno with the protection of Benevento's territory, a task that was complicated by the fact that even if the two rulers were inclined to assist Leo, neither of them could claim control over all of the bands of Normans in the area.[77] Drogo's assassination in August 1051[78] may have encouraged the pope to take a more active role in controlling the Normans, since it would take time for Drogo's younger brother Humphrey to consolidate his power as the new count.[79] Leo asked for military assistance from the German emperor and the king of France, neither of whom jumped at the chance.[80] With the assistance of Frederick of Lorraine, who had been appointed papal chancellor in that same year (1051), Leo set about gathering allies from among the southern Italian principalities, including Gaeta, the Marsi, Valva, and the March of Fermo.[81]

Leo also asked Guaimar V for his support, but the prince of Salerno absented himself, not wanting to alienate the Normans.[82] As it turned out, Guaimar was murdered shortly afterward (June 1052) during the unrest that followed a rebellion in Amalfi.[83] Guaimar's brother-in-law, who was involved in the conspiracy, was proclaimed prince in his place.[84] Guaimar's brother Guy, the duke of Sorrento, responded by seeking the help of the Normans on behalf of his nephew Gisulf, the son of Guaimar.[85] Humphrey, who had married Guaimar's (and Guy's) sister,[86] followed Guy to Salerno and forced the city to surrender (June 1052).[87] Guy and Humphrey installed Guaimar's son Gisulf (II) as the new prince of Salerno and he in turn reinvested the Normans with their territories.[88]

Meanwhile Leo and his chancellor Frederick were busy gathering support for an anti-Norman campaign. After meeting yet again with Henry III, Leo and Frederick returned to Italy in March 1053 with an army composed primarily of Swabians. After recruiting other contingents from Italian powers hostile to the Normans, the papal army began in June to push south, expecting to link up with Argyro and his Greek forces in Apulia.[89] But before the papal forces could effect their rendezvous, they encountered outside Civitate a Norman army that had been gathered from all of the Norman principalities and lordships. It was commanded jointly by Humphrey of Apulia, Richard of Aversa, and Robert Guiscard of Calabria.[90] According to Amatus, Leo absolved his troops and remitted the penance that they would normally have to perform for sins committed in battle.[91] When the fighting began on June 18 1053, the Italian contingent of the papal army fled, leaving the Germans to bear the brunt of the Norman assault. The Normans prevailed and took Leo prisoner, escorting him to Benevento where he was loosely confined for the next nine months.[92]

In January 1054, while still under house arrest in Benevento, Leo sent an embassy to Constantinople, headed by Cardinal Humbert and Frederick, the papal chancellor. Its principal business was to protest Patriarch Michael Cerularius's attacks against the Latin rite and his closure of Latin churches in Constantinople. But the embassy also carried a letter from Leo to Constantine IX Monomachus which called upon both the Greek and the German emperors to perform their proper functions as protectors of the church and expel the Normans from Italy.[93]

It is very difficult to determine what sort of agreement, if any, the pope and the Normans worked out at Benevento.[94] But Leo's unabated hostility toward the Normans after Civitate suggests that if the Normans did win some sort of papal recognition of their holdings in southern Italy,[95] it was granted under duress. In any case, Leo was finally allowed to leave Benevento for Rome in March 1054, with a Norman escort accompanying him as far as Capua. The pope died the following month. The embassy he had dispatched from Benevento stayed on in Constantinople until July, when Humbert dramatically excommunicated the patriarch and was anathematized in turn by Cerularius, thus initiating the so-called Schism of 1054. The proposed anti-Norman alliance never materialized.

The Normans of Melfi took advantage of their victory at Civitate and the delays in selecting a new pope to tighten their grip on Apulia. An entire year passed before Bishop Gebhard of Eichstätt was consecrated as Victor II (April 1055), the last in the series of Henry III's papal nominees. As Henry's chancellor, Gebhard had opposed sending the imperial forces that Leo had requested on the eve of Civitate,[96] and he seems to have begun his pontificate on good terms with the Normans,[97] but by the summer of 1056 he was on his way to Germany to request imperial aid against Norman encroachment.[98] As it happened, Henry III died unexpectedly in

September and Victor found himself occupied instead with the task of securing the succession of Henry's five-year-old son and namesake under the regency of Queen Agnes.

Henry III's death and the relative weakness of the German regency led Victor to search for a more dependable protector of reform party interests. He began to strengthen ties with Frederick of Lorraine's brother Godfrey who, by virtue of his marriage to the countess Beatrice,[99] had assumed control of Tuscany. This important territorial acquisition had placed Godfrey on a collision course with Henry III, who in 1055 had come south to confront his vassal. On that occasion Godfrey fled, prompting Henry to consider capturing his brother Frederick and holding him hostage. But Frederick eluded Henry by entering Montecassino as a monk. After Henry's death, Victor patched up relations between the imperial family and Godfrey and sent Humbert to Montecassino where he succeeded in convincing the monks to replace their newly elected abbot Peter with Frederick of Lorraine. He was consecrated as abbot and named cardinal by Victor in May 1057.[100] When Victor himself died two months later, the reform cardinals quickly elected the new abbot as pope and Frederick assumed the name Stephen IX.

Stephen's feelings about the Normans were predictably hostile. As Leo IX's chancellor and closest advisor, he had been present at the debacle of Civitate (1053) and had accompanied Humbert to Constantinople (1054) in his ill-fated attempt to secure Byzantine assistance for a new campaign against the Normans. As pope and abbot of Montecassino, Stephen began planning his own expedition against the Normans, to be financed in part by the treasure of Montecassino to which he had access.[101] Like Leo, he looked to both Germany and Byzantium for support. He sent envoys—including Desiderius, the acting abbot of Montecassino—to Bari where they were to consult with Argyro and then sail on to Constantinople. The accession of Isaac Comnenus (1057-59) and the fall of Michael Cerularius seemed to reopen the possibility of a papal-Byzantine alliance. The death of Humphrey in spring 1057 meant that Norman Apulia was preoccupied with the problems of succession. The dying Humphrey had designated his half-brother Robert Guiscard as regent on behalf of his young sons Abelard and Herman, but by August Robert had secured the allegiance of the Norman vassals and allowed himself to be acclaimed as the new count.[102] In the meantime Pope Stephen had traveled to Florence to consult with his brother, only to die there in March 1058. The embassy, still in Bari, was recalled and Desiderius, given a safe-conduct by Robert Guiscard despite his embassy's anti-Norman agenda, returned to Monte-cassino where he was elected abbot shortly after.[103]

The ensuing papal election resulted in a schism, with the aristocratic factions in Rome backing the bishop of Velletri as Benedict X, while the reform party, under the leadership of Hildebrand and Humbert, elected Bishop Gerard of Florence, who took the name Nicholas II. The reform party, looking for an effective protector,[104] decided to enlist the aid of the Norman Richard of Aversa, who had recently taken control of Capua (1058). It is likely that Desiderius, who had not only succeeded Frederick (Stephen IX) as abbot of Montecassino (1058-87) but had been named cardinal, was the driving force behind this radical change of papal policy.[105] Hildebrand went to confer with Richard in February 1059. Richard responded by sending troops to besiege the fortress of Galeria, where Benedict X had retreated. The fortress finally yielded and Benedict was compelled to renounce his claims to the papal see.[106]

During the Lentan council of April 1059, Nicholas II and the reform party passed the famous papal election decree which placed the process of selecting a pope in the hands of the cardinal bishops.[107] For this change to be implemented, the cardinals needed protection against the Italian and German factions that had traditionally played such a definitive role in selecting popes. In August 1059, Nicholas held another council at Melfi where he officially invested Richard with Aversa and Robert Guiscard with Apulia, Calabria, and—in anticipation of Norman campaigns across the straits—Sicily, in exchange for their homage as papal vassals.[108]

The text of Robert's oath at Melfi has survived.[109] Robert swore fealty to the church and to Nicholas, promising never to participate in any project aimed at harming the pope, nor to reveal things told to him by the pope in confidence. He agreed to preserve and respect papal territory and to pay the *pensiones* due to the pope for lands held from him. Robert promised to assure that the churches within his territory recognized papal jurisdiction, a reflection of the on-going competition between the Greek and Latin church for jurisdiction over southern Italy and Sicily.[110] Fur-thermore, Robert agreed to enforce the election decree, allowing the car-dinals to select future popes without outside interference. From that point on Robert officially styled himself "duke of Apulia, Calabria, and Sicily," a title that, according to William of Apulia, his half-brothers had not been entitled to use.[111]

Nicholas II's decision to install the Normans as papal vassals was, like his predecessors' efforts to resist them, a simple product of growing Norman power in the south. Guaimar V's assassination in 1052 and the eclipse of Salerno's hegemony in the region had opened the door for Richard to extend his authority. He immediately forced Capua to become a tributary[112] and when Pandulf VI died in 1057, Richard returned to lay siege to the city. In June 1058, Capua surrendered to Richard.[113]

Richard met Desiderius for the first time during the early stages of the siege of Capua, while Desiderius was still serving as prior of the monastery of St. Benedict in Capua. On that occasion Desiderius had managed to secure a promise from Richard to respect the property of the monastery during his assault on Capua.[114] As abbot of Montecassino,[115] Desiderius honored the new prince of Capua with a formal reception in November 1058 and enlisted his aid as the protector of the monastery. No doubt Desiderius's new relationship with Richard helped smooth the way for Nicholas II's recognition of the Normans as papal vassals at their famous meeting in Melfi the following summer.[116]

While Richard was consolidating his position in Campania, Robert Guiscard was busy making good his claim to the duchy of Apulia in the face of the first of many challenges posed by Humphrey's disinherited sons, Abelard and Herman.[117] Calabria also proved to be a thorn in Robert's side, ironically even more so after the task of its subjection had been passed down to the duke's youngest brother Roger, who had just arrived in Italy in 1057.[118] Roger was able to take advantage of the instability of his brother's rule to force him to accept his terms: according to Geoffrey Malaterra, Roger received half of all Calabria as well as the rights to Reggio whenever it fell to the Normans.[119] The city finally capitulated to Robert's and Roger's combined forces in the summer of 1059.[120] While Roger attended to the conquest of Squillace, the last of the Calabrian holdouts, Robert returned to Apulia and, as we have seen, met Nicholas II at Melfi.[121]

As Robert struggled to assert his authority over Apulia and Calabria, he secured an important diplomatic victory in Campania. Gisulf II, who had departed from the pro-Norman policy that had informed his father's rule and had placed his hopes in a new papally-sponsored expedition against the Normans, had been forced by the death of Stephen IX (1058) to rethink his stance. That same year he agreed to a marriage alliance with Robert—reminiscent of the ones that his father Guaimar had formed with the other sons of Tancred—whereby Robert would receive Gisulf's sister (Guaimar's daughter) Sichelgaita as his wife.[122] This led to Robert's repudiation of Alberada on the convenient grounds of consanguinity. The duke set aside lands in Calabria to support his ex-wife and their effectively bastardized son, Bohemond.[123]

Robert's campaigns in Apulia and Calabria prevented him from fulfilling his obligations as a papal vassal in the years immediately following the synod of Melfi. Insofar as any of the Norman rulers performed this function it was Richard, whose power base in Capua made it somewhat more likely that his interests and those of the papacy would coincide. When Nicholas II died in July 1061, the cardinals, led by Hildebrand, decided to elect Bishop Anselm of Lucca (Alexander II).[124] Knowing that this would not sit well with the Roman aristocracy, Hildebrand met with Richard of Capua and secured his services as a military escort.[125] After overcoming the resistance in Rome with not a little bloodshed, Richard— accompanied by Desiderius[126]—successfully delivered the newly elected pope to the Lateran palace on the first day of October. A few days later, Richard swore fidelity to Alexander II and then retreated.[127] The pope's position was, however, far from secure. Later that month the German regency, wary of the newfound independence of the reform party, sided with the Italian aristocrats and selected their own pope, Bishop Peter Cadalus of Parma, who took the name Honorius II.[128] The periodically violent stand-off in Rome would last until May 1064 when a synod was convened in Mantua and, in the absence of Honorius who refused to attend, formally recognized Alexander as pope.[129]

Though Norman forces participated in these struggles on behalf of Alexander II, Richard was more interested in extending his own hegemony than in performing his role as papal protector. Not content with the capitulation agreement of 1058 that had left the citadel of Capua in the hands of the Capuans, Richard besieged the city again in 1062 and accepted its unconditional surrender on May 21.[130] Richard's success in extending his power served, in fact, to alienate Alexander II, who had relied on Richard's military might to secure his position in Rome. When in 1066 Richard besieged and took Ceprano and raided the countryside up to Rome,[131] the pope appealed to Henry IV to intervene.[132] When that did not work out, he encouraged Richard's perennially rebellious former son-in-law William of Montreuil, who controlled Aquino, to break with Richard in 1068. The rebellion ended when William died in 1071 and

Richard was able to secure his son Jordan's succession to Aquino.[133]

The tension between Alexander II and Richard of Capua contrasted sharply with the amicable relationship enjoyed by Richard and Desiderius.[134] This situation sometimes complicated otherwise positive papal-Casinese relations.[135] But Rome and Montecassino managed for the most part to overlook their differences regarding the Normans. When the new basilica of Montecassino was dedicated in October 1071, Alexander II was there to perform the ceremony while Richard of Capua looked on as a distinguished guest.

III

According to Geoffrey Malaterra, Robert and Roger were pondering a Sicilian campaign even before they had secured Reggio and Squillace on the mainland (1059).[136] Apparently on that occasion, Robert sent Roger on a reconnaissance mission to Messina. But uprisings in Apulia in conjunction with the arrival of a Greek expeditionary force prevented the duke from undertaking any immediate campaigns in Sicily.[137] However, in February 1061, Roger was met in Calabria by the emir of Syracuse and Catania, Ibn Thimna, who sought to enlist Roger's aid against his rival Ibn Hawas of Castrogiovanni and Agrigento.[138] After reconnoitering the area around Messina with Ibn Thimna as his guide,[139] Roger spent March and April of 1061 preparing for an invasion. In May Robert Guiscard arrived in Calabria with reinforcements, but a Muslim fleet, dispatched from Palermo, prevented the Norman fleet from crossing. So Robert remained behind with the bulk of the Norman army as a decoy, while Roger crossed the straits with a much smaller force and managed to surprise and capture a practically undefended Messina.[140] The Muslim fleet retreated to Palermo, allowing Robert to cross over to Messina with the remainder of the Norman forces.[141]

Though Robert and Roger campaigned in Sicily the entire summer, moving through the island without encountering any serious opposition, they were unable to add to their Messinan toehold. Their efforts to subdue Ibn Hawas's army and take Castrogiovanni proved to be fruitless. But in December, on his way back from a raid directed against Agrigento, Roger was welcomed by the Greek Christian populations of the Valdemone and accepted the surrender of Troina.[142]

Shortly after, he crossed back over to Mileto, his Calabrian capital, and married Judith, the half-sister of Robert of Grantmesnil. Robert had been abbot of the Norman monastery of Saint-Evroul, until he was implicated in a plot against Duke William of Normandy. Forced into exile, he came to Rome to appeal to the pope and ended up being offered the abbacy of the Calabrian monastery of St. Eufemia, founded a short time before by Robert Guiscard.[143]

The following spring (1062) Roger and Ibn Thimna successfully beseiged Petralia, some thirty miles east of Troina. But later that season, after Roger had returned to Calabria, his Muslim ally was ambushed and killed. Hearing this, the Norman garrisons of Petralia and Troina abandoned their posts and retreated to Messina.[144] Roger was in no position to come to Sicily at that time, for he had once again broken with Robert, who, it seems, had been slow to hand over to his brother that portion of Calabria that he had promised him four years before.[145] When Roger finally returned to Sicily in mid-summer 1062, he headed straight for Troina and found to his relief that despite the retreat of the garrison the Muslims had not occupied the city. In the process of reestablishing the garrison, Roger alienated the local Greek Christian population who responded by rising up and, with the help of Muslim forces from a nearby fortress, besieging the count, his wife and his men for four months before order was restored.[146]

In the summer of 1063, Norman fears that Ibn Hawas was to receive reinforcements from Africa finally materialized.[147] Prevented from taking the fortress of Cerami by the timely arrival of Roger's nephew Serlo, the Muslims retreated to their camp. On the advice of Roussel of Bailleul—who fought for Roger before entering the service of the Greek emperor in Anatolia, for which he is more famous—Roger followed and the most significant single battle of the entire Sicilian conquest ensued. In the end, the Normans emerged victorious. From the spoils that the Normans collected from the Muslim camp, Roger sent four camels to Alexander II. The pope, in turn, bestowed upon Roger a papal banner.[148]

Among the dead at the Battle of Cerami was Kaid, the emir of Palermo, a casualty that presumably left that city in a vulnerable position. This and the fact that a Pisan embassy approached Roger in Troina that very summer (1063) proposing a joint operation against Palermo would seem to have made this a good time to act.[149] Roger's hesitation can only be explained in terms of his perennial lack of manpower, a situation that

precluded large-scale military operations unless Roger's forces were supplemented by his brother's. But 1063 was the beginning of a particularly
difficult period for the duke in Apulia. For it was in that year that Geoffrey of Conversano, Robert's brother-in-law and one of the more powerful Norman lords in his service, died, leaving behind a son, also named
Geoffrey, who rebelled against the duke and became yet another focal
point for Apulian dissent.[150]

With no hope of any immediate reinforcements from the mainland,
Roger contented himself with plundering expeditions until his brother
finally broke away from Apulia in early 1064 and joined Roger on a campaign aimed at securing Palermo. But the Normans accomplished nothing
in the months that they spent outside the city except to develop a great
distaste for the tarantulas that infested their camp.[151] After abandoning
the siege, they attacked Bugamo, destroyed it, and led its inhabitants away
in captivity to be relocated in Scribla.[152] By this time Robert was in a
hurry to get back to Apulia where the rebellion had intensified in his
absence.[153] Joining the young Geoffrey of Conversano[154] were Robert of
Montescaglioso,[155] Abelard,[156] Jocelyn,[157] Amico of Giovanazzo, and
Pereno of Durazzo.[158] It would take Robert four years to restore his
authority over the region and to make Geoffrey accept the overlordship of
the duke. No sooner was his position in Apulia secured than Robert, taking advantage of the Byzantine preoccupation with the Seldjuk Turks in
Anatolia, captured Otranto and initiated his long siege of Bari
(1068–71).[159]

Meanwhile Roger continued his raids in Sicily, accomplishing little
of lasting significance. While on a plundering expedition in the vicinity of
Palermo in 1068, Roger unexpectedly ran into a large African force at Misilmeri under the command of Ayub, the son of the caliph Temim.[160]
Despite the odds, the Normans prevailed. Among the spoils, Roger discovered carrier pigeons, which, according to Geoffrey Malaterra, he used
to send word to Palermo of the Muslim defeat.[161] This battle appears to
have been something of a turning point, weakening subsequent Muslim
resistance in Sicily and leading to Ayub's return to Africa. Little more is
known about Roger's exploits until he appeared in Apulia, perhaps as late
as 1071 to assist Robert at Bari.[162]

Robert had begun his siege of the city in August 1068,[163] construct-
ing a floating barrier of Norman ships chained together and connected at
each end to jetties extending from the shore.[164] The duke also established

contact with the leader of a sympathetic faction within Bari by the name of Argyrico who, in July 1070, arranged the assassination of the governor of Bari, Byzantius.[165] Robert had proved more fortunate when a similar attempt had been made on his life by a citizen of Bari who had managed to infiltrate the Norman camp.[166] When Roger finally came to Bari at his brother's summons, the people of Bari were awaiting the arrival of another imperial fleet. When it finally arrived from Durazzo—under the command of the Norman Jocelyn of Corinth who had participated in the earlier Apulian rebellion but had been forced to flee to Constantinople—it was Roger, at least according to Geoffrey Malaterra, who intercepted the flag ship and took Jocelyn prisoner.[167] Bari capitulated shortly after, in April 1071.[168] The surrender terms were very favorable to its citizens, allowing them to keep their property and have Argyrico as their governor.[169] At about the same time, Brindisi accepted Norman rule.[170] The surrender of these two key Adriatic cities effectively ended imperial challenges to Norman rule in southern Italy.

The brothers wasted no time before planning a new expedition against Palermo. Roger left for Sicily immediately after the fall of Bari while Robert spent June and July (1071) in Otranto gathering supplies and preparing a fleet.[171] Sometime prior to Robert's arrival, Roger had managed to secure control of Catania, which had been the center of his ally Ibn Thimna's emirate.[172] Robert joined Roger there and the two prepared a navy, ostensibly to be used for an expedition to Malta. Instead it sailed against Palermo in August. The Norman forces besieged the city by land and sea for five months.[173] Finally, in January 1072, they managed to make their way inside the walls, occupying part of the city.[174] The citizens sued for peace and swore on the Koran to pay tribute and do homage in exchange for permission to retain their law.[175] Robert and Roger oversaw the reconsecration of the former church of St. Mary, which had been converted into a mosque, and reinstated the exiled Greek archbishop.[176] Keeping Palermo for himself, Robert rewarded Roger with the Valdemone which he was to hold as a fief from the duke.[177] The as yet unconquered, southern half of the island was, at least according to Geoffrey Malaterra, granted to Robert's and Roger's nephew Serlo and to Arisgot of Pozzuole.[178] Serlo had been left behind in Cerami with instructions to defend against a possible counterattack by the Muslims in Castrogiovanni. But shortly after the fall of Palermo, Serlo was ambushed and killed on a hunting expedition by a Muslim contingent from Castrogiovanni.[179]

Robert's return to the mainland was greeted by another rebellion involving his nephews Abelard and Herman, among other disgruntled vassals.[180]

The timing of the rebellion suggests that Alexander II may have orchestrated it during his visit to consecrate Montecassino's new basilica in October 1071.[181] Papal efforts to counter Robert's growing power in southern Italy picked up after Hildebrand was elected pope in April 1073, though at first Gregory VII seemed more inclined to work with the duke rather than against him. Thus when it looked like Robert might not survive a fever that he had contracted, Gregory VII sent a letter of condolence to Sichelgaita, offering to invest her son Roger (Borsa) with the territories that Robert had ruled as a papal vassal.[182] And when the pope learned that Robert had recovered, he arranged through Desiderius to meet him, perhaps hoping to enlist Robert's support against Richard and other Norman lords—like Robert of Loritello, Robert's nephew[183]—whose northern campaigns were threatening papal territory in the Abruzzi. But this meeting, scheduled for August 1073, never took place thanks to Gregory's insistence that it be held within the city of Benevento and Robert's fear that if he complied he would be risking an ambush.[184]

From that point on, Gregory set out to isolate Robert, who for his part was preoccupied with a new rebellion in Calabria.[185] In September 1073 the pope was in Capua accepting homage from Richard as well as his promise to desist from any encroachment onto papal property.[186] At about this same time Gisulf II added his name to the growing list of papal allies.[187] The pope also secured a promise of assistance from Beatrice and her daughter Mathilda of Tuscany. In early February 1074, after Gregory had returned to Rome, he wrote to count William of Burgundy asking him, as a papal vassal, to mobilize an army that was to be used, in conjunction with the forces of other papal vassals like Raymond of Saint-Gilles, Richard of Capua, Amatus of Savoy, first to subdue Robert Guiscard and second to assist the Greek emperor against the Turks who had invaded Anatolia.[188] A short time later (March 1074), Gregory held his Lenten synod in Rome, attended by Beatrice, Mathilda and Gisulf, at which he excommunicated Robert Guiscard and called for a June campaign against him.[189] The allied forces gathered at Montecimino (near Viterbo), but a falling out between Gisulf and the Pisan contingent of Mathilda's troops led the army to disband before it had accomplished anything.[190].

At the beginning of 1076, Robert received an embassy from Henry IV. Henry, who had replaced Robert Guiscard as the primary focus of papal hostility as a result of the mounting controversy over the investiture of the archbishop of Milan, wanted Robert's support in the struggle with Gregory, offering imperial recognition of Robert's landholdings in exchange for his oath of vassalage. Little came of the embassy.[191] Gregory VII, who had been formally denounced by the German bishops at the Diet of Worms in January 1076, also began to reach out to the Normans. Whereas at his Lenten synod of 1075, he had reiterated his excommunication of Robert Guiscard, a year later (March 1076) the pope was writing to the bishop of Acerenza hinting that he was ready to lift his excommunication of Robert if the duke were willing to become an obedient servant of the church.[192]

Spurning both king and pope, Robert turned instead to Richard of Capua. With the mediation of Desiderius, the two came to terms, agreeing to hand over the lands that they had conquered from each other and promising mutual aid.[193] In May 1076 Robert laid siege to Salerno, assisted not only by Greek and Muslim contingents in his own army, but by the forces of Richard of Capua.[194] Apparently Robert was more than willing to negotiate a settlement, but Gisulf refused despite the active encouragement of Gregory VII, Desiderius, and his own sister (Robert's wife) Sichelgaita.[195] The siege wore on and the famine inside grew serious.[196] At some point during the siege, Robert was able to send troops to take control of Amalfi, as per the prior request of its citizens.[197] In October 1076 Robert and Richard left the siege to conduct campaigns to the north at the expense of Gregory,[198] returning to Salerno by way of Montecassino, where they were welcomed with a formal procession.[199] The besieging army finally succeeded in overcoming the resistance of Salerno's citizens and Robert entered the city in December 1076,[200] although Gisulf held out in the citadel until the following May.[201] At one point during the siege of the citadel, Robert was seriously injured by a stone hurled from the tower, but he recovered.[202] After swearing never to seek power in Salerno again, Gisulf was surrendered into Richard's custody and delivered to Gregory VII in Rome.[203]

In May 1077 Richard began his siege of Naples, this time with Robert playing the auxiliary role, providing a fleet to close off the city from the sea.[204] But again a speedy conquest proved elusive. In November, when news of the death of Landulf VI of Benevento reached Robert, the duke removed part of his contingent from the siege of Naples and used it to begin a new siege of Benevento (December 1077), which had been under papal protection since the pontificate of Leo IX.[205] Gregory responded at

his Lenten council in Rome in March 1078 with a violent new denunciation and excommunication of the Normans—specifically Robert Guiscard
and Robert of Loritello—who were involved in attacks against papal territory. Gregory went so far as to impose an interdict on the Norman territories, prohibiting the clergy in the Norman territories from performing the
mass. This time the censure apparently included Richard of Capua and his
son Jordan who had encroached into the Abruzzi.[206]

As it turned out, Richard became ill and died in April, 1078. This led
to a complete shift in the balance of power in the south. Richard's son
Jordan, concerned that the pope would not recognize his succession
because of the excommunication, had gone to Rome to seek Gregory's
pardon as soon as Richard became ill.[207] Jordan was restored to the good
graces of the church when he agreed to hand over the lands in question
that he and his father had conquered. When Richard died, the siege of
Naples was lifted and Robert had little choice but to give up on Benevento as well. Moreover Robert's perennially unruly vassals—led again
by Abelard—rose in revolt in Apulia in the autumn of 1078.[208] They were
not fully suppressed until spring 1080.[209]

While Robert was reasserting his authority over Apulia, Gregory
VII's position in Rome was becoming increasingly untenable. In his
Lenten synod of 1080 he excommunicated Henry IV for the second time.
The fact that he took the opportunity to reiterate his Norman excommu-
nications suggests that Gregory still regarded an alliance with Robert
Guiscard as an unsavory option.[210] But pressure from Henry and encouragement from Desiderius ultimately led him to absolve Robert Guiscard.[211] In late spring, Gregory left Rome and traveled to Ceprano, where
he met Robert, and, on June 6 1080, invested him with the territories conceded by Nicholas and Alexander, adding Salerno and Amalfi.[212] On June
29, he met with Robert again and accepted his oath of fealty.[213] Both
Robert and Jordan—who had taken his oath to the pope on June 10—
showed their appreciation to Desiderius by recognizing Montecassino's
holdings and adding a number of additional monasteries and churches to
them.[214] In 1080 Robert Guiscard also began work on a cathedral in
Salerno, his new base of operations.[215]

While Robert was consolidating his hold on southern Italy, Roger
was doing his best to extend his dominion in Sicily. The fact that Robert
Guiscard never returned to Sicily after the conquest of Palermo meant
that his brother's options were severely limited. In place of extended

sieges, the count had to rely on raids conducted from strategically placed fortresses, waiting for the right opportunity to force individual cities into submission. On the other hand, because the Muslim cities in the southern half of the island acted independently of one another and rarely in concert with the powers of the Maghrib, Roger did not face any overwhelming opposition. The Muslim campaigns, too, tended to resemble raids more than conquests. Nicotera was the focus of a maritime attack from Africa in 1074 and the count had to defend Mazara, which had capitulated shortly after Palermo's surrender, from a similar assault the following year.[216] In 1076 Benarvet, the emir of Syracuse,[217] took advantage of one of the count's trips to the mainland to launch an attack on Catania during which Roger's son-in-law Hugo was killed.[218] Roger responded with a series of harvest-season raids in the province of Noto that were so destructive they created a serious famine in Sicily. In 1077 the count opportunistically accepted the surrenders of Trapani and Castronovo.[219] Two years later, Taormina fell, after a rare siege.[220]

IV

In the wake of his acquisition of Salerno, Robert turned his attention to the other side of the Adriatic and began to prepare for an invasion of the Byzantine empire. Ostensibly he was defending the interests of his daughter who in 1074 had been betrothed to Constantine Ducas, the son and heir of the emperor, Michael VII Ducas.[221] When Michael was ousted by Nicephorus III Botaneiates (1078–81) in March 1078, Robert felt justified in intervening on behalf of the Ducas family and his daughter, who had been confined to a nunnery.[222] In 1080, as preparations for the Norman invasion were nearing completion in Otranto, a man claiming to be the deposed Michael Ducas appeared in Salerno.[223] This coupled with the news that Nicephorus had himself been deposed by Alexius Comnenus (1081–1118) only fueled Robert's enthusiasm for the campaign.[224] He was able to secure the blessing of Gregory VII,[225] despite the fact that the pope was in serious need of Robert's assistance. In October 1080, Rudolf of Swabia, Gregory's choice as king of Germany, had been killed and the army of Mathilda of Tuscany had been beaten at Volta by forces loyal to Henry.[226] In February 1081 Gregory wrote to Desiderius asking him to determine whether or not Robert Guiscard was prepared to commit himself and his resources to the defense of the pope.[227] In a second letter to Desiderius (May 1081), Gregory expressed his concern about rumors that Robert Guiscard and Henry IV had agreed to a marriage alliance.[228] But in truth, Robert would let neither the emperor nor the pope distract him from his Balkan project.[229] He sent only envoys to Rome.[230]

Robert sent Bohemond on ahead with part of the fleet to secure the area around Avlona.[231] After designating his son Roger Borsa as his heir and placing him in charge of his Italian holdings—with the support of Robert of Loritello and Gerard of Buonalbergo—Robert set sail from Otranto in May 1081 and quickly secured Corfu.[232] He then sailed north toward Durazzo, suffering the loss of many ships and provisions in a storm.[233] By mid-June Robert and Bohemond had begun their siege of the city.[234] Alexius Comnenus hastened to put together a relief force, buying time by enlisting the help of the Venetian navy.[235] In July the Venetians arrived and pinned down the Norman ships.[236] Alexius set out from Constantinople in August and made it to Durazzo in mid-October.[237] When the two sides engaged each other on October 18, the imperial troops almost pushed the Normans—fighting under the papal banner Robert had received at Ceprano[238]—into the sea, but, distracted by their premature quest for booty, they suffered a decisive reversal. George Palaeologus, the commander of the Greek garrison in Durazzo, was killed in the battle and Alexius was forced to flee for his life.[239] Robert then came to terms with Domenico, one of the Venetian leaders of Durazzo, and in February 1082 the Normans entered the city.[240]

Robert wrote of his success to Gregory, who at the time was hard pressed by Henry. The German king had set up his camp outside of Rome at about the same time that Robert had sailed from Otranto, though he had withdrawn after an unsuccessful attempt to win Roman favor.[241] Henry returned to Rome in March 1082 in the company of Guibert, the archbishop of Ravenna who had been elected pope (Clement III) by the German bishops. Henry lacked the manpower to install the new pontiff,[242] but the king's presence itself was enough to incite yet another rebellion on the part of Robert's allies and vassals. The players and the places involved in this newest Apulian rebellion were almost identical to those involved in the last.[243] Upon learning of this situation,[244] Robert, whose forces had advanced all the way to Kastoria, delegated the command of the Balkan expedition to Bohemond and Bryennius and left immediately for Italy, landing at Otranto in April 1082. He headed directly for Rome, but Henry had already retreated to Lombardy, so he returned to Apulia and, with his brother Roger's help, struggled to suppress the revolt.[245]

Meanwhile, in early June 1083, Henry's troops, which had returned to Rome yet again earlier that year, had managed to occupy the Leonine city,[246] forcing Gregory to retire to the Castel Sant'Angelo, where he awaited his deliverance at the hands of the Normans. The ensuing stand-off lasted until March 1084, when a number of cardinals and Roman aristocrats shifted allegiance to Henry and invited the king into the city. Henry occupied the Lateran palace and oversaw the denunciation of Gregory and the election of Clement III in his place. Henry then received the imperial crown from the new pope on Easter Day.

When Henry learned in May 1084 that Robert was approaching Rome with a formidable army, he retreated from the city.[247] After overcoming the imperial garrison in a pitched battle on the streets of Rome,[248] Robert made his way to the Castel Sant'Angelo, rescued the pope, and restored him to the Lateran palace. But in the process the Norman troops pillaged and burned the area around the Lateran palace and the Coliseum and killed many Roman citizens.[249] In July, he escorted Gregory, whose position in Rome had been rendered untenable thanks to the destructive behavior of his Norman allies, to Montecassino, Benevento, and finally Salerno, where he consecrated the new cathedral dedicated to St. Matthew and convened a council condemning Henry and Clement.[250]

Rather than pressing on toward Constantinople in his father's absence, Bohemond had pushed south to Joannina. There he had defeated a second imperial army in May 1082.[251] As a result, many other cities in the region surrendered to the Normans and by the end of autumn, Bohemond was besieging Larissa.[252] But the following spring (1083), Alexius was back and this time he succeeded in luring Bohemond and the bulk of his army away from the Norman camp at Larissa long enough for the Greeks to overcome the Normans that had been left behind to guard it.[253] Bohemond and his men returned to find Alexius and his men safely inside the city. Determining that the pillaged countryside could not sustain another siege, and being hampered by a lack of funds with which to pay his soldiers, Bohemond withdrew to Avlona and sailed for Italy, leaving Bryennius at Kastoria. Shortly thereafter a Venetian fleet managed to retake the poorly garrisoned Durazzo. A few months later, as a result of Alexius's promises to pay back wages if the Norman garrison came over to his side, Bryennius was forced to abandon Kastoria.

Undaunted by these reversals, Robert and his two sons prepared a new Balkan expedition that sailed from Brindisi in September 1084.[254] After a two month delay because of bad weather, they succeeded in repelling the Byzantine and Venetian fleets that were attempting to retake Corfu. The Normans then set up camp at Vonitsa to wait out the winter, but their ranks were thinned by an epidemic. Bohemond became ill and was forced to return to Italy to recuperate. The duke himself was stricken while on his way to Cephalonia to assist Roger Borsa in his effort to take the island.[255] On July 17 1085, Robert Guiscard died on Cephalonia. Knowing that Bohemond, Robert's first-born son—albeit by his since repudiated first wife—was already in Italy, Roger Borsa, the designated heir, abandoned the Balkan campaign and wasted little time in returning home with the body of his father. Robert was buried with his half-brothers in the church of the monastery of the Holy Trinity at Venosa.[256]

V

The tenuousness of Roger Borsa's position made the assistance of his uncle, Count Roger of Sicily, indispensible. In exchange for his help, the count asked for and received full jurisdiction over the Calabrian fortresses that he had formerly shared with Robert.[257] After reaching this agreement, the count returned to Sicily to resume a siege of Syracuse, which had been initiated in response to the emir Benarvet's raids against Nicotera and various ecclesiastical targets near Reggio and Squillace.[258] Shortly thereafter the city capitulated (1085). The emir's widow—Benarvet having drowned during the initial assault on the city—and son sought refuge in Noto.[259] Roger was, at this time, given a second opportunity to participate in a Pisan naval attack, this time aimed at the African coast adjacent to Sicily, but he declined out of respect for a treaty that he had previously arranged with the emir of that region, Temim.[260]

Count Roger and Jordan followed up their success in Syracuse with a siege of Agrigento (April 1086) which was, in the absence of its emir Hamud, garrisoned by forces loyal to his wife. The city opened its gates the following July.[261] From there the Norman army moved on to Castrogiovanni, where Roger secretly negotiated the city's surrender with Hamud. The emir and his family agreed to convert to Christianity and were relocated, having been given territory in Calabria near Mileto.[262] In control of all of Sicily with the exception of Noto and Butera, Roger set out to reorganize the ecclesiastical administration of the island, overseeing the construction of churches and appointing a number of bishops to key positions. These included Gerland of Savoy as bishop of Agrigento, Stephen of Rouen as bishop of Mazara, Stephen of Provence as bishop of Syracuse, and Angerius of Brittany as bishop of Catania. Count Roger then set out to revitalize monasticism in Sicily by importing large numbers of monks from the mainland.[263] Roger jealously guarded his control of ecclesiastical affairs in Sicily to the point that, in July 1098, he succeeded in securing for himself and his heirs the title of papal legate to Sicily.[264]

While the count was thus preoccupied with his Sicilian campaigns, Bohemond was doing everything he could to weaken his half-brother's position in Apulia. Using Oria as his base, he launched raids throughout the provinces of Taranto and Otranto. Due to a shortage of revenues, Roger Borsa had difficulty organizing an effective offensive against his half-brother. So in early 1086 the half-brothers negotiated a settlement whereby Bohemond would get Oria, Taranto, Otranto, and Gallipoli, plus the territory and feudal service of Geoffrey of Conversano.[265] Beginning in March 1086, Bohemond's name appears alongside Roger Borsa's on a number of ducal charters.[266] But this did not end Roger Borsa's difficulties with his half-brother. Miera, son of Hugh Falloc, had taken advantage of the death of Robert Guiscard and seized the ducal fortress of Maida, to go along with the lands he had inherited from his father. Subsequently he presented himself before Bohemond and did homage to him for his holdings.[267] For his own part, Bohemond successfully negotiated the surrender of the ducal city of Cosenza, promising to besiege and destroy the ducal fortress near the city. Roger Borsa again decided that a negotiated settlement was his best option and finally managed to get Bohemond to meet him. In the end, Bohemond received both Maida and Cosenza, though he quickly gave the latter to the duke in exchange for Bari.[268]

Roger Borsa's problems with Bohemond made it difficult for him to play a significant role in the selection of the new pope following Gregory VII's death in Salerno in May 1085. The antipope Guibert (Clement III) had steadily gained support since taking over the Lateran Palace in March of 1084. After months of negotiation, the reform party finally decided on the reluctant Desiderius of Montecassino, who came to Rome in May 1086 with Jordan of Capua and his army as an escort. But a few short days after his formal election and before his consecration, the new pope—Victor III—was forced out of the city by pro-imperial factions.[269] He responded by renouncing his own election and returning to Montecassino. There followed another period of indecision as different factions of the reform party supported different would-be popes. For his part, Roger Borsa was willing to offer his support to any candidate willing to respect his choice of Alfano as archbishop of Salerno. This turned out to be Victor who, after initially refusing to comply with the duke's wishes, finally relented out of fear that he would lose a powerful Norman ally. In March 1087, with the encouragement of Jordan, Victor convened a synod in Capua and reassumed the papacy. The following May, the Norman forces loyal to him escorted him north again, forcing Clement to abandon the Lateran palace. Victor was finally consecrated at that time. The situation in Rome was still not stable enough for him to stay there, so he divided the few months of life that he had left between Rome and Montecassino, where he died in September, 1087.[270]

Count Roger returned to Sicily in the spring of that year and undertook a siege of Butera. While there he received news that the new pope, Urban II, wanted to meet him at Troina. According to Geoffrey Malaterra, the pope wanted to discuss matters related to the Latin-Greek ecclesiatical schism. Urban, who already had the support of Jordan of Capua, probably also saw this as an opportunity to talk about the Sicilian church and to enlist Roger's aid against the forces loyal to Clement III that were keeping him out of Rome. After meeting with the pope, Count Roger returned to the siege and saw it to a successful conclusion, relocating the leaders of Butera to Calabria for security reasons.[271] In February 1090, Roger received an embassy from Noto—the last of the Muslim hold-outs in Sicily—suing for peace. Shortly afterward, the widow and son of the emir Benarvet left Noto for North Africa and Jordan entered the city. The Norman conquest of Sicily was essentially complete.

1090 also saw significant changes on the mainland, beginning with the death of Jordan of Capua in November. A short time later, Jordan's wife, acting as regent for her three young sons, was forced into exile in Aversa when Lombard factions took control of the city.[272] At the same time, Roger Borsa was having a difficult time imposing his authority over Apulia and Calabria. He was forced increasingly to rely on the assistance of his uncle, a situation that, like his treaties with Bohemond, cost the young duke a great deal of power. Thus while Count Roger was preparing for a naval campaign against Malta, he was forced to put down uprisings in Acerenza and Cosenza on behalf of his nephew.[273]   Once Roger had returned from the expedition, having made the Muslim ruler of Malta a tributary, he was obliged to assist the duke again, suppressing another rebellion in Cosenza.[274] When the city finally capitulated in July 1091, the count received a half share in its revenues.

1091 brought the death of the other Jordan, Count Roger's son, from a fever contracted in Syracuse. The fact that Roger had already lost his son Geoffrey to leprosy meant that he no longer had any direct male heirs.[275] But the following year (1093), Roger's third wife Adelaide gave birth to a son, Simon, who was immediately named heir.[276] Two years later, she gave birth to another son named Roger. That same year it looked as if Roger Borsa would succumb to a fever.[277] Bohemond responded to the news of the duke's failing health by soliciting oaths of fidelity from his vassals so that they would recognize him as regent on behalf of the duke's young son.[278] If Bohemond's intentions were to take control of the duchy himself, he was prevented by Roger's timely recovery.[279]

Duke Roger had recourse to his uncle's assistance again when the people of Amalfi rebelled in 1096.[280] The ensuing siege, by both land and sea, was subverted by the premature departure of Bohemond who, responding to Urban's famous appeal for an expedition to Jerusalem, saw his chance to resume his father's campaigns against the Byzantine empire.[281] But if in the short run the crusade seemed counter to ducal interests, it ultimately contributed to Apulian stability by removing Bohemond and a significant number of other perennially disruptive vassals from southern Italy.[282]

Count Roger also intervened on behalf of Richard, the son of Jordan of Capua, in his effort to enforce his claim to Capua. In exchange for his help, the count would receive Naples. For his part, Roger Borsa had actually managed to get the young Richard to swear homage to him in exchange for his support. The count arrived in 1098 with a large, mostly Muslim, army and made his way to Capua. During the siege Urban II came to Capua hoping to act as a mediator. His efforts came to naught and he predictably blessed the military efforts of the Norman coalition before retiring to Benevento. Shortly after, Capua surrendered and Richard (II) assumed control of the city as a vassal of the duke of Apulia.[283]

Two years later, on June 22, 1101, Roger died in Mileto. He was succeeded by his eight-year-old son Simon, under the regency of his widow, Adelaide. When Simon died two years later (1103), his younger brother Roger succeeded him. Though Roger II did not achieve his majority until 1112 or exercise any notable level of dominance in Sicily or Calabria until the 1120s, he did manage to secure, in 1128, his own succession to Apulia and Capua after the death of his cousin, Duke William (1111–1127), the son and heir of Roger Borsa. This, as it turned out, was the first step toward the establishment of the Norman "Kingdom of the Two Sicilies," which was recognized—under considerable duress—by Innocent II in 1139. The kingdom—which over time came to exercise its authority over all of the Norman principalities in southern Italy—would remain under Norman control until its absorption by the Hohenstaufen emperor Henry VI in 1194.[284]

Notes

1. For a recent overview of pre-Norman southern Italian history, see Barbara Kreutz's *Before the Normans: Southern Italy in the Ninth and Tenth Centuries* (Philadelphia: University of Pennsylvania Press, 1991).

2. CMCas 2.37, pp. 236–38; Lupus Proto. a. 1009, p. 57; *Ann. Barenses* a. 1011, p. 52; Amatus 1.26, p. 35.

3. Although there are a number of reports of Saracen raids in this general period, the only other sources that refer to an attack on Salerno place it in 1016. *Ann. Beneventani* a. 1016, p. 117; Lupus Proto. a. 1016, p. 57. It is conceivable that Melo coordinated his first rebellion with Saracen raids on Apulia. Lupus Protospatarius (a. 1009, p. 57) and the *Annales Barenses* (a. 1011, p. 53) report Saracen attacks in the very same entries that record Melo's first rebellion. Chalandon, *Histoire de la domination* 1:43.

4. Robert I did not, in fact, become count of Normandy until 1027. His predecessor Richard II ruled from 996 until 1026.

5. Amatus 1.17–20, pp. 21–27.

6. Monte Gargano was a logical enough focus of a Norman pilgrimage (though perhaps not as early as the second decade of the eleventh century: Einar Joranson, "The Inception of the Career of the Normans in Italy: Legend and History," *Speculum* 23 (1948), pp. 367–68). According to tradition, Aubert, the eighth-century founder of Mont-Saint-Michel, had brought back to France a piece of Michael's red cloak which he had acquired at Monte Gargano. AASS Sept VIII c. 76–79. See: Jean Décarreaux, *Normands, papes, et moines. Cinquante ans de conquêtes et de politique religieuse en Italie méridionale et en Sicile (milieu de XIe siècle-debut du XIIe)* (Paris: A. J. Picard, 1974), p. 24.

7. William 1.12–46, pp. 99–100.

8. This is the gist of the thesis offered by Joranson in his article: "The Inception of the Career of the Normans in Italy: Legend and History," *Speculum* 23

(1948): 353–96.

9. Joranson, "The Inception," pp. 370–71.

10. Glaber 3.3, pp. 98–99.

11. Adhemar 3.55, p. 178.

12. This is Hartmut Hoffmann's principal complaint about Joranson's thesis. Hoffman is more inclined to accept a version of Amatus's account. "Die Anfänge der Normannen in Süditalien," *Quellen und Forschungen aus italienischen Archiven und Bibliotheken* 49 (1969): 95–144.

13. CMCas 2.37, p. 239.

14. Lupus Proto. a. 1018, p. 57; William 1.92–94, p. 104; CMCas 2.37, p. 240.

15. William 1.97, p. 104; CMCas 2.37, p. 240; Lupus Proto. a. 1019, p. 57.

16. Where, according to Amatus (1.22–23, p. 30), other Normans attracted by the reports of the pilgrims had come.

17. Amatus 1.23, p. 32; William 1.136, 1.143–44, p. 107; CMCas 2:37 p. 240.

18. Odon Delarc, *Les Normands en Italie depuis les premières invasions jusqu'a l'avènement de S. Grégoire VII (859–862; 1016–1073)* (Paris: E. Leroux, 1883), p. 57.

19. Amatus 1.25, p. 34.

20. Technically referred to as Pandulf V. Hence Pandulf IV's son will be known as Pandulf VI.

21. Amatus 1.29, p. 39; CMCas 2.42, p. 246.

22. CMCas 2.41, p. 245; Amatus 1.31, p. 41.

23. Guaimar's wife, Gaitelgrima, was Pandulf's sister.

24. Amatus 1.34, p. 45; CMCas 2:56, p. 274.

25. CMCas 2.56, p. 275.

26. Amatus 1.34, p. 45; CMCas 2:56, p. 275.

27. Pandulf V fled to Rome. CMCas 2:56, p. 275; *Ann. Beneventani*, a. 1028, p. 178.

28. Amatus 1.41, p. 52; CMCas 2:56, p. 275.

29. According to Amatus (1.20, p. 25), he was a brother of Gilbert Buatère and one of the original Norman immigrants.

30. Amatus 1.42, p. 53; CMCas 2:56, p. 275; Ord. Vit. 4.13, 2:281.

31. William 1.180, p. 109.

32. See Chalandon, *Histoire de la domination* 1:75–76.

33. CMCas 2.56, p. 276.

34. CMCas 2:57, p. 277.

35. She was also the daughter of the ruler of Amalfi, who had married one of Pandulf IV's sisters.

36. Amatus 1.44–45, pp. 55–56.

37. Amatus 1.45, p. 56.

38. Amatus 2.4, pp. 60–61. Conrad's campaign may have been in part a response to requests for assistance on the part of Guaimar V. Amatus tells us that the wife of the duke of Sorrento—who happened to be the sister-in-law of Guaimar V—had been repudiated by her husband and so sought refuge in Capua, where Pandulf subsequently took advantage of her daughter. Amatus 2.3, p. 59.

39. CMCas 2.63, pp. 291–93; Amatus 2.5–6, pp. 62–63; Desiderius 1.9, p. 1123.

40. CMCas 2.63, pp. 292–93; Amatus 2.6, p. 63.

41. Amatus 2.6, p. 64.

42. Geoffrey 1.4–6, pp. 9–10; Amatus 2.8, p. 67. Humphrey probably came later than William and Drogo, as he is not mentioned in Amatus's account of the initial distribution of land in Apulia. Nor, for that matter, does his name appear in Geoffrey Malaterra's earliest references to the sons of Tancred in Italy (Geoffrey 1.9, p. 12). Tancred's sons by Muriella were William, Drogo, Humphrey, Geoffrey, and Serlo. His sons by Fressenda were Robert, Mauger, another William, Auvrai, Tancred, Humbert, and Roger.

43. Geoffrey 1.6, p. 10.

44. Amatus 2.8, pp. 66–67, 2.14, p. 72; William 1.202–5, p. 111; Geoffrey 1.6–7, pp. 10–11.

45. William 1.206–18, p. 111; Amatus 2.14, p. 72; Geoffrey 1.8, pp. 11–12.

46. Lupus Proto. a. 1038, p. 43.

47. Lupus Proto. a. 1041, p. 58. Amatus 2.18, p. 76; CMCas 2.66, p. 299; William 1.222–41, pp. 111–12.

48. Amatus 2.20, pp. 78–79; CMCas 2.66, p. 299; William 1.245, p. 112; CBN a. 1041, c. 1083.

49. Lupus Proto. a. 1041, p. 58.

50. *Ann. Barenses* a. 1041, p. 54; Geoffrey 1.9–10, pp. 12–13; Amatus 2.21–23, pp. 79–83; William 1.254–307, pp. 112–14; Lupus Proto. a. 1041, p. 58; CBN a. 1042, c. 1083.

51. *Ann. Barenses* a. 1042, p. 54; Lupus Proto. a. 1042, p. 58; Amatus 2.24–25, pp. 87–90; William 1.350–95, pp. 118–20; Geoffrey 1.10, p. 13.

52. Amatus 2.23, p. 76.

53. *Ann. Barenses* a. 1042, p. 55; Amatus 2.28, p.76; William 1.418–40, pp. 120–22.

54. *Ann. Barenses* a. 1042, p. 56; Lupus Proto. a. 1042, p. 58; William 1.479, pp. 124; Amatus 2.28. pp. 92–93.

55. Amatus 2.29, pp. 93–94.

56. That is, Guy of Sorrento's daughter. Amatus 2.29, pp. 93–94; CMCas 2.66, p. 300; CBN (a. 1045, c. 1083) refers to William as the *primus comes Apuliae* but Guaimar himself assumed the title of "duke of Apulia and Calabria" in February 1043: Ernesto Pontieri, *I Normanni nell'Italia meridionale*, 2nd ed. (Naples: Libreria scientifica editrice, 1964): 113; Chalandon, *Histoire de la domination* 1:105.

57. Amatus 2.31, pp. 95–96.

58. Son of the older Asclettin, Rainulf's younger brother and one of the original émigrés.

59. Amatus 2.32–34, pp. 97–101; CMCas 2.66, p. 301.

60. Amatus 2.36, pp. 103–4.

61. Amatus 2.35, p. 101; Lupus Proto. a. 1046, p. 43; Geoffrey, 1.12, p. 14; William 2.22–25, p. 132.

62. Amatus 2.35, pp. 101–2.

63. These difficulties led Richer to seek an audience with Henry III, whom he asked for assistance in reestablishing order in southern Italy. CMCas 2.69, p. 306.

64. CMCas 2.69–71, pp. 307–12; Desiderius 2.22, p. 1139; *Ann. Cav.* a. 1045, p. 189; Amatus 2.43, pp. 109–10.

65. Amatus 3.2–3, pp. 117–18; Hermann a. 1047, p. 126; CMCas 2.78, pp. 322–23.

66. Amatus, p. 118 n.; Pontieri, *I Normanni*, pp. 117–18.

67. Amatus 2.44, pp, 110–11.

68. Geoffrey 1.12, p. 14. Richard married Fredesenda, one of Tancred of Hauteville's daughters. Amatus 2.46, p. 112.

69. Amatus 3.12, p. 127; Pontieri, *I Normanni*, p. 136.

70. Amatus 3.13, p. 127.

71. Amatus 3.7, pp. 120–21; Geoffrey 1.12, p. 14; CBN a. 1048, c. 278.

72. Amatus 3.7, p. 121; Geoffrey 1.16, pp. 16–17.

73. Geoffrey 1.17, pp. 17–18; Amatus 3.10, pp. 122–25; cf. *Alexiad*, pp. 54–57.

74. Amatus 3.11, pp. 125–26.

75. For other references to early Calabrian campaigns, see CBN a. 1048, 1052, 1055, c. 1083–84.

76. Amatus 3.16, p. 130.

77. Amatus 3.17–18, pp. 132–33.

78. Lupus Proto. a. 1051, p. 59; William 2.75–76, p. 136; Geoffrey 1.13, pp. 14–15; Amatus 3.19, 3.22, pp. 133, 135–37.

79. Chalandon, *Histoire de la domination* 1:130.

80. Amatus 3.23, pp. 138–39.

81. Amatus 3.24, pp. 139–40.

82. Amatus 3.25, pp. 140–41.

83. Amatus 3.28, pp. 142–45.

84. Amatus 3.29, p. 146.

85. Amatus 3.30, p. 146.

86. Amatus 3.34, p. 149.

87. Amatus 3.31, pp. 147–48.

88. Amatus 3.32, pp. 148.

89. *Ann. Beneventani* a. 1053, pp. 179–80; William 2.70–74, pp. 134–36.

90. Amatus 3.40, p. 155; William 2.122–38, p. 138.

91. Amatus 3.40, pp. 154–56.

92. William 2.196–266, pp. 142-46; Bonizo, p. 589; Hermann a. 1053, p. 132; CBN a. 1053, c. 1084; CMCas 2.84, pp. 332–33; Amatus 3.40–41. pp. 154–58.

93. Leo IX, *Epistola* 103, PL 143:779–80.

94. Hermann's account, written in 1054 (five years before the Treaty of Melfi), is the best evidence that Leo and the Normans actually did arrive at some sort of agreement in Benevento.

95. Geoffrey 1.14, p. 15.

96. J. N. D. Kelly, *The Oxford Dictionary of Popes* (Oxford: Oxford University Press, 1986), p. 147.

97. Amatus 3.47, p. 163.

98. CMCas 2.86, pp. 335–36; *Ann. Rom.* p. 334; Amatus 3.48, pp. 163-64.

99. The widow of the marquis Boniface of Tuscany.

100. CMCas 2.91–92, pp. 347–51; Cowdrey, *Age of Abbot Desiderius*, pp. 57–58.

101. Amatus 3.49–50, pp. 165–67; CMCas 3.9, pp. 270–71.

102. Geoffrey, about whom little is known, was Robert's only surviving older brother. Robert had two younger ones in Italy at the time: William, count of the Principata, and Mauger, count of the Capitanata.

103. Kelly, *Popes*, p. 150; Benzo 2.15, p. 618; CMCas 2.97, p. 355; Amatus 3.52, pp. 169–70.

104. Godfrey was not as eager to help now that his brother was dead.

105. Cowdrey, *Age of Abbot Desiderius*, p. 117.

106. *Ann. Rom.* p. 335.

107. Traditionally the pope was elected by the "acclamation" of the clergy and nobility of Rome, but this played into the hands of local factions. Imperial intervention since the time of Otto I was based on the emperor's claim to the title "Patrician of Rome," that is, as a delegate representing the Roman people.

108. Bonizo, p. 593; William 2.387–405, pp. 152–54; CBN a. 1059, c. 1085; Romuald a. 1060, p. 406.

109. Léon-Robert Ménager, ed. *Recueil des actes des ducs normands d'Italie (1046–1127)*, I: *Les prémiers ducs (1046–1087)*, Società di storia patria per la Puglia, documenti e monografie, 45 (Bari: Grafica Bigiemme, 1980) pp. 30–32. See also Josef Deér, *Papsttum und Normannen. Untersuchungen zu ihren Lehnrechtlichen und kirchenpolitischen Beziehungen* (Cologne: Böhlau, 1972), p. 66.

110. Décarreaux, *Normands, papes, et moines*, pp. 83–84.

111. William 2.400–402, pp. 154. Interestingly enough, neither Amatus (4.3, pp. 182–85) nor Geoffrey Malaterra (1.34–35, pp. 23–24) mentions Melfi. They simply report that Robert began calling himself duke of Apulia and Calabria.

112. Amatus 4.8, p. 188.

113. Amatus 4.11, pp. 189–90; CMCas 3.15, pp. 378–79.

114. CMCas 3.8, p. 369.

115. He was installed on Easter, 1058, after Abbot Frederick of Lorraine's—or Stephen IX's—death in late March.

116. Amatus 4.13, pp. 191–92; CMCas 3.15, p. 379.

117. Romuald a. 1057, p. 405; William 2.368–72, p. 152.

118. Geoffrey 1.21–27, pp. 19–21.

119. Geoffrey 1.27–29, pp. 21–22; CBN a. 1058, c. 1058.

120. Geoffrey 1.34, p. 23; Amatus 4.3, pp. 182–84.

121. William of Apulia (2.382–83, 2.406–15, pp. 152–54) reported it differently.

122. Geoffrey 1.30, p. 22; Amatus 4.18, pp. 194–95; William 2.414–32, p. 154.

123. Amatus 4.23, p. 197.

124. Anselm of Lucca had studied at the Norman monastery at Bec.

125. Benzo 7.2, p. 270.

126. CMCas 3.19, pp. 385–86.

127. Chalandon, *Histoire de la domination* 1:213.

128. Kelly, *Popes*, pp. 153–54; *Ann. Rom.*, p. 396.

129. Kelly, *Popes*, p. 154.

130. Amatus 4.28–29, pp. 202–4; *Ann. Beneventani* a. 1062, p. 180; Romuald

a. 1062, p. 406.

131. Lupus Proto. a. 1066, p. 59; CMCas 3.23, p. 389.

132. Amatus 6.9, p. 270.

133. Amatus 6.24–29, pp. 286–89.

134. In 1066 the abbot began work on the new basilica and relied on the security provided by the Normans to expedite the completion of the project. Cowdrey, *Age of Abbot Desiderius*, p. 121.

135. Amatus 4.43, p. 214–16.

136. Geoffrey 2.1, p. 29.

137. CBN a. 1060, c. 1085.

138. Geoffrey (2.3, p. 30) and Amatus (5.8, pp. 229–30) both place the meeting in Reggio, though Amatus replaces Roger with Robert. Ibn al-Athir (Amari 1:275) has the meeting take place in Mileto.

139. Geoffrey 2.4–6, pp. 30–31. Amatus (5.9–10, pp. 231–33) has Robert Guiscard sending Geoffrey Ridel as the expedition leader along with Roger.

140. Geoffrey 2.8–10, pp. 31–32; Amatus 5.13–18, pp. 234–37.

141. Geoffrey 2.12, p. 33. Amatus 5.19, pp. 237–38.

142. Geoffrey 2.18, pp. 34–35.

143. Geoffrey 2.19, p. 35. The Grantmesnil family, an important one in Normandy, already had ties to the Hauteville clan: Robert of Grantmesnil's brother William had married one of Robert Guiscard's daughters. For more on Robert, see Ord. Vit. 3, 2:94–104.

144. Geoffrey 2.22, p. 36.

145. Geoffrey 2.21, 2.24–27, pp. 35–36, 37–39.

146. Geoffrey 2.29–30, pp. 39–41.

147. Geoffrey 2.32. pp. 41–42. Ibn al-Athir (Amari 1:448) says the relieving force from Africa was led by Ayub, son of the Zirid caliph Temim of Kairouan.

148. Geoffrey 2.33, pp. 42–45.

149. Geoffrey 2.34, p. 45. The subsequent and abortive Pisan attempt occurred on August 18, 1063 (*Annales Pisani*, MGH SS 19). Amatus (5.28, pp. 255–56) claims that Robert Guiscard solicited Pisan aid against Palermo while he was involved in Apulia.

150. CBN a. 1063, p. 1085.

151. Geoffrey 2.36, pp. 46–47; Amatus 5.26, pp. 246–48; Lupus Proto. a. 1065, p. 59.

152. Geoffrey 2.36, pp. 46–47.

153. Geoffrey 2.37, p. 47.

154. Robert's nephew, son of his sister.

155. Geoffrey's brother (Robert's nephew).

156. Robert's nephew, son of Humphrey.

157. Later, after entering imperial service, known as Jocelyn of Corinth.

158. Amatus 5.4, pp. 224–27; CBN a. 1064, c. 1085; William 2.450–53; p. 156.

159. Geoffrey 2.40, pp. 48–49; Amatus 5.27, pp. 248–55; CBN a. 1069, c. 1085; Lupus Proto. a. 1069, p. 60).

160. According to Ibn al-Athir, Ibn Hawas and Ayub had suffered a falling

out, the former being killed some time later (Amari 1:448). Hence, apparently, Roger's reference to the change of leaders in his speech to his men at Misilmeri (Geoffrey 2.41, p. 50).

161. Geoffrey 2.41, pp. 49–50.

162. Geoffrey 2.43, pp. 50–51.

163. Amatus 5.27, pp. 248–55; William 2.480, p. 158.

164. Geoffrey 2.40, pp. 48–49; William 2.522–27, p. 160; Lupus Proto. a. 1071, p. 60.

165. Lupus Proto. a. 1071, p. 60; William 2.532–39, pp. 160–62; Amatus 5.27, p. 251.

166. Geoffrey 2.40, pp. 48–49; William 2.543–71, p. 162.

167. Geoffrey 2.43, p. 51; Amatus 5.27, p. 253; William 2.540–42, 3.111–31, pp. 162, 170.

168. Lupus Proto. a. 1071, p. 60; William 3.142–44, p. 172.

169. William 3.145–62, p. 172.

170. CBN a. 1071, c. 1085.

171. Geoffrey 2.43, p. 51.

172. Amatus 6.14, pp. 276–77.

173. Amatus 6.17–19, pp. 278–82; William 3.204–81, pp. 174–78.

174. Lupus Proto. a. 1072, p. 60; CBN a. 1072, c. 1086; William 3.297–320, p. 180.

175. Geoffrey 2.45, pp. 52–53.

176. William 3.332–36, p. 182. This archbishop was replaced by the Latin Auger in April 1083.

177. Geoffrey 2.45, pp. 52–53. Amatus (6.21, p. 283) reports that Robert gave all of Sicily to Roger except half of Palermo, half of Messina, and half of the Valdemone.

178. Geoffrey 2.46, pp. 53–54.

179. Geoffrey 2.46, p. 54.

180. Amatus 7.1, 7.5, pp. 292–93, 296–97; William 3.355–66, pp. 182–84.

181. Pontieri, *I Normanni*, pp. 203–4.

182. Amatus 7.7, p. 297.

183. Amatus 7.31, pp. 326–30. Robert Loritello was the son of Robert Guiscard's brother Geoffrey.

184. Amatus 7.9–10, pp. 298–302.

185. Amatus 7.18, 7.20, 7.25, 8.24, pp. 310–11, 313–14, 316–17, pp. 373–74.

186. Gregory VII, *Register* 1.21a, 1.25, pp. 35–36, pp. 41–42. Amatus 7.10, p. 300.

187. Amatus 7.12, p. 303.

188. Gregory VII, *Register* 2.46, 2.49, pp. 169–71, 188–90. See H. E. J. Cowdrey, "Pope Gregory VII's 'Crusading' Plans of 1074," in *Outremer: Studies in the History of the Crusading Kingdom of Jerusalem Presented to Joshua Prawer*, ed. Benjamin Z. Kedar et al. (Jerusalem: Yad Izhak Ben Zvi Institute, 1982), pp. 27–40. Gregory had received request for military aid from Michael VII Ducas in June 1073.

189. Gregory VII, *Register* 1.85a; Amatus 7.12–13, pp. 303–6; Bonizo, p. 602.

190. Amatus 7.13–14, pp. 305–7; cf. Bonizo, p. 604.

191. Amatus 7.27, pp. 320–21.

192. Gregory VII, *Register* 3.11; 3.15, pp. 271–72, 276–77.

193. Amatus 7.28–29, p. 322.

194. Amatus 8.14–15, pp. 354–57; William 3.425–27, p. 186.

195. Amatus 8.13, 8.15, pp. 353, 357.

196. Amatus 8.16–20, pp. 357–60; William 3. 427–44, p. 186.

197. William 3.475–76, p. 190; Amatus 8.8–9, pp. 348–50; Geoffrey 3.3, p. 58.

198. Amatus 8.22. p. 361; Gregory VII, *Register* 4.7, p. 305.

199. Amatus 8.22, p. 365.

200. Amatus 8.24, p. 366.

201. Amatus 8.24, 8.26–28, pp. 366, 367–69; William 3.445–50, p. 188.

202. Amatus 8.24, p. 366; William 3.451–55, p. 188.

203. Amatus 8.30–1, pp. 371–72; William 3.457–64, p. 188.

204. Amatus 8.25, pp. 366–67.

205. Amatus 8.32, p. 372; CMCas 3.45, p. 423; *Ann. Beneventani* a. 1077, p. 181.

206. Gregory VII, *Register* 5.14a, pp. 368–71; Amatus 8.33, pp. 372–73.

207. Amatus 8.33, pp. 372–73; CMCas 3.46–47; Chalandon, *Histoire de la domination* 1:251.

208. William 3.509–27, p. 192.

209. William 3.540–685, pp. 194–202; CBN a. 1079, c. 1086; Lupus Proto. a. 1080, p. 60.

210. Gregory VII, *Register* 7.14a, pp. 479–81.

211. CMCas 3.45, pp. 423–4.

212. Gregory VII, *Register* 8.16, pp. 525–26.

213.Gregory VII, *Register* 8.1a, pp. 514–15; see also Romuald a. 1080, p. 408; William 4.28–32, pp. 204–6; Bonizo p. 612. For the text of the oath, see Deér, *Papsttum und Normannen*, 116.

214. Cowdrey, *Age of Abbot Desiderius*, pp. 139–40.

215. William 4.71–2, p. 208; Gregory VII, *Register* 8.8, p. 521.

216. Geoffrey 3.8–9, p. 61.

217. Amari was unable to identify this emir. Michele Amari, *Storia dei musulmani di Sicilia*, 2nd ed., 3 vol. (Catania: R. Prampolini, 1933–39), 3:149 n.

218. Geoffrey 3.10, pp. 61–62.

219. Geoffrey 3.11–12, pp. 62–64.

220. Geoffrey 3.15–18, pp. 66–67.

221. *Alexiad* 1.12, pp. 57–58.

222. William 4.1–5, 4.73–75, 4.122–27, pp. 204, 208, 210.

223. Lupus Proto. a. 1080, p. 60; CBN a. 1081, c. 1086; Geoffrey 3.13, pp. 64–65; William 4.162, p. 212; *Alexiad* 1.12, pp. 58–60.

224. In December 1080, Robert sent an embassy to Constantinople to protest the treatment of his daughter, but before the legate could return, Nicephoras had been replaced by Alexius Comnenus (April 1081).

225. Gregory VII, *Register* 8.6, p. 519.

226. Cowdrey, *Age of Abbot Desiderius*, p. 145.

227. Gregory VII, *Register*, 9.4, p. 534.

228. Gregory VII, *Register* 9.11, p. 538; William 4.171–75, p. 213.

229. Nor the fact that the new emperor, Alexius Comnenus, was a long-time supporter of Michael Ducas.

230. William 4.177–78, p. 214.

231. *Alexiad* 1.14, p. 66.

232. CBN a. 1081, c. 1086; William 4.185–207, p. 214; Geoffrey 3.24, pp. 71–72; *Alexiad* 1.16, p. 69.

233. William 4.218–24, p. 216.

234. Lupus Proto. a. 1081, p. 60; *Alexiad* 3.12, pp. 132–33; William 4.243–56, pp. 216–18.

235. William 4.275–81, p. 218; *Alexiad* 4.2, p. 137.

236. William 4.295, p. 220.

237. *Alexiad* 4.5, p. 143; Lupus Proto. a. 1082, p. 61; Geoffrey 3.27, pp. 73–4.

238. William 4.408–9, p. 226; Romuald a. 1081, p. 409.

239. *Alexiad* 4.6, p. 150; William 4.432–33, p. 226.

240. *Alexiad* 5.1, p. 155; William 4.449–505, p. 228.

241. Henry, *Epistola* 16, pp. 74–76.

242. Henry, *Epistola* 17, pp. 76–82; Bonizo 9, pp. 613–14.

243. Geoffrey 3.34, pp. 77–78; William 4.506, p. 230.

244. Gregory was one of the ones who wrote him: Gregory VII, *Register*, 9.17, p. 541.

245. Geoffrey 3.34–36, pp. 77–79; Lupus Proto. a. 1082–83, p. 61; William 4.528–29, 5.106–8, 5.116–19, pp. 232, 242.

246. That portion of the city, containing the Vatican and Castel Sant'Angelo, which had been fortified by Leo IV after the Muslim sack of 846.

247. Geoffrey 3.34–37, pp. 77–80; Bonizo 9, pp. 614–15; Bernold a. 1084; William 4.547–49, p. 234; CMCas 3.53 434–35.

248. Bernold a. 1084; LP 2.290.

249. Bonizo.

250. *Ann. Beneventani* a. 1084, p. 182; William 4.554–57, 5.121–24; p. 234, 242; Geoffrey 3.37, pp. 79–80; CMCas 3.58, p. 438; Bernold a. 1084. According to Peter the Deacon (CMCas 3.53, pp. 434–35), Desiderius was with Gregory every step of the way until his death.

251. William 5.6–19, p. 236.

252. William 5.26, p. 236.

253. William 5.35–49, p. 238.

254. William 5.129–39, p. 242.

255. William 5.154–227, pp. 244–48.

256. William 5.401, p. 258.

257. Geoffrey 3.42, p. 82.

258. Geoffrey 4.1, p. 85.

259. Geoffrey 4.2, pp. 85–86.

260. Geoffrey 4.3, pp. 86–87.

261. Geoffrey 4.5, pp. 87–88.

262. Geoffrey 4.6, p. 88.

263. Geoffrey 4.7, pp. 88–90.

264. Geoffrey 4.29, pp. 106–8.

265. Geoffrey 4.4, p. 87.

266. Chalandon, *Histoire de la domination* 1:289.

267. Geoffrey 4.9, pp. 90–91.

268. Geoffrey 4.10, p. 91.

269. Roger Borsa's release of the imperial prefect of Rome, whom his father had captured during his expedition to Rome, seems to have been the precipitating factor behind the unrest. Roger's motives for this are unclear.

270. CMCas 3.65–67.

271. Geoffrey 4.13, pp. 92–93.

272. Geoffrey 4.26, p. 104.

273. Geoffrey 4.16, pp. 94–96.

274. From this point on, the count's Sicilian forces would include a large Saracen contingent. Geoffrey 4.17, pp. 96–97.

275. Geoffrey 4.18, pp. 97–98. Roger was married three times: (1) to Judith, daughter of William of Evreux, who gave birth to Adelaide and Emma; (2) to Eremburga, daughter of William of Mortain, who gave birth to Geoffrey and Jordan (Geoffrey 4.14); and (3) to Adelaide, daughter of Marquis Manfred, who gave birth to Simon and Roger. Other daughters are mentioned in the sources but without reference to their mothers' identities.

276. Geoffrey 4.19, p. 98.

277. Geoffrey 4.19, p. 98.

278. Louis was ten at the time (1093): Geoffrey 4.22, pp. 99–101.

279. Geoffrey 4.20, pp. 98–99.

280. Geoffrey 4.23, p. 101.

281. Geoffrey 4.24, pp. 102–4.

282. Chalandon, *Histoire de la domination* 1:302.

283. Geoffrey 4.28, p. 106.

284. For a recent and cogent overview of this period of Norman-Italian history, see Donald Matthew, *The Norman Kingdom of Sicily* (Cambridge: Cambridge University Press, 1992).

2. The Papacy and the Normans

The bishop of Rome and the abbot of Montecassino were the two church leaders most affected by the Norman conquests in southern Italy. This being the case, it is not surprising that the earliest recorded images of the Normans in that region come from papal and Casinese sources. Nor is it difficult, given the nature of early Norman activities in the south, to understand why such sources would consistently underscore the violence, barbarity, and political illegitimacy of the Normans. Such antagonistic portraits of the Normans would, in fact, dominate the literature of the period until the abbots and popes in turn realized that it made more sense to work with the Normans than to plot against them. In the case of Montecassino, this realization came in 1058, in the wake of Richard of Aversa's conquest of Capua. In the case of Rome, it was not until 1080 that Gregory VII definitively tied his fortunes with those of Robert Guiscard. We will discuss the evolution of Casinese images of the Normans in the next two chapters. Here our concern is to reconstruct and contextualize the images of the Normans that have come down to us in the papal sources.

If Raoul Glaber and Adhemar of Chabannes are to be believed, Benedict VIII (1012–24) was the first pope to become involved with the Normans in Italy. According to their accounts, the Norman Rodulf had come directly to Rome from Normandy, having incurred the wrath of his duke, and was then sent south by Benedict VIII to help in the the struggle against the Greeks. Such a scenario, as we have already observed, is plausible enough given what we can surmise about papal concern over recent Greek campaigns in Apulia and Calabria. But as it turned out, the same fears about the unification of southern Italy that might have led Benedict to embrace Rodulf and his like ultimately made Benedict's successors wish the Normans had never set foot in Italy. For once the Normans began creating their own lordships at the expense of the Greeks and Lombards, they became a source of papal concern every bit as worrisome as the Greeks and Lombards had been at different times in the past. Papal policy with regard to southern Italy remained consistent, at least for the time being: prevent its consolidation in the hands of any one single ruler. But by mid-century it was not the Greeks or the Lombards but the Normans who were threatening to achieve this dangerous level of hegemony in the region.

Leo IX was the first pope to confront the Norman problem. His attempt to resolve it militarily led to the rout of his papal army by an allied Norman force at Civitate in 1053. This defeat was a particularly hard one for many contemporary observers to swallow. At least one—the anonymous author of the appropriate entry in the papal catalogue—would not even admit that Leo's army had lost.

> With his admonition and preaching, Leo removed all of the Normans and the Franks who dwelled in the region of Apulia so as to destroy their pride, for their pride had grown to such an extent that they placed all of that region under their dominion, leaving the vicars of blessed Peter with nothing there under their own jurisdiction or dominion. *After the victory had been won* and all of the land had been handed over to Leo's dominion, the confessor of Christ returned to the city [of Rome] and passed on to Christ.[1]

The author's deft use of the ablative absolute—*victoria facta*—allowed him to avoid identifying the winner in the struggle, while simultaneously leaving the impression that it must have been Leo if, as the account made clear, the lands in question were finally restored to his dominion. In fact the idea that the territory was "handed over to Leo's jurisdiction" would appear to have been a simple exaggeration of Norman willingness to hold their land as a papal fief.

The other contemporaries who wrote about the battle of Civitate *did* acknowledge Leo's defeat but felt obliged to explain why it had happened. Some attributed it to the pope's unusually direct participation in the campaign, for Leo had not only organized the army but had accompanied it to battle. For those who supported Leo's efforts against simony and nicholaitism, however, this moralization of his defeat was unacceptable. They tended instead to assume an apologetic stance, trying to vindicate Leo by creating a context within which his dubious behavior would seem more reasonable. With few exceptions, this meant making the Normans look as bad as possible.

Probably the earliest account of Civitate is the letter that Leo himself wrote from his confinement to the emperor Constantine IX Monomachus in January 1054, in an attempt to win his support for a new anti-Norman campaign.[2] In the letter Leo attempted to justify his actions, explaining that he was simply reacting to Norman aggression against innocent people and churches in southern Italy. He had tried everything to make the Normans change their ways, but nothing had worked. Knowing full well that "princes carry swords not without reason but that for ministers of God, vengeance in anger is evil," Leo decided that he would best be able, as he put it, to "liberate the sheep of Christ" if he consulted with the secular powers whose task it was to punish malefactors. So he arranged to meet with the Byzantine catapan Argyro, "not because I was opting for the death of any Normans, or of any men, or that I was even entertaining it, but so that they, who had seemed so little frightened by divine judgement might immediately be brought back to their senses by human terror." But as it turned out, before Leo and his retinue could effect their rendezvous with Argyro, the Normans suddenly attacked. Leo did not bother to go into the painful details of the battle itself.

It is clear from the apologetic tone and content of the letter that Leo knew his own level of involvement in the expedition was, at least prima facie, open to criticism. He defended his actions on three separate grounds. First, he assured the emperor that he had not violated the proscriptions against clerical use of arms.[3] As Leo described it, he was simply on his way to confer with Argyro. If his retinue—Leo used the word *comitatus*—looked like an army it was only to frighten the Normans. Secondly, Leo portrayed his actions as being consistent with the pastoral duties of a bishop. "In so far as I am the vicar of the Apostolic See," wrote Leo, "I have labored to fulfill, with the small measure of my humility and ability, the dispensation committed to me, according to the divinely inspired words of Paul: 'Woe to me if I shall not have evangelized: the greatest necessity compels me to.'"[4] By "evangelization," Leo seems to have been referring to the shepherd-like security with which a bishop is supposed to provide his flock. Finally, and for our purposes most significantly, Leo exaggerated the threat posed by the Normans. He told the emperor that he had seen

an undisciplined and alien people with incredible and unheard of rage, rise up in every direction against the church of God with more than pagan impiety; killing Christians and afflicting many with novel and horrible tortures leading to the very expiration of their lives; sparing, with respect for the fragility of humanity, not infants, old people, or women; despoiling, burning, and tearing down the churches of the saints, recognizing no distinction between the holy and the profane.

Given the sheer magnitude of the threat that the Normans posed to the "church of God," Leo reasoned, it was perfectly understandable that he, as pope, should personally take charge of the church's defense. More specifically, if the Normans could be depicted as violators of the Peace of God—which by the time he was writing had spread to virtually every corner of Latin Christendom—then Leo could present his abortive expedition as something resembling the episcopally-sanctioned "posse" that was supposed to bring such malefactors to justice.

Leo was not the only one who felt compelled to defend direct papal involvement in the debacle at Civitate. Another was Archdeacon Wibert of Toul, who had known and worked closely with Leo in his pre-papal life as Bruno, bishop of Toul, and who wrote his *Vita Leonis IX* after the pope's death in 1054. Wibert had read Leo's letter and in fact quoted from it at length as he tried to place the actions of the pope—"that most pious shepherd concerned about the sheep committed to him by God and mercifully sympathizing with the unheard of affliction of the people of Apulia"—in a pastoral context.[5] Like Leo, Wibert did not dwell on the battle itself. Instead he developed the dénouement, recounting what happened when the victorious Normans—whom he bluntly referred to as that *pessima gens*—came to get the pope in the town of Civitate, where he was awaiting news of the battle. Much to the astonishment of the Normans, Leo lived up to his name and passed right through their midst "like a confident lion" on his way to Benevento. His fearlessness, Wibert wrote, "transformed the hearts of the Normans to his service, and, kissing his footsteps, they undeservedly sought his indulgence." As testimony to their change of heart, the Normans set about burying those whom they had killed in a nearby, dilapidated church, which they then reconstructed so that it might serve as a proper burial ground for such "martyrs," as Wibert termed them, who had "chosen to undergo a faithful death for the sake of the faith of Christ and the liberation of an afflicted people." According to Wibert, the Normans were so "terrified" by the signs, revelations, and miracles that graced these holy bodies, that they "dispensed with their cruelty and henceforth treated the peoples with whom they lived amicably as compatriots and served the venerable pope faithfully in complete subjection as long as he lived."

Notice how Wibert, in his desire to present Leo in the best possible light, shifted the focal point of his account of Civitate from the battle itself to the subsequent reconciliation. This allowed him to downplay the military victory won by the Normans and to underscore the moral victory won by Leo. Despite the loss of his army, the pope nevertheless demonstrated the courage and confidence of a successful commander, an attitude which transformed the haughty victors into docile, penitent losers. And, even more significantly, the power of the Normans on the battlefield was upstaged by the power of God working his miracles through the very ones that the Normans had supposedly vanquished.

The monk Hermann of Reichenau authored another contemporary account of the events at Civitate, but within the context of a chronicle rather than a papal biography. He was, as a result, not specifically concerned about salvaging Leo's reputation at the expense of the Normans. His *Chronicon*, a particularly valuable source of first-hand information about Henry III's reign, ends in 1054, making it likely that he was at work on the entry for 1053 at about the same time that Leo was writing to Constantine.[6] Hermann reported that Leo came to Henry seeking help against "the violence and injuries of the Normans, who held for themselves by compulsion and force the property of St. Peter, having conquered a great deal of it." The pope's goal was "the elimination of their nefarious and inextricable sins from that region and the liberation of the inhabitants from them." According to Hermann, Henry complied, sending a large number of "Teutons" with Leo to Rome.

Already preparing the reader for what lay ahead, Hermann noted that the motives of the Germans who followed the pope were not as pure as they might have been. Some were only following the orders of their superiors; others were hoping for some monetary gain; and others, "sinful and impudent," had been "expelled from their homeland as a result of various crimes." But Leo was in no position to quibble. "He clemently and graciously received all of them with the great compassion of his customary mercy, because he seemed to need their strength for the coming battle." But the pope was not, according to Hermann, entirely blameless for what happened at Civitate. For as he "moved his army against the Normans," his opponents sued for peace. "They promised to be subject to him and to serve him, and they said that they wanted to hold as a benefice from him whatever they had previously invaded and unjustly usurped for themselves." But Leo would not even entertain such an offer, insisting that they retreat completely from the property they had "seized from St. Peter." This was unacceptable to the Normans: "They refused to do what was proposed to them, regarding it as an impossibility because they had held that territory for a long time, and announced that they would rather go to war and defend with arms the land they had acquired through the exercise of arms even if it meant their deaths."

Hermann's Teutonic sympathies pervade his account of the ensuing battle. As he described it, the German contingent was about to overcome the Norman vanguard when the unexpected arrival of Norman reinforcements coupled with the flight of the Italian troops turned the tide and the "enemy won an exceedingly cruel victory." Like Leo, Hermann felt obliged to offer some tentative explanation for what he regarded as a "hidden judgement of God." There were, as he saw it, only two humanly comprehensible reasons for the Norman victory, the first being Leo's involvement in a "carnal fight for transitory things" rather than a spiritual struggle "more fitting for a priest." The second: the motives of the "nefarious men" who rushed to Leo's side "for the sake of the remission of their sins or in pursuit of an avaricious quest."

Compared to Leo's account, Hermann's is much less hard on the Normans. It is true that he regarded their "violence and injuries" as the precipitating factor in the incident. But he did not transform them into any paradigm of secular despotism or rapine. On the contrary, he attributed to them an understandable and reasonable reluctance to sacrifice the lands that they had struggled for so long to control. In contrast to Wibert's version, Hermann's was much more critical of the pope. He seemed to side with the Normans when they offered to hold their lands as papal vassals, underscoring the obstinacy of Leo, whose unwillingness to compromise spoiled a perfect opportunity for a peaceful settlement.

The six years that passed between the Battle of Civitate and the Synod of Melfi saw, as we noted in the previous chapter, a number of attempts on the part of Leo IX and his successors to generate imperial interest in another anti-Norman campaign. As Henry III's chancellor, Bishop Gebhard of Eichstätt had opposed imperial involvement in Leo's anti-Norman campaign. But as Pope Victor II, he decided that Leo may have had the right idea after all. Only the brevity of his pontificate prevented him from orchestrating a new alliance. His successor, Stephen IX, who, as Frederick of Lorraine, had been with Leo at Civitate, also planned an anti-Norman expedition with Greek and German support. But he too died before his plans came to fruition.

Nicholas II broke new ground when he decided that the Normans might, in fact, prove to be a useful counterbalance to the Italian aristocracy not to mention the as-yet minor German king, Henry IV, whom he anticipated would not endorse an election decree that effectively removed him from the process of selecting the pope. The text of the oath that Robert Guiscard swore to Nicholas at Melfi has survived:

> I, Robert, by grace of God and St. Peter, duke of Apulia and Calabria and, once both of these are subdued, future duke of Sicily, from this hour on will be faithful to the holy Roman church and to you, lord Pope Nicholas. I will not be part of any plan or action from which you might lose either life or limb or be captured with evil deceit. I will not divulge to your injury any counsel with which you have entrusted me and which you have forbidden me to reveal. I will assist the holy Roman church in holding and acquiring the *regalia* of St. Peter and his possessions in so much as I am able against all men. I will help you so that you may securely and honorably hold the Roman papacy and the land and principate of St. Peter, and I will not seek to invade or acquire it, nor will I presume to plunder without your explicit approval or that of your successors, except that which you concede to me or is conceded to me by your successors. I will, with good faith, be diligent about the *pensio* with regard to the land of St. Peter which I hold or will hold, as it has been established, so that the Roman church will have it annually. And I will hand over to your jurisdiction all of the churches that remain under my dominion along with their possessions, and I will be their defender in fidelity to the holy Roman church. And if you or your successors should leave this life before me, I will assist, as I am instructed by the greater cardinals, Roman clerics and laymen, so that a pope can be elected and ordained to the honor of St. Peter. I will observe all of the above written to the holy Roman church and to yourself with good faith, and I will observe this fidelity to your successors, ordained to the

honor of St. Peter, who will invest me with what was conceded to me by you. Thus may God and these holy gospels assist me.[7]

As Josef Deér has shown, the first part of the oath (here, the first four sentences) closely resembles the first part of the oath normally sworn to a pope by a metropolitan bishop.[8] But the second part is very different. In place of the episcopally-specific section regarding the proper treatment of papal legates and expectations about synodal attendance, Nicholas inserted a prohibition against military encroachment on papal territory and promises not only to promote papal jurisdiction over Norman churches but to protect the papal election process. There is, in short, little in the wording of this oath, aside from the recognition of Robert's titles, that served to place the Normans on any higher level of respectability. The tone is negative and proscriptive, explicitly spelling out what the Normans, as papal vassals, should *not* do.

While the Treaty of Melfi might appear to have been a real watershed in papal-Norman relations, its tangible effects were, as we saw in the first chapter, few. The problem with the treaty, as Deér has observed, was that while the popes regarded it as an act of investment *gratia Sancti Petri* that justified papal expectations of Norman service, the Normans—particularly Robert Guiscard—seemed to see it solely as a means of securing some form of legitimation for their conquests.[9] As a result papal visions of utilizing the military might of its new vassals for its own purposes never really materialized. It is true that Richard of Capua responded to requests for assistance from Nicholas II and Alexander II by sending troops to Rome. But his own territorial interests in the Ceprano region ultimately tainted his relationship with the papacy.

For our purposes, the important point in all this is that despite the official alliance forged between Nicholas II and the Normans at Melfi in 1059, there is no evidence of any commensurate change in papal attitudes toward the Normans. In fact by the time of Hildebrand's succession to the papal see in 1073, the hostility between Rome and the Normans—at least those of Apulia—was as intense as it had been during the days of Leo IX. Even Gregory's positive relations with Capua were predicated on Richard's cooperation in papal efforts to subdue Robert Guiscard.

In early 1074 Gregory—following the precedent established by Leo IX—set out to organize an international expedition against Robert. In February he wrote to William of Burgundy, requesting his help against the Normans, "who are rebellious toward us." Gregory asked William to pass the word on to Raymond of Saint-Gilles, Richard of Capua, and Amatus of Savoy, who had also promised to help, so that they would come and "pacify the Normans." Once this had been done, Gregory hoped that he and the army would be able to move on to Constantinople "to assist the Christians, who, greatly afflicted by the most frequent attacks of the Saracens, have been beseeching us in vain to extend to them the hand of our assistance."[10] The language of this letter is significant in a number of ways. First of all, the identification of the Normans as *qui nobis rebelles sunt* suggests that Gregory saw himself as a feudal overlord and Robert as a contumacious vassal, deserving punishment at the hands of his other, more faithful vassals.[11] Second, the letter essentially equates the Normans with the "Saracens" who, in the wake of the Battle of Manzikert (1071), were posing a serious threat to the territorial integrity of eastern Christendom.

Gregory's expedition came to naught and early the following year (January 1075) he wrote to Hugh of Cluny, informing him of his many woes, among which the Normans figured prominently: "Among the secular princes, I know of none who place the honor of God above their own, or justice before their search for wealth. I contend that those among whom I live, namely the Romans, the Lombards, and the Normans, are, as I have often said to them, in a certain way worse than the Jews and the pagans."[12] Again the equation of the political enemies of the pope with the religious enemies of Christendom suggests that Gregory was searching for a more accommodating context within which to frame his hostility toward Robert Guiscard.

It was Gregory's breach with Henry IV that encouraged him to reconsider his antagonistic stance toward the Normans. In March 1076, he instructed Archbishop Arnald of Acerenza to absolve Roger and encourage him to continue his struggle against the "pagans" of Sicily. Gregory also told Arnald that "if duke Robert should choose to be obedient like a son of the holy Roman church, I am prepared to receive him with paternal love and with his counsel to maintain justice with him, to release him wholly from the chains of excommunication, and to number him among the divine sheep."[13] Robert apparently responded to the overture with a list of concessions that he expected from Gregory, effectively closing the door, at least for the time being, on their reconciliation.[14]

Gregory's relations with the Normans took a turn for the worse when, in the spring of 1076, Robert and Richard finally managed to form the alliance that Gregory had always feared. By autumn 1077, Robert had displaced Gisulf II as prince of Salerno and had turned his attention to Benevento. In late winter 1077, Gregory excommunicted "all Normans who labor to invade the land of St. Peter," including "those who besiege Benevento and who try to invade and plunder Campania."[15] Gregory reiterated this condemnation at the Roman synod of March 1080, and imposed an interdict on Norman churches.[16] It was not until Henry IV had overcome his rivals for the German crown once and for all that Gregory was forced, at Ceprano, to offer Robert reconciliation on the duke's own terms.

Gregory's conflict with Henry IV, like that of Leo IX against the Normans, spawned a number of treatises written by defenders of papal policy. While these works naturally focus on the events surrounding the Investiture Controversy, they are not entirely bereft of references to the Normans. For one thing, such sources could hardly avoid making occasional reference to Robert Guiscard in so far as he, from time to time, found himself on a stage otherwise dominated by pope and king. More fully developed, however, are the portraits of the Normans to be found in portions of these treatises devoted to earlier stages in the history of the reform papacy. For in their search for precedents for Gregory's opposition to simony as well as his willingness to resort to military means to protect papal interests, the apologists naturally turned to the pontificate of Leo IX. And when they did, they resurrected and refitted papal views of the Normans that dated back to the Battle of Civitate.

The bishops Bonizo of Sutri and Bruno of Segni were both protégés of Gregory VII, promoted to their respective sees at his nomination. Both suffered for their close association to Gregory when they were captured and imprisoned by imperial forces in 1082. Bonizo managed to escape and sought refuge with Mathilda of Tuscany, under whose protection he wrote his *Liber ad Amicum*, addressed to an anonymous friend and designed as a justification for papally-sponsored military activity in the wake of Gregory's death in Norman "exile" in 1085. Bruno was ultimately released and continued to serve as a papal advisor under Victor III and then Urban II. It was probably during Urban's pontificate (1088-99) that Bruno wrote his *Libellus de Symoniacis*, praising the efforts of Leo IX in inaugurating the struggle against simony.

Bonizo explicitly stated at the outset of the *Liber ad Amicum* that he intended to address the question: "whether it was and is permitted to engage in armed struggle for the sake of Christian doctrine."[17] He may or may not have been aware that Peter Damian had posed this same question some twenty years before in a letter to Bishop Olderic of Fermo. The violence in Italy in Peter's own day—exacerbated by the schism between Honorius II and Alexander II—had "moved some [to ask] whether the leaders of the church ought to avenge themselves, rendering evil for evil in the manner of secular men." Peter's answer, buttressed by passage after passage from the New Testament, was an unambiguous, "no":

> If anyone should object to this on the grounds that Pope Leo [IX] involved himself in military campaigns and yet was a holy man, I would respond that Peter did not secure his apostolic principate on these grounds, . . . nor did David come to merit the oracle of the prophets because he invaded the land of another man.[18] Such actions are not to be judged to be good or bad on the basis of the merits of those engaging in them, but according to their own qualities. Do we read that Gregory [I], who was subjected to great plundering and violence by the ferocity of the Lombards, either did or taught such things in his writings? Did Ambrose wage war against the Arians who were cruelly attacking him and his church? Were any of the holy popes given to rising up in arms?[19]

Bonizo, who wanted to place Leo's actions in a more complimentary light, approached the question differently. In fact, he essentially ignored it altogether, assembling examples from the past that illustrated a very different point: that it was the fate of the church to suffer violence at the hands of worldly powers. Bonizo began by citing examples from the Old and New Testaments illustrating the long tradition of believers suffering for their faith: "Be not surprised if the world hates you."[20] Bonizo then turned to post-scriptural Christian history, beginning with Constantine, to show how even when church and empire were no longer opposed to one another, the former continued to suffer occasional violence from heretics and schismatics on the one hand[21] and barbarian invaders on the other.[22] The empire properly defended the church from both of these challenges, attentive to its well-being.[23] The Carolingian and Saxon kings and emperors followed suit.[24]

As Bonizo approached the eleventh century, his original line of argument became even more obscure, lost in his detailed re-creation of the papal reform. Bonizo applauded Henry III, that "wisest and most completely Christian of men," for extricating the papacy from the hands of local Roman families who had made it "seem like it was theirs by some hereditary right."[25] He dwelled on Leo's campaign against simony at some length, making certain to place the young deacon Hildebrand at his side from the outset.[26] Then he turned to Civitate. "That most formidable people of the Normans, who had extracted Apulia and Calabria from the dominion of the Greeks," attacked Benevento, forcing its citizens to offer their city to St. Peter in hopes of papal assistance. "Once this was done, [Leo], as a result not only of the attacks against the territory of the holy Roman church, but of the harsh afflictions which [the Normans] brought to the Christians, was moved first to strike them down with the sword of excommunication. Then he determined that they should be attacked with the material sword. But in accordance with the providence of ineffable God—whose counsel is a great abyss[27]—the Normans emerged victorious from the battle."

> What more shall I say? God showed with signs and miracles that those who, fighting for justice, had been laid low in battle were pleasing to him, and when he deigned to include these ones among the saints, he made a great pledge to any in the future who might come and fight for justice.[28]

There are a number of noteworthy points to be made about Bonizo's understanding of the battle of Civitate. Perhaps the most interesting is that there is hardly a trace of the sense of guilt, embarrassment, and disillusion that permeated the more contemporary accounts of the battle that we considered above. Rather than following their lead and speculating as to why such an apparently holy venture had gone awry, Bonizo, operating from a vantage point some forty years after the events he described, could instead point to the "signs and miracles" that had purportedly graced the bodies of the "martyrs" of Civitate and recast the event into an occasion for celebration. Bonizo reiterated this point at the very end of the *Liber ad Amicum*: "Let us consider our own times and see what the Omnipotent has conferred on those who fought against the Normans under Pope Leo. He crowned them with glory and honor and showed by means of signs and prodigies that they were pleasing to him."[29] The battle was not, by

Bonizo's reckoning, a defeat for the papal alliance, but simply one more in a long line of God-given opportunities for good Christians to demonstrate their dedication to the church by suffering for it. By so doing they had not only followed the well-worn path of their persecuted and martyred forbears, but they set themselves up as models for new generations of Christians—such as those in Gregory VII's own day—to "come and fight for justice."

Describing Civitate in this light served Bonizo's purposes well in that it set the stage for a sympathetic treatment of Gregory's conflict with Henry IV. This was, after all, the real point of his book. In the wake of what would otherwise have appeared to be Gregory's unqualified defeat and ignoble flight, Bonizo offered proponents of the reform movement a more positive way of looking at the events that had just unfolded before them. If it was still too soon to expect the "signs and miracles" verifying God's support of Gregory, Bonizo's readers could take heart in the example of Leo at Civitate, realizing that Henry's apparent victory was simply another God-given opportunity for defending the Christian faith.

Bonizo's recasting of Civitate inevitably affected the image of the Normans. Again, as in the case of Leo's letter to the emperor, we see the juxtaposition of "Norman" and "Christian" as if the former were not a subset of the latter. In light of Bonizo's understanding of the history of the church, it made sense that he should see the Normans at Civitate as occupying the same functional niche as the "barbarian" Lombards and Saracens: non-Catholic invaders who threatened papal interests in Italy.

Nonetheless, the Normans of the *Liber ad Amicum* were spared much of the negative language that Bonizo used when describing these previous "threats to Christendom." Bonizo reserved the epithet *pessima gens* for the Saracens and did not posit a *rabies normannica* to parallel the *rabies langobardica* of the past. The earlier invaders of Italy conjured up for him apocalyptic images of the tenth horn of the beast and seemed to have been "extracted from the sheath of the Lord's fury." The Normans did not.[30]

This "softening" of the generic image of the "barbarian threat to Christendom" was probably a function of Bonizo's recognition that however difficult the Normans had proved themselves to be at Civitate, they did ultimately come to the aid of Gregory VII when he was hard pressed in Rome by Henry's troops. This would explain why, despite the spotty record of the Normans as papal protectors after 1059, Bonizo made the most out of the few times that the Normans "pulled through" and down-played those occasions when they did not. In the wake of the Synod of Melfi—where "the venerable pontiff [Nicholas II], protected by God, went to Apulia and released the Normans from the bonds of excommunication and handed over to them, by means of investiture, all of Apulia and Calabria as well as the lands of St. Peter that they had previously invaded, with the exception of Benevento"—the Normans are depicted as defenders of the church (just as the emperors had once been) "quickly liberating the city of Rome from the tyranny of its captains."[31] Predictably, Bonizo passed over without comment Richard's incursions into papal territory in 1066, Gregory's excommunication of and campaign against Robert in 1074, and the lifting of the censure at Ceprano in 1080.[32] On the other hand, he described at some length the efforts of Gregory's enemies in 1074 to enlist Robert's aid to expel the pope from Rome, enticing the duke with promises of the imperial crown. According to Bonizo, the "most prudent duke" declined:

> You will not be able to persuade me to arm myself against the pope. It is evil to believe that the pope could be deposed through your treacheries or those of any others, when he was enthroned by the election of the clerics and acclamation of the Roman people, after the papal throne had become vacant, and was consecrated to the altar of St. Peter by the cardinal bishops.[33]

Despite his excommunication, Bonizo's Robert comes across as being true to his word at Melfi, upholding the papal election decree against any who would dare to subvert the process. He becomes, in short, a paradigmatic papal vassal whose deference to the pope stands in marked contrast to Henry's heavy-handedness.

Bruno of Segni, another ardent supporter of Gregory VII, wrote his *Libellus de Symoniacis* to commemorate Leo IX's inauguration of the struggle for reform that he felt had culminated in the pontificate of Gregory VII. Again it is important to realize that Bruno was looking back to Leo's years from the perspective of someone whose conception of reform was shaped by personal experience with Gregory VII. In fact, if we can believe Bruno, Gregory was himself Bruno's principal source of information about Leo. Near the beginning of the *Libellus*, Bruno wrote:

Now let us come to those things which the Lord accomplished through [Leo], not that we want to record everything that we have heard or found written. The blessed Pope Gregory, of whom we made mention above, used to tell us many things about this man, on the basis on which I have reported the most significant events from those which I remember having heard about. Whenever he spoke to us listeners about this matter, he would chastise us and me especially—or so it seemed to me, as he fixed his eyes intently upon me— saying that we were allowing the deeds of Leo to perish in silence and that we were not recording those things that would promote, for many listeners, the glory of the Roman church and provide an example of humility.[34]

This passage suggests that the Leo that emerges from the *Libellus de Symoniacis* is as close to Gregory VII's own recollection of Leo as we are likely to get. By extension, the Normans that Leo encountered at Civitate, as described by Bruno, would also reflect something of Gregory's own view, shaped not only by his close ties to Leo, but, at some level, by his own ambivalent feelings about Robert Guiscard.

"When the blessed Leo was in Rome and was ruling the apostolic see in peace," wrote Bruno, "many came up from the territory of Apulia with their eyes put out, their noses cut off, and their hands and feet amputated, having been miserably subjected to the cruelty of the Normans." Leo, "that meekest of men, full of pity and mercy," sympathized with the affliction of the Apulians and, in an effort to "humble the pride of that people," organized a small army to do battle against the Normans. Bruno conceded that while Leo "had the zeal of God, he perhaps did not act in accordance with wisdom," for he chose not simply to send the army "in the defense of justice," but to accompany it.

Like the other pro-papal commentators, Bruno was at a loss for words when trying to explain the defeat.

[Leo's forces] were able to say, in their death, what our savior said in the midst of his passion: "They do not have power over us unless it is has been given to them from on high."[35] But how is it that the good are vanquished and the bad do the vanquishing? "O the height of God's riches of wisdom and knowledge: how incomprehensible are his judgements, and sought after his methods?"[36] Those who fought for justice were defeated and those who fought against justice were victorious.[37]

The people whom Leo met on his way to Benevento and later as he returned to Rome shared this sense of profound disillusion.

> Suddenly word spread, it filled the land, and everywhere it told about the battle that had occurred, that the knights of Christ [*milites Christi*] and the army of saints had been defeated. Then the pitiable pope returned to Benevento, a city always faithful and familiar to the blessed Peter. Hearing of the arrival of the pope, the entire town rushed to meet him, men and women, adolescents and virgins, the old in the company of the young, not in procession, but in tearful lamentation. They stood astonished, watching from a distance as the pope approached, preceded by bishops and clerics with sad faces and bowed heads. Afterwards the venerable pope went among them and blessed them with his hand raised. The shouting and the wailing was carried up into the heavens and all the earth resounded with grief and sorrow. Amidst such a procession he entered the city and with such psalmody he came to the church. After remaining in Benevento for some time, he made his way back to Rome and in each town [through which he passed] the wailing and the tears began anew. How could anyone who had seen him leave with such a noble army and then return with only his clerics manage to hold back his tears?[38]

There is not the slightest hint of reproach for Leo in all of this. Though Bruno had questioned the wisdom of the pope's decision to accompany the troops to the battle, there is no second guessing of Leo's judgment after the defeat. The tears in Benevento are not for a pope gone astray, but for a holy army defeated by an unholy one. The people who lamented Leo's fate did not interpret the battle as a lesson in humility, but as an opportunity for martyrdom: "Precious in the eyes of the Lord is the death of his saints," wrote Bruno. "It is most firmly to be believed and by no means to be doubted that all who die for the sake of justice will be gathered among the martyrs.[39]

On the eve of his death, the Leo of the *Libellus de Symoniacis* even experienced a vision confirming the martyrial honors won by the dead at Civitate:

I vehemently rejoice that I saw there among the martyrs of Christ those brothers and friends of mine who followed me to Apulia and died in defense of justice. They were well decked out, holding palm fronds in their hands, so that through this those who thought that they had been defeated would realize that they were the victors.[40]

These saints invited Leo to join them: "Come, our beloved, and dwell with us, for we have received this great glory through you." On the basis of this vision, Leo predicted that he would die within three days and told the people around him: "If after the third day I am still in this life, you will know that what I have seen was not real." Leo did die three days later,[41] thus verifying the vision and confirming that the defeat at Civitate was in fact a martyrial "victory." The final words that Bruno put in Leo's mouth established a legacy that Gregory VII would have been particularly comfortable with: "I, [Peter's] unworthy vicar, beseech your immense clemency, that you absolve from all of their sins and lead to the repose of the saints those servants, my brothers, who were killed for love of justice."[42]

The pro-papal accounts of the Battle of Civitate, taken as a group, suggest the influence of various interpretative models. The references to pagans terrorizing Christians on the one hand and to martyrdom on the other point in the direction of the passionaries. These highly stylized accounts of the trial and execution of Christian confessors during the Great Persecutions of the mid-third and early fourth centuries provided easily adaptable paradigms not only of heroic Christian victims but of bestial pagan persecutors—the Roman magistrates—who regularly "raged" and seethed against the confessors in their futile efforts to subvert their determination to remain faithful to God. In some of the *passiones*, the Roman magistrates are described as being so impressed by the fortitude of the confessors and the miracles that grace their bodies that they actually converted on the spot. The fact, then, that Leo attributed an "incredible and unheard of rage" to the Normans and that Wibert portrayed them as being "converted," in a manner of speaking, by the undaunted fortitude of the pope and the display of miracles that accompanied the burial of the papal troops, suggests that they might have had martyrological paradigms in mind when they described the Battle of Civitate.

But on the other hand the *passiones* did not offer much in the way of justification for military resistance to persecutors of the church. Being a martyr meant submitting passively to the violence inflicted by the oppressor, and there was certainly nothing passive about Leo's or Gregory's armies. A more serviceable model in this regard was to be found in the accounts of invasion of Christian territory by non-Christian (or at least non-Catholic) forces—accounts which were, by the way, themselves influenced by the martyrologies.[43] Under such circumstances, one could at least make a case, à la Augustine, for a *bellum justum* on the grounds that fighting off such an invader amounted to an acceptably defensive action.

One of the effects of applying the "pagan invader of Christendom" model to the Normans was to "dechristianize" them. Leo's letter to the emperor is a case in point. In his words, the Normans were "an undisciplined and alien people" rising up "against the church of God with more than pagan impiety." By berating them for having "killed Christians," he implied that they were not themselves Christians. Finally, when Leo asked the emperor to assist him in a new campaign against the Normans, he described his mission as none other than the "liberation of Christianity." There is, in short, nothing in his letter that would suggest to an uninformed reader that the Normans were Christian, and much to suggest that they were not.

Leo's biographers also contributed to this "paganization" of the Normans. By treating the casualties at Civitate as martyrs, Wibert, Bonizo, and Bruno implied that the unfortunate papal soldiers had been killed in defense of Christendom. This in turn implied that the Normans whom they fought were threats to Christendom; that they were themselves, in some sense, pagans. Equally suggestive in this regard is a bizarre portent reported by Wibert at the outset of his *Vita Leonis IX*.

> It is said that . . . there was a dog in the territory of Apulia that was in the habit of barking out the human words, "*Deus meus*." But is it really so incredible that a brute animal in that region should be invoking the mercy of God in this way, when the religion of Christ has almost perished there and its inhabitants have been subjected to the power of an alien land?[44]

This thinly veiled reference to the Normans, designed to prepare the reader for the confrontation at Civitate which Wibert would recount further on, portrays the Normans as a threat to the very practice of Christianity in Apulia.

Given the fact that the Normans in Italy were neither ethnically nor etymologically far removed from the Northmen who had regularly visited their destruction on the northern and western coasts and riverbanks of Europe in the ninth and early tenth centuries, one might have expected Leo and Wibert to depict the Norman conquests in Italy as if they represented a new phase of Scandinavian aggression. The Northmen, who regarded monasteries as particularly attractive concentrations of booty, certainly qualified, from a monastic perspective, as a pagan threat to Christendom. But interestingly enough the papal sources never make this connection. Instead they invoke the model of the Saracens who, as a result of their conquest of Sicily in the ninth century and their subsequent raids directed against the Italian mainland, offered a more geographically immediate variation on the same theme.

Some two centuries before the Battle of Civitate, Pope John VIII (872–882) had addressed a number of letters to secular rulers outside Italy asking for assistance in defending papal territory from Saracen incursions. "We exhort you," wrote John to Count Boso of Vienne in 876, "and we beseech you not to put us off any longer, not to allow the people of God to be torn to pieces by these Agarenes who, thundering by the will of God, have covered the land like locusts so that practically all of its inhabitants have been carried off or given over to plunder or the sword, or forced into solitude, into the dens of beasts."[45] In a separate letter to Charles the Bald, John reiterated:

> How many times and in what ways have we suffered at the hands of the impious people of the Saracens? . . . Oh the pain! While the enemies of the cross congratulate themselves, the company of the faithful is consumed with great suffering, the blood of the Christians is spilled, and the people devoted to God are laid low by the endless slaughter.[46]

The rhetoric is similar enough to Leo's to suggest that, if he did not actually consult John's correspondence, he had such appeals for assistance against the Saracens in mind when he wrote to Constantine.

John VIII was also, as it turns out, one of the first popes to offer spiritual inducements to encourage campaigns against the Saracens. In a letter to the bishops within the realm of Louis the Stammerer, John explicitly stated that

With regard to those who were recently killed in defense of the holy church of God and for the standing of the Christian religion and the republic, as well as those who will fall for the same cause, we respond with boldness and with the piety of Christ our lord, that they can obtain indulgence for their sins [*indulgentiam delictorum*] because those who fall in battle while fighting vigorously against pagans and infidels are received into the peace of eternal life.[47]

John was simply elaborating on a similar promise made by Leo IV in 853 to the participants in a Frankish expedition against "the enemies of the holy faith and the adversaries of all lands," the Saracens, that

the kingdom of heaven will not be denied to any of them killed while struggling faithfully in this war. God Omnipotent knows that if any of you die, since you have died on behalf of the truth of the faith and the salvation of the soul and the defense of the fatherland of the Christians, a reward prescribed by him will follow.[48]

These precedents are particularly significant, because when Wibert, Bonizo, and Bruno bestowed the palm of martyrdom on the soldiers killed at Civitate they were extending a concept of papal indulgence that had hitherto been enunciated only in relation to campaigns against the Saracens in Italy. In their efforts to explain papal involvement in the debacle at Civitate, then, it would appear that Leo and the apologists effectively transformed the Norman defense of Apulia in the face of a papal military offensive into another Saracen attack against Christian Italy.

One account of Civitate that we have yet to consider explicitly ties the image of the Normans to that of the Saracens. The author(s) of the *Annales Romani*, a series of brief papal biographies that survives as an appendix in one of the extant versions of the *Liber Pontificalis*, actually referred to Leo's opponents at Civitate as "Agarenes" rather than Normans! The account related how Leo asked Henry "to come down into Apulia and liberate its inhabitants from their servitude to the Agarenes." In the battle, the Germans were wiped out, "though many on the side of the Agarenes were killed too." But no sooner had they won their victory than "the princes of the Agarenes became full of sorrow."[49] The term *Normanni* does not appear at all in the text. It is clear that the author knew that Leo's opponents were not actually Saracens, for later the account describes how Leo "absolved them of their anathema," something that Leo could not have done if his opponents had not been Christian. Like Leo and the apologists, the author seems to have referred to the Normans in this way for apologetic reasons: to vindicate Leo for his questionable choice of tactics.

The choice of "Agarene" as a synonym for "Norman" was, from this apologetic perspective, a particularly apt one. Although the term was almost always used in a literal sense to designate the Arabs—the supposed products of Abraham's union with his handmaid Hagar—it could be used metaphorically to indicate any assailant of the "chosen people," the products of Abraham's union with his wife Sarah. In Genesis, after all, the angel of the Lord promised the outcast Hagar that she would at least have the satisfaction of being the progenitor of a great, indomitable people: "You shall conceive and bear a son and you shall call him Ishmael. . . . He will be a fierce man, with his hand raised against everyone and the hands of everyone raised against him in turn."[50] The Normans could thus be considered "Agarenes" in so far as they had fulfilled the prophecy revealed to Hagar and "raised their hands" against the church.

On the other hand, actual instances of the use of the term *Agareni* to describe peoples other than the Saracens are very rare in this period, thus adding to the pointedness of this particular identification. One of the contributors to the annals of St. Gall referred to the Hungarian invaders of Germany as *Agareni*, in place of the usual *Ungari* or *Ungri*. But Ekkehard, a late tenth-century monk of the same institution, was critical of this identification: "Those who regard the Hungarians as Agarenes stray a long way from the path."[51]

The papal apologists we have been considering knew that the Normans were not in fact Saracens. They understood that there was little in the way of historical justification for identifying the two outside of the simple chronological fact that the Norman depradations in southern Italy began just as the Saracen assaults subsided. Presumably they also knew that the threat posed to the church by the Normans was of a rather different order than the one posed by the Saracens; the two converged only in so far as they challenged papal authority in the south. But from the perspective of papal propaganda, it made perfect sense to blur the distinction between the two, thus transforming an ambiguous Christian threat to papal hegemony in southern Italy into an unambiguous "pagan threat to Christendom."[52]

Notes

1. LP 2:275; PRV 1:94.
2. Leo, *Epistola* 103, PL 149:779–80.
3. Proscriptions that Leo had, in fact, reiterated at the Council of Rheims in 1049 (PL 143:1437). Carl Erdmann, *The Origin of the Idea of Crusade*, tr. Marshall W. Baldwin and Walter Goffart (Princeton, NJ: Princeton University Press, 1977), p. 123.
4. 1 Corinthians 9:16.
5. PRV 1:163–66.
6. Hermann a. 1053. The relevant passages can also be found in PRV 2:107–8.
7. For the original text, see Ménager, *Recueil* 1.6, pp. 30–32, and Deér, *Papsttum und Normannen*, p. 66.
8. Deér, *Papsttum und Normannen*, pp. 66 ff.
9. Deér, *Papsttum und Normannen*, pp. 107–24.
10. Gregory VII, *Register* 2.46, pp. 169–71.
11. Archbishop Alfano of Salerno, a supporter of Gregory's anti-Norman campaign, took this opportunity to write a pair of odes to Gisulf of Salerno and his brother Guido, encouraging them to participate in Gregory's expedition. In the one addressed to Guido, Alfano waxed nostalgic about Salerno's hey-day under Guido and Gisulf's father, Guaimar V. He went on to lament the fortunes of the city in the wake of Guaimar's murder:

> But after your father, the father of this country, was run through with swords in the midst of his own people, Whatever he had held before in this noble life perished in an instant and became smoke and shadow. For as a plague is wont to do to a flock of sheep, debilitating them by means of foul air, So a multitude of the people of the Gauls struck the region of Salerno once its prince had died.

Alfano, "Ad Guidonem fratrem principis Salerniatni," ed. M. Schipa, *Archivio storico per le province napoletane*, v. 12 (Naples, 1887), p. 774. See also: Anselmo Lentini, "Le odi di Alfano ai principi Gisulfo e Guido di Salerno," *Aevum* 31 (1957), pp. 230–40.

12. Gregory VII, *Register* 2.49, pp. 188–90.
13. Gregory VII, *Register* 3.11, pp. 271–72.
14. Gregory VII, *Register* 4.7, p. 305.
15. Gregory VII, *Register* 5.14a, pp. 368–71.
16. Gregory VII, *Register* 7.14a, pp. 479–81.

17. Bonizo 1, p. 571.

18. 2 Kings 11.

19. Peter Damian, *Epistola* 8.9, PL 144:316.

20. 1 John 3:13; Bonizo 1, p. 572.

21. Bonizo 2, p. 573.

22. Bonizo 2, p. 575.

23. Bonizo 2, pp. 576–77.

24. Bonizo 3–4, pp. 577–82.

25. Bonizo 5, pp. 584–87.

26. Bonizo 5, p. 588.

27. Psalm 35:7.

28. Bonizo 5, p. 589.

29. Bonizo 9, p. 620.

30. Bonizo 2, p. 575.

31. Bonizo 6, p. 593.

32. Bonizo 7, 9, pp. 599, 602, 604.

33. Bonizo 7, p. 604.

34. Bruno 3, p. 548. Cf. Bruno 4, p. 549.

35. John 19:11.

36. Romans 11:33.

37. Bruno 5, p. 550.

38. Bruno 6, p. 550.

39. Bruno 6, p. 550.

40. Bruno 6, p. 551.

41. Bruno 6, p. 552.

42. Bruno 6, p. 551.

43. Jerome's description of the Visigothic sack of Rome and especially Victor of Vita's account of the Vandal invasion of North Africa provide good early examples of this type of literature. For an overview, see Courcelle, *Histoire litteraire*, pp. 25–26, 84–85, 118, etc.

44. PRV 1:153.

45. John VIII, *Epistola* 8, MGH *Epistolae* 7:7–8.

46. John VIII, *Epistola* 22, MGH *Epistolae* 7:20.

47. John VIII, *Epistola* 150, MGH *Epistolae* 7:126.

48. Leo IV, *Epistola*, MGH *Epistolae* 5:601.

49. LP 2:333; PRV 2:94.

50. Genesis 16:11–12.

51. *Annales Sangallenses maiores* a. 888, 899, 902, 908, 909, 910, 943, and 955, MGH SS 1:77–79.

52. It should be noted that this loose, rhetorical identification between the Normans and the Saracens was not confined to the papally-oriented accounts of the Battle of Civitate. Gregory VII's idea of using his vassals' armies first against the Normans in southern Italy and then against the "Saracens" threatening Constantinople shows that he regarded both opponents as legitimate foci of papally-sanctioned warfare. From Gregory's perspective, the Normans and the Saracens

posed similar and simultaneous threats to Christendom (broadly conceived) and the same army that subdued one could legitimately be employed to neutralize the other. Gregory's letter to Hugh of Cluny, claiming that the Romans, Lombards, and Normans were "in a certain way worse than the Jews and the pagans," again identifies the Normans as a threat to Christendom. Gregory VII, *Register* 2.46, 2.49, pp. 188–90, 169–71.

3. Montecassino and the Normans

The abbots of Montecassino, like the bishops of Rome (at least from the time of Leo IX), initially regarded the Normans as a threat to the security of their position in southern Italy. Only later, after coming to terms with the Normans, did they begin to regard them as a potentially positive force. As a result the Casinese "views of the Normans" that have made their way down to us reveal the same basic shift from the Normans as antagonists to the Normans as protagonists that we saw in the papal documentation. Yet there are significant differences between the images produced in Montecassino and Rome. Part of this, as we shall see, is a reflection of differences in the nature of the sources themselves. For in place of the letters and apologetic biographies that dominate the pertinent papal materials, Montecassino offers miracle stories and chronicles. But beyond this there is also the fact that Montecassino embraced the Normans much sooner and much less ambiguously than the papacy ever did, creating an environment conducive to the production of the first, full-scale narrative history of the Normans. Before turning to these sources, however, we should provide a context for them by considering the situation and history of the monastery that produced them.

Montecassino's geographical position placed it within a number of overlapping spheres of influence.[1]   One was that of the Latin empire. When Charlemagne defeated the Lombard armies of King Desiderius in 773–774 and assumed the title of *rex Langobardorum*, Montecassino, which had been the principal monastery within the Duchy of Benevento, became an important imperial monastery. As such, it was expected to offer hospitality to the emperors whenever they were in the area.[2] Sometimes such visits provided an occasion for significant imperial intervention in monastic affairs, such as the replacement of an abbot. But Montecassino's distance from the transalpine centers of the Carolingian and German empires meant that such visits—and therefore such examples of imperial interference—were relatively rare. In the first half of the eleventh century,

Montecassino played host to the emperor only three times: to Henry II in 1022, Conrad II in 1038, and Henry III in 1047.

The papacy also exercised some influence over Montecassino. Like his father Pepin III, Charlemagne recognized some form of papal jurisdiction over southern Italy in general on the basis of the papal claims advanced in the Donation of Constantine.[3] Otto I in 962 and Henry II in 1020 confirmed these papal privileges. When Nicholas II invested the Normans at Melfi (1059) with the territories they had conquered in southern Italy, he was simply exercising this imperially recognized jurisdiction. According to Casinese tradition, however, the popes had forged ties specifically to Montecassino long before their alliance with the Franks. When the monastery was sacked for the first time during the Lombard invasion, Gregory I (590–604) welcomed the itinerant community to Rome and allowed its members to construct a monastery adjacent to the Lateran palace, where they remained for over a century.[4] Later Gregory III (731–41) played a key role in encouraging Abbot Petronax (c.718–49/51) to revive the monastery at Montecassino.[5] According to Leo Marsicanus, Zacharias (741–52) granted the new monastery exemption from local episcopal control. Whether or not this exemption was in fact granted at such an early date, Victor II recognized it in 1057 and each of his successors followed suit. Like the emperors, the popes had an interest in who held the position of abbot. Humbert's active role in securing the election of Frederick of Lorraine to succeed Richer shows how intimate papal involvement could be.

At a local level Montecassino and its domain, the *terra sancti Benedicti*, fell primarily within the political sphere of the Lombard principality of Capua. The proximity and relative power of Capua made it a more immediate and perennial source of concern for Montecassino than either the empire or the papacy. When the monastery was destroyed for the second time by the Saracens of Garigliano in 883, the monks relocated first to Teano and then to Capua in 914.[6] The Capuan princes helped the monks build a new monastery within the city itself and there the community remained until the monastery at Montecassino was finally rebuilt in 949 under Abbot Aligernus (948–85) with the approval of Pandulf I of Capua.[7] This Capuan "exile" set the stage for a century of intimate Capuan involvement in the affairs of Montecassino. At best, the princes of Capua proved that they could serve as effective protectors, enforcing the immunity of Casinese territory from the jurisdiction of the counts of Teano,

Aquino, and the Marsi.[8] The princes of Capua recognized Casinese immunity in 925, 952, 961, 963, 967, and 1040. And when the Lombard dynasty in Capua gave way to Norman rule, Richard and Jordan followed suit in 1058 and 1080.

But the strength and proximity that made Capua a potentially effective protector of Casinese liberties could also make it a threat to the monastery. The line between protection and manipulation was very thin.[9] As we saw in the first chapter, Pandulf IV's brother Atenulf served as abbot for eleven years until Henry II intervened in 1022, deposing Pandulf and forcing Atenulf to flee the monastery. In an effort to undermine the alliance to Byzantium that the two brothers had forged, Henry placed Capua under the jurisdiction of Guaimar IV of Salerno and oversaw the election of Abbot Theobald (1022–36). But in 1032, some years after Pandulf's restoration, Theobald was effectively replaced by Basil, who worked closely with Pandulf to restore Capuan control over the Casinese domain. Conrad II intervened in 1038, supervising the deposition of Basil and the election of the Bavarian Richer (1038–55), who then had to struggle to regain direct control of the Casinese domain.

The arrival of the Normans did not fundamentally alter these relationships. In their dealings with Montecassino, the Normans tended to fill niches that had previously been occupied by others. We have already described how Abbot Atenulf enlisted some of the Norman survivors from the battle of Cannae (1018) to man Casinese fortresses and protect the monastic domains from encroachment by the counts of Aquino. Pandulf IV seems to have added to the number of Norman castellans on the *terra sancti Benedicti* after his restoration in 1036. In the following decade Richer, aligned with German interests, dislodged these Normans (1045) and, by so doing, rooted out the last vestiges of Capuan control over the Casinese domain. But when Richard of Aversa took control of Capua (1058), the new abbot Desiderius set out to re-establish the traditionally close working relationship between Montecassino and Capua, now under Norman rule.

It is very difficult to recapture a Casinese "view of the Normans" from the period preceding Desiderius's enlistment of Richard as the protector of Montecassino (1058). The earliest extant sources describing the interaction between the Normans and the monastery date from twenty years after this watershed in Norman-Casinese relations. Desiderius's own

Dialogi de miraculis sancti Benedicti was written between 1076 and 1079.[10] And the *Historia Normannorum* of Amatus of Montecassino dates from between 1078 and 1080. But while each of these authors recounted the "early years" of Montecassino's interaction with the Normans from chronological vantage points well beyond 1058, it is clear that they had at their disposal sources of information—particularly oral ones—that reached back into the period in question. Since we have reserved the next chapter for Amatus, we will confine our attention here to the *Dialogi de miraculis sancti Benedicti,* before moving on to consider even later sources that have something to say about this early period.

Desiderius modeled his *Dialogues* on Gregory I's more famous book of the same name.[11] The point of Gregory's work was ostensibly to prove that the church in his day, far from being bereft of holy men (in comparison to apostolic times), was in fact full of them. He supported this observation by recounting miracle stories that involved contemporary Italian churchmen, both regular and secular. Desiderius had a more specific purpose in mind when he wrote his own *Dialogues.* As he told his interlocutor, the deacon Theophilus, his intention was to record the miracles that God "desired to be accomplished in praise of his name in this monastery of Montecassino," miracles which were "either done within my memory or reported to me by my elders."[12] To this end, Desiderius promised four books, the first two being dedicated to miracles that had occurred at the monastery itself, and the two remaining ones to those that had graced affiliated institutions. The text that has come down to us breaks off in the middle of the third book, altogether lacking the fourth. But fortunately for our purposes, the stories with which we are concerned—those that deal with Montecassino itself—fall within the first two apparently complete books of the *Dialogues.*

Among the accounts that Desiderius incorporated into his work are seven which specifically involve divine protection of the monastery from outside aggression. In the abbot's own words, such miracles showed "how omnipotent God, with the right hand of his divinity, always tears this monastery from the hands of tyrants and protects it from the attack of enemies through the merits of the blessed father Benedict."[13] It is within this subcategory of miraculous interventions that we find the early Norman castellans predictably cast as aggressors against Montecassino. Unfortunately the Normans figure in only two of these seven "protection" anecdotes, the remaining five featuring other local aggressors. But this, in and of itself, is information, for the five stories that do not involve the Normans allow us to put the image of the Normans projected in the other two in some kind of perspective. The diversity of aggressors, in other words, makes it easier not only to recognize the generic characteristics that the Normans shared with every such "tyrant," but to appreciate how the particular tyranny of the Normans differed from the tyrannies exercised by other regional powers. Before considering the Norman anecdotes, then, it behooves us to take a look at the stories that involve other aggressors against the monastery.

The first of these recounts the abortive Saracen assault on Montecassino in the wake of the more famous sack of St. Peter's in 846.[14] Desiderius described how the Saracens had set up their camp on the other side of the river Liri, "so that at daybreak they could utterly destroy the monastery, take whatever they might find there as booty, and—in their great thirst for blood—decapitate any monks that they encountered." The monks were terrified and spent the night praying for deliverance. Finally Abbot Bassacius experienced a vision in which he learned that the monks had nothing to fear because "the most holy father Benedict had secured their well-being from Almighty God." The next day, a great storm came, swelling the river with its rain and thus preventing the Saracens from crossing.[15]

The remainder of the "protection" stories all date from the eleventh century. Not surprisingly, given Montecassino's perennial difficulties with Pandulf IV of Capua, two of the accounts involve him. In the first Pandulf is described as

> a most powerful and rich man who, by means of his thievery and the shedding of human blood, subjected to his dominion cities and towns, cruelly carrying off the estates of others dwelling nearby, and who insatiably raped, slaughtered, plundered, and tore good churches asunder for a long time without any mercy. Then after he had made off with the great riches, seizing them from the churches of Christ, he, driven by sacrilegious cupidity, removed all of the fortresses, villas, and estates of his monastery, so that he left to the monks not so much as a single peasant to till the fields nor even any fields for a peasant to till. Moreover, he carried off the entire treasure of this monastery and he remained hidden in a keep, which he had constructed on a hill not far from the city of Capua, named after St.

Agatha the martyr, in which he had placed a great amount of spoils taken from orphans, widows, churches, and poor people.[16]

In short, Pandulf had abused every aspect of his role as monastic protector, the litany of his transgressions leaving none of the proscriptions associated with the Peace of God unviolated.

Finally, as the story continued, God was moved by the "tears and voices of the small children, the widows, and the poor, as well as by the prayers and invocations of the servants of God." He responded by inspiring the emperor Conrad to come to Italy "to avenge his churches and to pluck them from the hands of tyrants." In the face of Pandulf's intransigence, Conrad passed through Montecassino en route from Rome to Capua, asking the monks to pray to God and St. Benedict on his behalf, "since he had come to that region for no other reason than to tear [Benedict's] monastery from the hands of that most cruel tyrant." In answer to their prayers, Conrad found that as he approached Capua Pandulf's troops dispersed before his very eyes and the stolen property was restored to Montecassino.

The second episode involving Pandulf supposedly took place a short time after his death in 1049. Returning after a long day of hunting, Sergio V of Naples ordered one of his retainers, a boy named Pythagoras, to stay behind and collect the nets that he had used to secure his prey. Having done so, Pythagoras was heading home when he came upon a pair of mysterious monks who escorted him to a terrifying lake. There he saw Pandulf in chains, being tortured by two black demons who were repeatedly submerging him in the lake. When the boy asked what Pandulf had done to deserve such punishment, the victim himself responded, between dunkings: "Although, my boy, many and infinite punishments have been prepared for me as a result of my countless sins, I am suffering the punishment that you see now for no other reason than that I, before my death, failed to return the golden chalice that, driven by sacrilegious greed, I took from the monastery of blessed Benedict." Desiderius went on to explain to Theophilus that his example should serve as a warning "so that whoever might hear of this will be terrified and thereafter restrain his thoughts and his hands from the plundering of churches."[17]

Of the other miracle accounts that fall into this "protection from tyrants" category, one describes a Capuan nobleman, also named Pandulf, who tried one night to seize the Casinese fortress of Conca only to become so disoriented by the darkness that he was unable even to enter the fortress before the morning light had spoiled his plans.[18] Another tells of some thieves who managed to break into the monastery's cellar and fill their bags with food, but then found that their sacks had become too heavy to carry. Abandoning them in their flight, the thieves were later apprehended and brought back to the monastery, where, instead of being punished, they were mercifully given food and drink and sent on their way.[19]

The two remaining episodes of this type involve the Normans. The first describes "a certain Norman, swollen and inflated in pride," who, "in a frenzied state of mind," came upon some of the monastery's fishermen. "Since [the Normans as a people] are avid for rapine and insatiably anxious to seize the property of others," this Norman grabbed one of the fishermen, ordering him to draw in his nets and hand over his catch. When the fisherman resisted, saying that his intention was to feed the monks, not the Normans, he was thrown into the sea. The Norman, "avid for the booty of fish," began to pull in the net himself and gather his catch. But suddenly "he fell from the boat into the water and, sinking into the sea, gave up his soul. But, wonderful to relate, before the waves washed his dead body ashore, the fisherman who had been thrown into the water succeeded in swimming ashore unharmed."[20]

The other miracle story involving the Normans comes at the end of the second book. It tells how Abbot Atenulf, concerned about the threat posed by the count of Aquino, "installed some of the Normans, who had at that time come to Italy at the invitation of our princes, on the property of this monastery, so that he might protect them from the aforementioned count." At first the Normans served their intended purpose well: "They began nobly and faithfully to defend everything belonging to the monastery and, in the manner of strenuous knights, they pushed the enemy back on all sides." They carried on in this manner *satis honeste* during Atenulf's abbacy, but then the "Norman cohort, which had been enlisted for our defense, began, little by little, to be unfaithful and adverse to us. Driven by sacrilegious greed, they turned to our perdition and, like a crawling crab, brought us, by this means and that, under the domination of their law." After their "barbaric avarice" had removed all but a handful of local estates from Casinese control, St. Benedict finally decided to intervene. First he appeared to a peasant in a dream, in which he was seen driving the Normans from his land with a rod. Then, as testimony to the truth of the vision, a group of Normans was attacked *nutu Dei* in San Germano, some being killed and others captured. The rest, besieged at the fortress of San Andrea, finally surrendered when "they realized that they were fighting against the right hand of God," and were sent back to Aversa. "This was done so that from that time on, through the merits of St. Benedict, this land on which we dwell, might remain undamaged by their attacks and secure under the protection of this saint."[21]

Desiderius assured the readers of his *Dialogues* that, for those events that he did not actually witness, he relied on reports by *senioribus nostris*. Given the fact that Desiderius did not join the community at Montecassino until 1055, the stories that concern us would all have reached Desiderius second hand, making them part of an oral tradition at Montecassino into which Desiderius tapped for material. It is impossible to know for sure how faithfully he recorded these stories. Of the two that involve Normans, neither reveals any obvious signs of tampering. In the fisherman episode, the Normans as a people are depicted as being "avid for rapine and insatiably anxious to seize the property of others," while the particular Norman in question, "swollen and inflated in pride" and "in a frenzied state of mind," lived up to this image of his people by trying to steal the fish. Similarly, the Normans of San Andrea are "driven by a sacrilegious greed" to bring the monastery under their control. There is, in short, no indication that Desiderius adapted this negative image of the Normans to fit the more positive role that they were playing vis-à-vis Montecassino by the time he was writing the *Dialogues*.

Nor would we have expected him to do so. The point of the stories was to illustrate—in an anecdotal fashion designed to be entertaining as well as instructive for a monastic audience—Benedict's ongoing concern for the institution he founded. In each case, the monks were depicted as innocent victims and Benedict as their defender. The only role left was that of the oppressor and regardless of his identity—Pandulf, a petty thief, or a Norman castellan—his characteristics were largely predetermined and stylized to fit the specific narrative requirements of this type of story. Hence we see the same characterizations repeated again and again. The aggressors against Casinese property were invariably "tyrants" who were "driven by sacrilegious greed."

Having said this, it is also clear that it was Pandulf who epitomized these qualities for Desiderius, his oral sources, or both. The lengthy, somewhat abstract, survey of his abuses at the beginning of his first episode and the re-creation of his sufferings in the underworld are unparalleled in the accounts of the other "tyrants." At the other extreme we find the thieves in the pantry whose transgression elicited mercy rather than punishment. The Normans fall into an intermediate category somewhere between the horrible Pandulf and the hungry thieves. Perhaps this is a function of Desiderius's own relations with the Normans: he may have pared down an original diatribe that rivalled the one aimed at Pandulf. There is simply no way of knowing.

One additional source that may help us in our attempt to reconstruct a Casinese "view of the Normans" prior to 1058 is the *Chronica monasterii Casinensis* of Leo Marsicanus. Leo, a member of the ruling family of the Marsi, entered Montecassino as a child in the early 1060s and trained to be one of its librarians and archivists. In this capacity he authored the *Chronica monasterii Casinensis* at the request of Abbot Oderisius (1087-1105). Leo's prefatory letter indicates that Oderisius had originally asked him simply to write a life of Desiderius, his predecessor, but later decided that the scope of the work should be broadened to include Desiderius's predecessors as well.

Leo's letter, dedicating the book to Oderisius, was written while the abbot was still alive, that is, before 1105. But Leo had not at that time accomplished all that he had set out to do. Neither of the two extant redactions of his work is complete. The first includes only book one, covering the period from the foundation of Montecassino by Benedict (around 529) to the death of Maielpotus (948), and book two, from the accession of Aligernus (948) to the death of Frederick (1058). The second redaction makes some progress into a third book, entirely dedicated to Desiderius (1058–87), but breaks off in 1075. We know that sometime between 1102 and 1107, Leo was appointed cardinal bishop of Ostia by Paschal II, a position he held up to his death in 1115.[22] Perhaps his new duties prevented him from finishing the *Chronica*.

The second redaction of the *Chronica monasterii Casinensis* is more than simply an extension of the first. At some point after Leo had written the first two books and dedicated the as yet uncompleted work to Oderisius, he apparently came across a copy of the *Historia Normannorum* of Amatus. How it was that Leo, the monastery's librarian, could have been ignorant of Amatus's work when he began the project remains a mystery. But when he finally did become aware of it, he retraced his steps and incorporated pertinent passages from Amatus into what he had already written. From then on, as he composed the third book, he regularly consulted Amatus for information about the Normans.

Though Leo wrote the *Chronica* long after the Normans had become the protectors of Montecassino, it can still be of some use in reconstructing earlier images of the Normans. For one thing, because Leo wrote the first redaction without access to Amatus's *Historia Normannorum*, it provides us with a view of Montecassino's past that, while later than that provided by Amatus, was nonetheless independent of it. Some of the sources, both oral and written, were no doubt the same. Some were different. Furthermore, because Leo chose to write a chronicle as opposed to a fully narrativized history like that of Amatus, he would have had less reason to edit out or modify early episodes in Norman-Casinese relations to fit a preconceived notion about where such relations were heading. This second point cannot, however, be taken too far. Though Leo's work is clearly more of a chronicle than Amatus's work, it is not, as we shall see, entirely without its narrative elements.

Before we move on to consider the pre-1058 Norman episodes in Leo's chronicle, it behooves us to consider some structural aspects of the work as a whole. The divisions within Leo's *Chronica* reflect what he seems to have regarded as a recurring cycle of consolidation and dissolution in Casinese history. Leo's heroes were Petronax, Aligernus, and Desiderius, each of whom shared Benedict's status as *fundatores* and *constructores* of Montecassino, each having restored the monastery after it had been "violated" by outside forces.[23] Within forty years of its foundation (c. 529), Montecassino suffered the first of these setbacks. "The Lombards who had recently . . . invaded Italy [568] . . . entered the monastery [577] at night as the brothers slept, and ravaged everything."[24] The monks fled to Rome, where they were welcomed by Gregory I and allowed to construct a monastery adjacent to the Lateran palace. "And they inhabited it for almost 110 years because the monastery at Casino remained destroyed."[25]

Finally "omnipotent God in his mercy decreed that the monastery of St. Benedict be restored, and that the monastic regimen that it had taken up at the time of its foundation, be propagated from that same place on the basis of the same rule throughout the world."[26] The task of reconstruction fell on the able shoulders of Abbot Petronax (c.718–49/51), whom the "divinely inspired" Gregory IV "admonished to go to the fortress of Casino, and to the monastery of St. Benedict which had been destroyed so many years ago, and zealously occupy himself with its restoration." In 720, Petronax and his monks returned to Montecassino and set about restoring its buildings and resuming their monastic regimen there in accordance with their founder's rule. Gregory IV granted the monastery immunity from all episcopal authority save that of Rome.[27] By this time, the local Lombard powers were more than willing to assist them in their efforts. Gisulf II of Benevento (742–751/52), who "found the monks, who lived there at that time in the service of God, living so religiously next to the body of the holy father Benedict," was so moved that he granted vast adjacent lands to the monastery as a perpetual gift [744].[28]

The next great threat to the existence of the monastery came in 883, after the Saracens had established themselves in a fortress on the Garigliano River. Not only did they destroy the monastery, but they killed many monks, including the abbot Bertharius himself. They tried to burn down the church of San Salvatore in San Germano as well, but although they lit a number of fires, they were foiled by "some judgement of God."[29] The remaining monks made their way to Teano where the community remained until 914. In that year their newly elected abbot John, a former archdeacon of Capua, moved the community to Capua.[30] With the support of the princes Landulf and Atenulf, John oversaw the construction of a new monastery of St. Benedict in Capua, and made an attempt to reconstruct the one at Montecassino as well.[31]

This second period of exile lasted until the accession of Aligernus (948–85), who, "began to restore that place which had been burned down by the Saracens since the time of Abbot Bertharius, and which had remained neglected, destitute, and practically deserted for sixty-seven years."[32] Apart from the monastery proper, Aligernus also set about to reconstitute the *terra sancti Benedicti*. As a result, he and his successors found themselves at odds with the rulers of Teano, Aquino and the Marsi.

It was in response to subsequent incursions by the counts of Aquino that Abbot Atenulf (1011–22) decided to "accept some of the strongest of the Normans and establish them in the fortress which is called Piniatarium not far from the city of San Germano, for the protection of the monastery."[33] Leo also reported that Atenulf ransomed the Norman prisoners of Boioannes, presumably to use them in the same way.[34] When, in 1032, the newly restored Pandulf of Capua removed Abbot Theobald and placed his own men over the monastery, he "distributed the rest of the fortresses and villas belonging to the monastery among the Normans who adhered to him and to others among his followers," in particular the fortress called Vantra in San Germano itself.[35] It is not clear whether Leo meant that Pandulf actually dispossessed the Casinese Normans and gave the fortresses to other Normans in his service or, as seems more likely, he simply won the fidelity of those Normans who were already there.

The *Chronica* provides virtually no information about the Normans of the *terra sancti Benedicti*[36] until their run-in with Abbot Richer in 1045. Ironically, one of the few references to these Normans fulfilling their function as protectors appears right before the rift, when Richer successfully employed the Normans against the counts of Aquino and again against the Aquinan fortress of Sant'Angelo.[37] But in the very next section of the chronicle, Leo set off on an extended account of the rebelliousness of the Casinese Normans.

In light of the pattern apparent in the first two books—disastrous intrusions by outside invaders followed by periods of restoration—the problems with the Normans would seem in Leo's mind to have paralleled those posed by the Lombards and the Saracens in earlier periods. But this time the outcome would be different. Instead of a monastery being destroyed and its community being forced into exile, the invaders would be successfully repelled and the vicious cycle broken once and for all by the strong hand of Abbot Richer, opening the door to a new era of renewal, and a new relationship with the Normans under Desiderius (1058–87). It was with this structure in mind that Leo incorporated what he knew—based on Desiderius's *Dialogues* as well as other written and oral sources—about Norman-Casinese relations before 1058. Not surprisingly, given the parallelism that Leo cultivated between the Norman threat and those posed by the Lombards and Saracens in earlier periods, and given Leo's interest in setting the stage for the triumphant abbacy of Desiderius, Richer's campaign against the Normans receives much more attention and is developed at much greater length in the *Chronica* than in the *Dialogues*.

Leo's *Chronica* describes in detail how Richer responded to the unauthorized fortification of San Andrea undertaken by the Normans. When it was clear that they "did not want to give him any obedience or reverence," Richer took counsel with his monks and decided to prepare an ambush.

A few days later, the count [of the Normans] by the name of Rodulf came to the abbot's *curia* [in San Germano] accompanied by not a few of his soldiers, and, depositing his arms outside the church, he entered it along with his men to pray. Then the men of the monastery, seizing the horses and arms [of the Normans], closed the doors of the church and began to ring all the bells at once. Hearing this all the men of the land were frightened, not knowing what had happened and thinking that the Normans had come to capture or kill the abbot. They rushed [to the church] armed with various weapons and, having opened its doors, they entered and attacked the Normans who were armed only with swords. The Normans fled toward the altar, as they tried to defend themselves, imploring in vain the faith of God which they, by demeaning it, had broken. Fifteen of [the Normans] were killed and the rest fled. The count was the only one they took alive. They ordered him confined to the monastery.[38]

The men of the monastery then circulated throughout the *terra sancti Benedicti* compelling everyone they met to swear fidelity to the abbot. Then they summoned the counts of the Marsi, identified as *monasterii fideles*, who came to help them besiege San Andrea where the Norman count's wife had taken refuge with the treasure and the rest of the soldiers. After fifteen days, the besiegers began to grow impatient. But the monks roused their spirits:

> Why do you endure such long delays? Why do you waste time doing nothing? Rise up and attack the stronghold together! Do not be afraid of anything! Your fight is against the enemies of God, against perjurors and thieves. God will be present and the most holy father Benedict will confuse the adversaries of the faith and offer victory to us, who have taken up this just cause.[39]

"Ignited with shame as well as anger," the beseigers rushed at the stronghold and finally breached its walls.

> When the Normans realized this, not being able to do anything more against the will of God, they surrendered themselves into the hands of the monks and handed over the stronghold. They themselves, scarcely guarded by the monks, fled unarmed to their fellows in Aversa. They left all their horses, arms, and treasure behind for their opponents.

The victory of the Casinese forces would have been short lived if the Normans of Aversa had had their way. They were "ready to avenge the injuries done to their fellows" and launch a full scale attack on the monastery. But Guaimar of Salerno convinced them not to. "So with the land restored in its entirety to the property of St. Benedict and to the merits of his law, from then on it rested, as a result of the mercy of God, from the infestation of the Normans in the year of our Lord 1045."[40]

This successful recovery of monastic territory from the Normans and Montecassino's subsequent "rest" from Norman encroachment marked, for Leo, the beginning of the end of the "foundation-destruction-refoundation" cycle that had dominated the first five hundred years of Casinese history. From now on there would be no setbacks. To underscore the significance of this moment, Leo paused to lend a supernatural aura to the events he had just recounted. He reported a dream that a peasant named Jerome had experienced the night before the assault on San Andrea. Jerome had imagined himself walking along a road when suddenly there appeared a monk with a staff in his hand walking beside him. When they reached a fork in the road where the path broke off toward San Andrea, the monk invited the peasant to rest with him awhile and began to speak:

> Long ago, I lived with the brothers on that mountain over there, building upon it the monastery of Cassino. But when the brothers became so disobediant and ungrateful to me that I was no longer able to bear their disturbances, I left them and went to Jerusalem, and there I remained with blessed Stephen for forty and more years. But now, called back by their frequent requests and prayers, I have returned. If they have indeed corrected their ways, I will dwell with them. But if not, I will immediately return by the road on which I came.[41]

The monk, asked to identify himself, confirmed that he was none other than Benedict himself and got up to resume his journey. As he proceeded along the road to San Andrea, he explained "that there is much for me to do in that stronghold on the morrow." Leo was quick to point out that the peasant woke up and immediately informed an archpriest named Mainard what he had seen.

Leo also claimed that there were some still alive at the time that he was writing who claimed "to have seen in the midst of the most intense part of the conflict, a certain monk bravely fighting against the Normans and earnestly urging on his own men." Moreover, Leo reiterated Desiderius's account of the other peasant who had a dream a few days later, in which he saw Benedict chasing the Normans out of the territory, beating them with the staff he carried in his hand.[42]

The siege of San Andrea was the beginning of the end of the Norman threat. It was not, the *Chronica* informs us, the end itself. Though Guaimar and Drogo came to Montecassino asking that the errant count Rodulf be absolved, Richer was not convinced that his trouble with Rodulf and his like was over. "Suspicious of the iniquity of the Normans," he ordered the strengthening of the fortresses protecting the monastery's lands, making provision for the protection of the peasant population.[43] Richer's instincts served him well. For, according to Leo, Pandulf VI— son of Pandulf IV—approached the Normans who had been expelled from the *terra sancti Benedicti* and enlisted their aid for an attack on the monastery's holdings, promising to restore them to their fortresses. As Pandulf and the Normans camped on the edge of the Casinese domain, Richer and the monks prayed, knowing that "unless impeded by God, [their enemies] would lay waste the entire territory."[44] Their prayers were answered when Count Atenulf of Aquino offered his services as protector and checked Pandulf's offensive (1047).

Still Rodulf was not to be restrained. "After these things, the above mentioned Rodulf, count of those [Normans] who had been expelled, acting as one of a race insatiable in its avarice, forgot the vow that he had made so lightly and came with certain accomplices in his iniquity into this land to ravage it." But on the morning of his raid, he was found dead.

> As a result of this, great terror rushed among the remaining Normans so that they did not presume to enter this territory any longer for the sake of either invasion or depredation. Finally, in manifest vengeance of this holy place, one hundred fifty of the count's Norman soldiers were consumed by various forms of death in various places over the next two years.[45]

With this, the Norman role as the most recent in a long line of aggressors against Montecassino finally ended once and for all. Later, when eulogizing Richer, Leo, mirroring the language of Desiderius, would credit him with "tearing the lands of the blessed Benedict, with the help of God, from the hands of the Normans."[46]

Like Desiderius, Leo Marsicanus knew that the problems between the Normans and Montecassino would ultimately give way to good relations. Yet, again like Desiderius, he does not appear to have altered the earlier image of the Normans to fit the later one. He did not, for instance, try to hide the fact that the Normans of Aversa would have attempted to avenge the injuries done to Rodulf had they not been restrained by Guaimar of Salerno. There is thus no reason to believe that the detailed account that Leo offered of Richer's campaign against the Normans as well as the visions that heralded its success, were not based on more or less "authentic" products of the collective, primarily orally-transmitted memory of Montecassino, a memory that, while no doubt subject to adaptation and embellishment between 1058 and the time Leo was writing, nonetheless was rooted in the years immediately after 1045. Leo inserted these monastic anecdotes into a broader narrative structure, but there was nothing inherent in this particular framework that would have forced him to tamper with the stories as they came down to him. If anything, his choice of structure helped preserve a more complete record of the pre-1058 "view of the Normans," for it elevated Richer's campaigns to regain control over the monastic domain to the position of a climactic prelude to Desiderius's abbacy. Though Leo was as scandalized as Desiderius by the crimes against Montecassino committed by Pandulf IV,[47] for Leo it was the Norman depradations that took center stage precisely because they were the last threat to the monastery before the election of Desiderius.

Notes

1. Cowdrey, *Age of Abbot Desiderius*, pp. xxix–xxxiii.
2. Décarreaux, *Normands, papes, et moines*, p. 41.
3. See Deér, *Papsttum und Normannen*, pp. 51–106, for a detailed reassessment of the basis for papal claims to southern Italy.
4. CMCas 1.2, p. 21.
5. CMCas 1.4, pp. 23–25.
6. CMCas 1.53, pp. 135–36.
7. CMCas 1.53–54, 2.1, pp. 137–39, 166.
8. CMCas 2.1, pp. 166–67.
9. Manso, Aligernus's successor, had been a member of the Capuan ruling family before being promoted to the abbacy by Pandulf I's widow. Décarreaux, *Normands, papes, et moines*, p. 43.
10. See the calculations of G. Schwartz, in Desiderius, p. 1113.
11. Gregory, in turn, had modeled his on the *Dialogues* of Sulpicius Severus.

12. Desiderius, prologue, p. 1116.

13. Desiderius 1.9, p. 1122.

14. This account may, in fact, be an interpolation given that is much earlier in date than the others.

15. Desiderius 1.2, pp. 1118–19.

16. Desiderius 1.9, p. 1123.

17. Desiderius, 1.13, pp. 1125–27. Compare this to Peter Damian's story about a hermit looking out of his window one night and seeing "many black men like Ethiopians" walking by carrying hay. Asked what they were doing, they responded that they were "evil spirits" and were going to stoke the fire in preparation for Pandulf, who was about to die. Upon Pandulf's death, Vesuvius erupted as testimony to the truth of the vision. Damiani, *Opuscula* 19.9, quoted by Bartholomaeus in Amatus, p. 128 n.

18. Desiderius 1.10, p. 1124.

19. Desiderius 1.11, pp. 1124–25.

20. Desiderius 1.11, p. 1124.

21. Desiderius 1.22, pp. 1138–39.

22. CMCas p. viii.

23. CMCas, *Epistola*, p. 9; CMCas 3 prologue, p. 362.

24. CMCas 1.2, p. 20.

25. CMCas 1.2, p. 21.

26. CMCas 1.4, pp. 22–23.

27. CMCas 1.4, pp. 24–25.

28. CMCas 1.5, p. 25.

29. CMCas 1.44, p.114.

30. CMCas 1.53, pp. 135–36.

31. CMCas 1.53–54, pp. 137–39.

32. CMCas 2.1, p.166.

33. CMCas 2.38, p 241.

34. CMCas 2.38, p.241. Leo's observation that Atenulf had negotiated this agreement with the Normans *necessitate coactus* hints at the difficulties that this relationship would pose for the monastery.

35. CMCas 56, p. 277.

36. CMCas 2.68, p. 304.

37. CMCas 2.69–70, 307–8.

38. CMCas 2.71, pp. 309–10.

39. CMCas 2.71, pp. 310–11.

40. CMCas 2.71, pp. 311–12.

41. CMCas 2.72, pp. 312–13.

42. CMCas 2.72, pp. 313–14.

43. CMCas 2.73, p. 315. An early case of *incastellamento*: Cowdrey, *Age of Abbot Desiderius*, p. 3.

44. CMCas 2.74, p. 316.

45. CMCas 2.75, pp. 317–18.

46. CMCas 2.89, p. 341.

47. CMCas 2.79, 2.81, 2.84, pp. 534–35, 328–29, 331–33.

4. Amatus of Montecassino and the Normans

The running conflict between the papacy and the Apulian Normans—which lasted, in one form or another, from 1053 until 1080, when Gregory VII had no choice but to enlist Robert Guiscard's aid against Henry IV—was not conducive to sympathetic treatments of the Normans in Italy. As we have seen, contemporary observers who wrote about Civitate found that they could blunt potential criticism of Leo's actions by emphasizing the threat that the Normans posed to the security of southern Italy. Even Hermann of Reichenau, who blamed the pope for his unwillingness to compromise, did not doubt that the Normans were guilty of "nefarious and inextricable sins" against the people of Apulia.[1] Despite the official papal recognition of Norman legitimacy at Melfi in 1059, relations between Rome and the Normans—especially between Gregory VII and Robert Guiscard—remained tense and the papal rhetoric, uncomplimentary.

Nor was there any reason, based on the early history of Norman-Casinese relations, to expect that the Normans would be treated any more sympathetically by the monks of Montecassino. Abbot Atenulf's (1011-22) plan to employ the Normans as monastic protectors by installing them in the fortresses of the *terra sancti Benedicti* proved to be short-sighted. By the time Richer became abbot in 1038, the Norman castellans were operating quite independently of the abbot's wishes, ultimately forcing him to turn to local counts to expel the Normans from Casinese territory.

But with the accession of Desiderius as abbot in 1058 the situation changed dramatically. Richard of Aversa's siege and acquisition of Capua that same year, and his subsequent campaign to subdue the area in and around the principality, meant that he enjoyed a level of regional hegemony that Montecassino could not easily resist. Yet at the same time, Richard's new position as prince of Capua was precarious and the abbey of Montecassino offered a potential source of legitimacy that Richard lacked. Not surprisingly, then, while Richard was besieging Capua, he paid a visit to Desiderius and was enlisted as the newest protector of Montecassino. As we have already observed, the available evidence does not indicate that Richard applied himself to his new role with any great vigor. But his relations with Montecassino remained close enough for him to be one of the guests of honor at the dedication of Desiderius's new basilica on October 1, 1071. And they were close enough seven years later for Desiderius to commission a Casinese monk named Amatus to write the very first history dedicated specifically to the Normans in Italy.

Very little is known about Amatus. Peter the Deacon, who was responsible for continuing Leo Marsicanus's *Chronica monasterii Casinensis* up to 1139, included Amatus in his list of distinguished Casinese scholars in the late 1070s. He identified Amatus as a "bishop and monk of this monastery," who authored the verse *De gestis apostolorum Petri et Pauli* and the *Historia Normannorum*, dedicated to Gregory VII and Desiderius respectively.[2] Peter referred to Amatus's literary efforts a second time in his *Liber illustrium virorum Casinensis archiesterii*, referring to Amatus as a *versificator admirabilis* and adding to his list of writings the *De laude Gregorii VII* and the *De duodecim lapidibus et civitate coelesti Hierusalem*, neither of which has survived.[3] Two Casinese necrologies refer to the death of an Amatus, *episcopus et monachus* on March 1. Though the year is not recorded, the fact that one of the necrologies was written before 1101 perhaps provides a terminus ad quem for Amatus's death.[4] There was an Amatus who served as bishop of Pesto-Capaccio (south of Salerno) between the years 1047–58.[5] If the two were indeed one and the same—and this is by no means clear—then he must have entered Montecassino after retiring from his see in 1058 and was a rather old man by the time he set himself to writing the *Historia Normannorum*.

Internal evidence makes it possible to pinpoint, more or less, the years in which Amatus wrote the *Historia Normannorum*. For all intents and purposes, the history ends with the death of Richard of Capua, which we know occurred on April 5, 1078. The fact that Amatus's stated purpose for writing was to commemorate the deeds of Richard and Robert suggests that he—or more likely his patron, Desiderius—was prompted to do so by Richard's death. It is also likely that Amatus spent no more than two years working on his *opus*. For although he mentioned Gregory VII's excommunication of Robert on March 3, 1078,[6] he said nothing about their reconciliation at Ceprano in July 1080, an event which, given his apparent respect for Gregory VII as evidenced by his other literary projects, he would have eagerly recorded if he had still been writing at the time.[7]

Unfortunately, the original Latin version of the *Historia Normannorum* is lost.[8] The text survives only in an early fourteenth-century French translation. The preface to this version tells us that the translation was commissioned by a certain "conte de Militrée," whose identity is as obscure as the location of his county. It would seem, however, given his interest in Amatus's subject and the language of the translation, that the translator had some connection to the Angevin dynasty that ruled the kingdom of Naples at the time.[9] It is important to note that the translator did not simply translate Amatus's work, but often abridged it and commented on it in an (often misguided) effort to clarify words or allusions for the benefit of his readers. The version of the *Historia Normannorum* that we have is, in other words, potentially a poor imitation of the original. There is some cause for optimism, however, for Leo Marsicanus had access to the Latin original of Amatus's work when he wrote his second redaction of the *Chronica monasterii Casinensis* and incorporated a number of passages into his own work. If his borrowings can be regarded as true to their source, the French version would not seem to be hopelessly corrupt.[10]

In the dedicatory preface addressed to Desiderius, Amatus apologized for the fact that he, a monk, had devoted himself to writing a history of secular events. He pointed, in his own defense, to the precedent set by Paul the Deacon, author of the famous *Historia Langobardorum*, who was himself a monk at Montecassino. But even without Paul's example, Amatus felt that he could justify his decision to write a history of Richard and Robert on two grounds. First of all, claimed Amatus, the deeds that he was recounting were not simply the deeds of men; they were deeds "that had been conceded by the dispensation of God to be done through these men."[11] In fact, Amatus explained, he had been inspired to write the *Historia Normannorum* because it seemed to him that Richard of Capua and Robert of Apulia had "fulfilled the words spoken by God with regard to Cyrus, king of Persia":

I have taken him by his right hand so that the people would be subjected before his face and the kings would flee in his presence. I will go before him and I will humble the most glorious of the land and I will fight against the bronze door, and I will break the chains of iron; I will open the doors before him and no one will be able to keep them closed to him.[12]

The choice of the Persian king Cyrus is a suggestive one. Not only was Cyrus traditionally regarded as an extremely powerful ruler, but he was respected as a foreign king who was nonetheless chosen by God to assist in the return of the Jews to their promised land.[13] Amatus's presentation of Richard and Robert as new "Cyruses" suggests that he wanted his readers to see the Normans as a similarly powerful, alien force chosen by God to assist the church.

Indeed the second of Amatus's excuses for authoring a secular history—to wit that Richard and Robert deserved to be memorialized for their generosity and devotion towards Montecassino—fits nicely into this picture. If Cyrus served as the terrestrial force behind the restoration of Israel and the rebuilding of the temple, Richard and Robert could be seen as protectors of Montecassino, "restoring" the monastery after centuries of secular interference. It was easy for Amatus to apply this model to Richard, who, once he had taken over Capua, was officially installed as protector. Robert, who for most of the period covered by Amatus's history was geographically far removed from Montecassino, did not fit the model as closely. As we shall see later, Amatus dealt with this problem by transforming Robert's "protector" role into one that concerned not just Montecassino, but the church as a whole.

These two lines of defense provide a preview of the basic trajectory that Amatus would follow in his efforts to present the Normans in the best possible light. On the one hand, he would interpret their military and political success not simply as a function of their skill, but as the fulfilment of some inscrutable providential plan. And on the other, he would give pride of place in his account to the role of the Normans as protectors of the monastery and defenders of Christendom.

The *Historia Normannorum* proper opens with a brief discussion of the origins of the Normans as a people. "At the far end of France," wrote Amatus, "there is a plain full of trees and various fruits. In that narrow place lived a great multitude of people"—the Normans—"who were very robust and strong."[14] As it happened, however, the Normans found their territory in France to be insufficient to support their growing population.

So they "abandoned the little that they had" and "left for different parts of the world" in their effort to support themselves. But the Normans did not come to these new lands as mercenaries, for "it was not [their] custom...to place themselves in the service of another, but like the knights of old, they wanted to have every people subject to them and under their lordship. They took up arms, broke the ties of peace, and formed great armies and great knighthood."[15]   Already we see indications that the aggressiveness and cruelty that characterized the Normans in the papal sources is being transformed into something more positive, more heroic. Amatus's Normans are not cruel; they are "robust" and irresistable in their quest for domination.

Amatus could describe the Normans this way because he had already decided that they were exercizing this military aptitude within a divinely-sanctioned, providential context. This is clear from Amatus's brief overview of the activities of three Norman emigrés whose *Wanderlust* took them to places other than Italy: William the Conqueror in England (1066), Robert Crespin in Spain (1065),[16] and Roussel of Bailleul in Anatolia (1071). Though at first glance it may seem odd that, of the three, William should receive the least attention when his efforts yielded the only politically enduring result,[17] in fact it makes perfect sense if we take into account Amatus's concern with the workings of providence. For despite the respective failures of Robert Crespin and Roussel to establish themselves in Spain and Anatolia, the simple fact that they were fighting Muslims rather than Christians made it easier to see the hand of God at work.

As Amatus described it, Robert Crespin's expedition was organized "by the inspiration of God" in response to the "detestable folly of the Saracens," who had "occupied Spain and subjected the Christians."[18] Prior to the battle, Crespin and his men "called for the assistance of God and He was present to give help to those who had requested it. Because God's faithful prayed for victory in battle, a great part of the Saracens were killed. And they gave thanks to God for the victory that he had given to his people."[19]   Leaving a garrison in the city of Barbastro, Crespin returned north to gather a larger army to resume the conquest of Spain.

> But the devil, armed with subtle malice, was envious of this good beginning of the [Christian] faith and began to consider how to respond to it. And he introduced into the minds of the Christian knights the fire of love [of fame]. And those who had become proud

fell. Christ was angered because the knights gave themselves over to the love of fame. Therefore, because of their sins, they lost what they had acquired and were chased out by the Saracens.[20]

Pride "going before the fall" was, of course, standard fare for the medieval chronicler. But this particular motif would see relatively little action overall in the *Historia Normannorum*, Amatus apparently finding it difficult to distinguish easily between the kind of pride that ensued from a love of fame and the kind that one would expect to accompany the "robustness" that he so admired in the Normans.

Roussel's activities in Anatolia were as ill-starred as Crespin's, yet equally well-intentioned and divinely-directed. "An honest knight, true and faithful," Roussel entered into imperial service to fight the Turks. But "as a result of a righteous judgement of God, they were victorious [at Manzikert] and there was a great slaughter of Christians."[21]

Amatus's account of the earliest Norman activity in Italy fits nicely into this narrative scheme: a desire for domination coupled with an awareness of their own participation in something of grander proportions. "In the year before the year 1000," recounted Amatus, " forty valiant [Norman] pilgrims appeared in [that part of] the world. They had come from the Holy Sepulchre of Jerusalem, where they had adored Christ and arrived at Salerno, which was being besieged by Saracens."[22] According to Amatus, Salerno had been made a tributary of the Saracens, and was, at the time the Normans arrived, delinquent in its payments and suffering the consequences. "The pilgrims from Normandy arrived and could not tolerate the injuries of the Saracen lords nor the fact that the Christians were subject to the Saracens." So they armed themselves with weapons and horses provided by Guaimar IV and fought, "not for the sake of reward but because they could not stand the pride of the Saracens." The subsequent Norman victory delivered the people of Salerno from their "servitude to the pagans."[23] The grateful citizens offered gifts to reward them and to entice them to stay and continue to defend the Christians, but "the Normans did not want to take money for that which they had done out of their love for God," so they left.[24] Guaimar, duly impressed, immediately sent to Normandy to see if he could enlist the aid of other such men to help defend his city.

Amatus's *Historia Normannorum* is the only eleventh-century Italian source which specifically ties the arrival of the Normans to the depredations of the Saracens. It is not inconceivable that the Normans actually performed this service. We know from independent sources that the Muslims did attack Salerno in 1016. And other sources do describe the first Normans in Italy as pilgrims. But on the other hand, the narrative convenience of having the Norman "debut" in Italy involve a "holy war" against the Saracens makes one skeptical about the veracity of the account. Such an opening act allowed Amatus to place Norman involvement in Italy as a whole within the framework of an extended, if interrupted, campaign against the Saracens. This in turn permitted Amatus to locate the more mundane aspects of Norman motivation—specifically their drive to dominate—within an acceptably religious context. By dominating the Saracens, they were not only fulfilling their own nature as Normans, but they were correcting what was, from Amatus's perspective anyway, an unnatural political situation: Saracen dominion over Christians.[25]

But as convenient as the Salerno episode was for Amatus's narrative, the fact of the matter was that there were precious few other instances of conflict with the Saracens in the first forty-five years of Norman involvement in Italy. The Normans who responded to Guaimar's invitation were, according to Amatus, quite different from the ones who had inspired the prince to seek recruits in Normandy in the first place. Gilbert Buatère and his four brothers were motivated, Amatus tells us without a hint of embarassment, not by the "love of God" but by the wealth of Italy, a "land of milk and honey and such beautiful things."[26] Moreover, Gilbert was a fugitive, wanted by Count Robert of Normandy for the murder of one of his viscounts.[27] Finally, Gilbert and his brothers were not enlisted to protect Salerno against Saracen raids; instead they were employed by Melo of Bari in his rebellion against the Greeks.[28]

Despite the fact that Gilbert's motives and circumstances contrasted so sharply with those attributed to the original liberators of Salerno, Amatus did not hesitate to present him and his brothers in a favorable light: "They came armed, not as enemies, but as angels,"[29] and, under Melo's command they repeatedly put the imperial armies to flight before finally being crushed by a large Greek army that had gathered "like bees" at Cannae (1018). Even in defeat, the Normans proved their mettle, being "ready to die rather than flee."[30]

Amatus was equally sympathetic in his rendering of the efforts of the Normans of Comino, under the command of Melo's nephews, against the rival Lombard forces of Peter of Sora. Outmanned, the Normans "wanted to flee, but they had no one to receive them. When they saw that there was to be no other aid, they called on the assistance of God, by means of whose help"—Amatus knew from his reading of Deuteronomy—"one man can pursue a thousand and ten thousand can be put to flight by two."[31] Peter of Sora's troops, on the other hand, "confided in their own strength and did not seek any other assistance." The Normans predictably came out on top.[32]

In order to be able to describe these Norman mercenaries as "liberators" and "angels" who "called on the assistance of God," Amatus had to extend the idea of the illegitimacy of Saracen rule and apply it to the Greeks and Lombards as well. Since the Greeks and the Lombards were not, like the Saracens, "pagans," and therefore not automatically disqualified from exercising dominion over Christians, Amatus had to find other grounds for their illegitimacy. In the case of the Greeks, he relied on three devices. First, he depicted the Greek "yoke" in Apulia as an oppressive one that their Apulian subjects wanted nothing more than to remove. Second, he described the Greeks as militarily weak: despite their superior numbers they were no match for the Normans on the field of battle. Whereas Amatus's Normans were valiant, strong, and hardy, like lions, his Greeks were "womanly."[33] Third, and most important, even though they were superior warriors, the Normans of the *Historia Normannorum* knew better than to place their trust solely in their martial abilities. They understood that they could win nothing without the help of God. This, more than anything else, gave them a right to Apulia, a right that the Greeks had forfeited by being too ready to place their trust in numbers. It was precisely on this basis that Amatus was able to give something of a religious dimension to the struggle for control of Apulia despite the fact that both of the contestants were Christian.[34]

Amatus's rendition of the role of the sons of Tancred in the ultimate Norman takeover of Apulia shows how he made use of these narrative devices to undercut the legitimacy of Greek rule in the region. It all began in 1038, when the Greeks were organizing an expedition to conquer Sicily and requested assistance from Guaimar V of Salerno. He obliged by sending the brothers William, Drogo, and Humphrey at the head of a Norman contingent. "To tell the truth," observed Amatus, "the hardiness and prowess of that small band of Normans was of greater value than the whole army of Greeks."[35] Thanks to the efforts of the Normans, the Christian forces managed to take Syracuse. But the Greek leader of the expedition, George Maniakes, in his bid for the imperial throne, shamefully abandoned the enterprise before it was finished and as a result Syracuse was lost.[36] No doubt Amatus was preparing the reader for the later Norman-led campaign in Sicily that would enjoy the priority such a noble enterprise deserved and as a result achieve more lasting results.

According to Amatus, the "proud commander" Maniakes also selfishly deprived the Lombard commander Harduin of a horse that he had claimed as his share of the spoils, thus precipitating Harduin's withdrawal from the expedition.[37] Back in Apulia, Harduin made common cause with the local Lombards, "suffering from the mistreatment they had sustained from the lordship of the Greeks and the injuries that had been inflicted on [Lombard] wives and women." Harduin fanned the flames, hoping to use Lombard disaffection as an avenue for vengeance.[38] He specifically sent to Rainulf of Aversa for Norman assistance, promising "to increase the honor of [their] majesty and lordship." In his recreation of Harduin's appeal for help, Amatus returned to the theme that he had developed at the beginning of the *Historia Normannorum*: that the Normans needed space. Harduin compared the Normans of Aversa to "mice living in a hole," while reminding them that the Greeks, whom he characterized as "effeminate men," occupied a "rich and spacious land."[39] This was all that the Normans needed to hear. When they arrived at Melfi, ready to take up their new post, Harduin informed the locals that the Normans had come "not as enemies, but as good friends" to help remove their yoke.[40] The ease of their subsequent conquest of Venosa, Lavello, and Ascoli led the Normans to believe that they, "trusting in the power of God and in their own bravery," were well on their way to controlling Apulia.[41]

When the Greek army assembled at Olivento (1041) to suppress the rebellion, the catapan Doukeianos "revelled in the great number of men," even though, as Amatus hastened to point out, they fought "like women."[42] When the imperial army hesitated to attack, seeing no honor in beating an enemy so "few and poor," Amatus's Normans responded: "If you will not deign to come to us, certainly we will take the battle to you because we place our trust more in the mercy of God than in the size of our army."[43] Indeed the Greeks were put to flight by the numerically inferior rebel forces. The emperor, concerned lest he be "deprived and chased [by the Normans] from the dignity of [his] empire," responded to the defeat by digging deeper into the imperial treasury to pay for an even bigger army. To the horror of Amatus, he even considered diverting church funds should his own resources prove insufficient.44 When the two armies met again at Montepeloso, the Normans not only got the upper hand, but God intervened by miraculously causing a river to swell over its banks, trapping the retreating Greeks.45 With that, according to Amatus anyway, Apulia was pacified. It is important to note that throughout his account of the rebellion, Amatus cultivated the impression that the Normans actually spearheaded the rebellion, when in fact, as Amatus himself admits at one point, they constituted only part of a larger force under Lombard command. His pejorative comments about Greek reliance on mercenaries also helped to mask the fact that the Normans performed essentially the same function under Harduin.46

Amatus's treatment of the Lombards was more complicated than his portrayal of the Greeks, partly because the Normans actually benefitted, in the early stages of their involvement in Italy, from the patronage of some Lombard leaders, notably Guaimar IV and Guaimar V of Salerno and Sergio V of Naples. But ultimately, of course, Richard would take over Capua and Robert would conquer Salerno, thus displacing two long-standing Lombard dynasties. Amatus observed: "Since, as some say, 'one cannot rise to greatness if another does not fall,' when we speak about the rise of these two princes [Richard and Robert], we will show how others princes and lords fell."47 It is not surprising, given this change of regime and his high opinion of the Normans, that Amatus would locate the cause of this eclipse of Lombard rule in Capua and Salerno in the decadence of individual Lombard leaders.

The role that Amatus developed for Pandulf IV of Capua was as much a function of the heavy-handedness with which he "protected" the *terra sancti Benedicti* after his release from exile in 1024 as it was a product of the fact that Capua was predestined to fall to Richard. "When [Pandulf] recovered the glory of his principate, he took to heart neither the fear of God nor the misery [that he had suffered] in prison. Instead, 'on the advice of evil ones, he stood on the path of sinners and sat in the seat of sinners and of pestilence.'"48 Abusing his power as protector over Montecassino, Pandulf found himself "doing battle against God and against the holy." He confined the imperially invested Abbot Theobald to the Benedictine priory in Capua and replaced him with his own man, Basil.49 "He chased away so many monks with his iniquity" that there were barely enough to perform the liturgy, and he "vilely treated" the few that remained.[50] The administrator of the monastery disposed of its revenues and property in accordance with Pandulf's instructions, allowing him to stockpile provisions while the monks went hungry. As if this were not enough, Amatus accused Pandulf and his men of "placing the young boys who lived there in the vice of lust."[51] Nor did Pandulf confine his abuses to Montecassino. He mistreated Abbot Hilarius of Volturno[52] and he made his own bastard son Ildeprand a priest so that he could appoint him archbishop of Capua to replace the imprisoned Atenulf.[53] "The preaching of the priests was not heard and ears were closed so as not to hear the word of the Gospel, like a serpent that turns a deaf ear to the voices of those who would charm it."[54] Though scandalized by such abuses, Amatus seemed to have found Pandulf to be a particularly satisfying character to develop. Because Amatus knew that Pandulf would ultimately be removed from power—in other words, that justice would be done—he not only felt comfortable dwelling at great length on the excesses of the prince, but he peppered his account with biblical passages and prophetic allusions that heralded his demise.

Given the lack of any consistent Norman posture vis-à-vis Capua, it would have been difficult for Amatus to juxtapose Pandulf and the Normans the way he had the Greeks and the Normans. For one thing, it was Pandulf's brother, Abbot Atenulf, who first installed the Normans as castellans in the *terra sancti Benedicti*.[55] And while it was true that Sergio of Naples, concerned about Pandulf's return to power, had allied himself to the Norman Rainulf, "a man adorned with all the virtues that befit a knight," giving him his sister and the strategically-situated town of Aversa, Amatus could not hide the fact that when Sergio's sister died a short time later, Rainulf turned around and married Pandulf's niece![56] Although other unidentified Normans did respond to an appeal by Guaimar against Pandulf,[57] it was the emperor Conrad who forced the recalcitrant prince of Capua, "full of every sin and iniquity," back into exile (1038) and who put Guaimar in charge of Capua.[58] Only then did Rainulf, whom Conrad recognized as the lord of Aversa, begin to act in ways consistent with Amatus's storyline. He "persevered in loyalty to the prince [Guaimar]. The Normans exhausted themselves in increasing their honor and dedicated themselves to suppressing the pride of the prince's enemies."[59]

But even though Amatus could not develop any direct, adversarial relationship between Pandulf and Richard in the way that he had between the Apulian Normans and the Greeks, he certainly intended the image of Pandulf as an abuser of Casinese liberties to serve as a foil for his subsequent description of Richard's relationship with Montecassino. Because Amatus ultimately wanted to portray Richard as the ideal monastic "protector" upholding the interests of the monastery, narrative balance dictated that he depict Pandulf as the quintessential secular violator of monastic liberties.

Rainulf's alliance with the evil Pandulf was only one of a number of narrative "inconveniences" that Amatus faced in his effort to depict the early years of the Normans in a positive light. When Rainulf died in 1045 and his nephew and successor Asclettin followed him to the grave shortly afterward, Guaimar V overlooked the count's other nephew, also named Rainulf, when appointing a successor. Rainulf rebelled with the support of the Normans of Aversa as well as of Pandulf, who emerged yet again from exile hoping for an opportunity to turn the tables on Guaimar.[60] But the Melfi-based Normans under Drogo—"a singularly wise knight with a fear of God,"[61] who had succeeded his brother William as count of Apulia in 1046—remained loyal to Guaimar. "Let us advance against our enemy and put down his audacity," said Amatus's Drogo to Guaimar, "Let us show him our power and let the outcome of the battle undermine the pride of this presumptuous one."[62] If Rainulf and Pandulf had taken the field against Drogo and Guaimar, not only would Amatus have had to deal once again with an alliance between the hated Pandulf and Norman Aversa, but he would have had to find a way of explaining a war between the two principal Norman enclaves in Italy. As it turned out, Drogo interceded on Rainulf's behalf and Guaimar responded by recognizing him as the legitimate count of Aversa.[63]

It was even more difficult for Amatus to avoid compromising his protagonists when in 1045 hostilities arose between Abbot Richer of Montecassino and the Normans who were the abbey's "protectors." Amatus described the situation this way: "In those times the Normans inhabited and held the lordship of the fortress of St. Benedict, which lies behind the monastery of Montecassino. From it they inflicted injury on the poor. The abbot [Richer] considered how he might dislodge them."[64] He invited the Normans to come to San Germano and, once they had put down their arms and entered the church, he had them ambushed. Unable to defend themselves, some were killed and others captured. Richer then used the monastic treasure to organize an army which, in Amatus's

words, "fought to defend the land of God." In the course of the subsequent battle, Benedict himself appeared as the standard bearer[65] and the
Normans were defeated. From then on, the monastery was secure from
depredation. Though Amatus made it clear that his sympathies were with
Montecassino, he avoided castigating the Normans as a group for the
actions of those who opposed the monastery. The fact that the hostilities
predated the arrival in Italy of Richard and Robert made it easier for Amatus to dispense with this dark episode in Norman history and get on with
his story.

The conflict between Leo IX and the Normans posed a problem for
Amatus's narrative of similar magnitude, for by that time (1053) Amatus's
heroes, Richard and Robert Guiscard, were not only in Italy but were in
command of two out of the three Norman armies at Civitate. Moreover,
Amatus had a very high opinion of the reform-minded Leo, bestowing
unrestrained praise on him for his campaign against simony and carefully
enumerating the miracles that graced his holy endeavors.[66] Amatus was
also thoroughly impressed by Leo's insistence on the principles of the
Peace of God and on these grounds he seemed to condone Leo's criticism
of the Normans. Amatus wrote:

> Afterward [Leo] went to Melfi to oppose the actions of the powerful
> Normans. There he asked them to desist from their cruelty and stop
> bothering the poor. He showed how God is persecuted when the
> poor are persecuted and how God is pleased when the poor are treat-
> ed well. He commanded that they faithfully protect priests and the
> property of the church. He encouraged them to do good and to make
> offerings to God, to be continent and chaste toward their neighbors,
> and [to practice] every virtue.[67]

Amatus tried to insulate Drogo from this general criticism of the Normans by depicting him and Guaimar as being more than willing to "do as
the pope commanded" and protect Benevento from harm.[68] The problem
was that Drogo could not control all of the Normans, thus forcing Leo to
look for other ways "to defend the city and beat down the pride of the
Normans."[69] When Leo heard that Drogo had been assassinated (1051),
Amatus was quick to point out that Leo cried and said a mass for him.[70]

With Drogo out of the picture, Amatus seemed ready to side with
Leo once and for all in his effort to "confuse" and "disperse" the Nor-

mans.[71] Leo requested German troops from Henry and "promised to give absolution for their sins and great gifts if they succeeded in delivering the land from the malice of the Normans."[72] But just when it seemed that Amatus had made up his mind to embrace the papal cause once and for all, he began to lean over in the direction of the Normans. He criticized Frederick of Lorraine, the papal chancellor, for focusing entirely on the "malice of the Normans and not on the iniquity of the others who lived in those parts."[73] He attributed to Frederick a boast—"if I had a hundred effeminate knights, I would do battle against the entire Norman cavalry"[74]—that served to place him in the same uncomplimentary category vis-à-vis the Normans that the Greeks had occupied during the Apulian revolt. Finally when Leo invited Guaimar to join his anti-Norman coalition, the prince declined on the grounds that the Normans were his most valuable "treasure"; that "he had grown in honor on the incorruptible prosperity of their good will."[75] All that he could offer to the pope was a prophetic warning: "You will find what you are looking for, O wretched one! You will become food for the devouring lions [a play on Leo's name?] . . . you will find out what power and strength there is in them. Go and test the folly of the Normans and you will find that the words that God spoke to David will be fulfilled in them: 'One attacks a thousand, and two move 10,000.'"[76] Guaimar's warning was echoed by the words of St. Matthew, who appeared in a vision to the archbishop of Salerno on the eve of the battle:

> For it has been ordained in the presence of God that whosoever shall oppose the Normans will be put to flight by them; either they will all die or they will suffer great affliction. For this land has been given to the Normans by God. Because of the perversity of those who used to hold it and the paternal ties that God has with the Normans, the just will of God turned the land over to them. For both the law of God and the law of the empire command that the son succeed to the patrimony of the father.[77]

Guaimar's warning and the archbishop's vision reemphasized the two key Cyrus-like characteristics of the Normans that had led Amatus to write about them in the first place: they were militarily formidable and favored by God.

Amatus softened the subsequent confrontation between the holy pope and the divinely-favored Normans as much as he could. To their credit, Amatus's Normans were extremely reluctant to take the field against Leo. They sent a message of peace to him offering to hold the lands that they had conquered as his vassals, while pointing out that they had been duly invested with the territory by the emperor.[78] "But the pope would not talk" and Frederick only reiterated his intention to destroy them.[79] As the two sides prepared for battle, Amatus persisted in blurring the lines separating the protagonists and the antagonists. The same paragraph that described Leo dispensing absolution to his troops depicted the famished Normans, "following the example of the apostles," picking stalks of grain, rubbing them between their hands and eating them to assuage their hunger.[80] Finally, though the Normans routed the papal forces, they took no joy from it. Instead they gently reassured the shaken Leo, took him to Benevento, and catered to his every need.[81]

Leo IX was not the only pope who made Amatus's task as a Norman apologist difficult. Amatus seemed relieved to report that Victor II, who succeeded Leo IX in 1055, "did not promote emnity against the Norman knights but, acting on wise counsel, made peace with the Normans in friendship."[82] But he neglected to tell his readers that Victor subsequently changed his mind and solicited help from Henry against the Normans.[83] When Victor died a year later, his successor Stephen IX picked up where he had left off. This and the fact that the new pope was none other than the recently appointed abbot of Montecassino, Frederick of Lorraine, would seem to have complicated Amatus's task yet again.[84] But the fact that Stephen, without the consent of his former monastic brothers, appropriated the resources of Montecassino to help finance his campaign against the Normans soured Amatus on him.[85] Thus he incorporated into his account the dream of a fellow monk, in which St. Benedict himself appeared to assure him that the illicitly removed treasure would be restored.[86] Indeed Stephen's own death prevented him from organizing his anti-Norman campaign, thus preserving the abbey's wealth.[87] Amatus never got past Stephen's unorthodox appropriation of monastic funds to address the licitness of his anti-Norman policy. Finally Alexander II, echoing the words of Leo IX, appealed to Henry IV "to advance against the cruelty of the Normans in response to the affliction of those who live in their midst." But rather than elaborating on the precise nature of the afflictions administered by the Normans, Amatus used the episode to illustrate the corrosive effects of pride. By refusing to cooperate with

Henry and deciding to "go it alone," Godfrey of Lorraine doomed from the very beginning the effort to dislodge Richard.[88] Once again Amatus felt no obligation to address the issue of whether Richard deserved to be dislodged.

Amatus's task as a historian with a dual allegiance to the church and the Normans was simplified when he reached 1058, the year in which Desiderius was elected abbot of Montecassino and Richard annexed Capua—"not out of any greed for gold or silver, but out of a desire for honor."[89] According to Amatus, Desiderius took it upon himself to establish closer ties with the Normans of Aversa. When, during his siege of Capua, Richard visited Montecassino "to give thanks to the Lord St. Benedict,"

> He was received with a procession as if he were a king. The church was decorated as if it were Easter. The lamps were lit and the court resounded with songs in praise of the prince. He was led into the chapter and put in place of the abbot, even though he did not want to do this. His feet were washed many times by the abbot who committed to him the care and defense of the monastery. And he was asked by the abbot and by all of the monks to permit no man or enemy to do injury [to the monastery]. He granted peace to the church and promised to wage war against its enemies. He said that he would never be at peace with those who sought to take church property.[90]

From that point on, everything that Richard accomplished could be portrayed as an outgrowth of his relationship to Montecassino. When, in 1062, the recalcitrant citadel of Capua finally yielded to Richard, he, like one of the wiser Old Testament kings, "attributed the prosperity, power, and victory that came to him to the mercy of God rather than to his own power."[91]

> From that hour on [Richard] began to love and honor the church of St. Benedict at Montecassino more fervently. And he held its abbot Desiderius in reverence and commended himself to the prayers of the monks. He gave Abbot Desiderius a mitre of gold adorned with gems. He enriched the monastery with fortresses placed all around it. One man refused because he did not want [Richard] to put a fortress

on that territory which lay close to the monastery. But the prince saw that the fortress which had been begun was completed and the violence of that proud man was subjected to the abbot.[92]

In passages like these, Amatus effectively recast Richard in the mold of a monastic protector, transforming him into the embodiment of a monk's idea of the proper exercise of secular lordship. This served the needs of Amatus as a sympathetic historian of the Normans by allowing him to place Richard's military exploits within the legitimizing context of Richard's role as the protector of Montecassino. Instead of fighting for power, Amatus's Richard fought to promote peace.

And so Richard's campaigns take on a providential air. In his struggles with William of Montreuil, Richard was protected by "divine law" and the "judgement of God."[93] When his son Jordan rebelled after being invested with Aquino, Richard "put all his hope and all his faith in God and in St. Benedict," and through his power managed to regain control of Aquino peacefully.[94]

> And when the prince saw that the merit of St. Benedict had aided him in all his needs—for he had managed to take control of Aquino without a battle—he summoned the abbot and informed him of his intention: that he wanted to reward the monastery. Because he had been protected from his enemies and had achieved victory over them by means of the merit of the Lord St. Benedict and through the prayer of the brothers that dwelled in the monastery,

he offered the lordship of Aquino to Montecassino, claiming that he was only giving to Benedict what Benedict had given to him.[95]

Richard's close working relationship with Desiderius made Amatus's task, as a Casinese historian writing a sympathetic history of the Normans in Italy, an easy one. Robert Guiscard, on the other hand, provided him with a better opportunity to demonstrate his historiographical dexterity. There are a number of reasons for this. For one thing, Robert's Apulian and Calabrian power base lay at some distance from the monastery, making him much less a factor in Casinese affairs than Richard. Only when Robert took over Salerno in late 1076 did he find himself in close contact with the monastery and Desiderius. Moreover, Robert's behavior as a petty castellan in Calabria before acceding to the duchy of Apulia in 1057 flatly contradicted Amatus's ideas about the proper exercise of secular authority. In Amatus's own words, Robert's "poverty forced him to follow the path of a thief."[96] Finally, Robert spent his later years locked in a bitter struggle with Gregory VII that left him, more often than not, in a state of excommunication.

Amatus relied on a number of narrative devices to smooth over these blemishes in Robert's biography, so as to render him a more appropriate protagonist for his *Historia Normannorum*. He dealt with the "brigand" phase of Robert's career by turning it into a "before picture" designed to impress his readers with how far Robert, as duke of Apulia, had come. "His knights were few. He lacked essential goods. He had no money in his purse. And since he lacked everything, except for charity, which he had in abundance, he lived as did the children of Israel in the desert."[97] "He went wherever he thought he could find bread. He plundered continually, as it pleased him. What he had once done in hiding, he came to do out in the open."[98]

Of particular interest in this regard is Amatus's rendition of Robert's dealings with Peter, the Greek governor of Bisignano, "whom [Robert] regarded as a father, he in turn treating [Robert] as a son." At the end of one of their regular visits, Peter leaned over to kiss Robert, only to have the Norman grab him around his neck, carry him off to his fortress, and hold him for ransom. Amatus moralized what must have originally been a very entertaining fireside anecdote by having Robert experience pangs of guilt about his treacherous treatment of a friend. From Amatus's point of view, it was not Robert but Robert's poverty that was the precipitating factor. If anyone was to blame it was Peter, who, in his abundance, should have anticipated Robert's needs and, like a father, voluntarily offered his assistance to his "son."[99]

"Having spoken of the hunger, poverty, and solitude of Robert Guiscard" during those early years in Calabria, Amatus then set out to relate "how, through the mercy of God and the great multiplication of very strong men, [Robert] was exalted and how he subjected and overcame the proud."[100] The first step was Robert's marriage to Alberada, the young aunt of the Norman castellan Gerard of Buonalbergo, who brought with her a particularly attractive dowry in the form of two hundred knights: "This was the beginning of the increase of every good to Robert Guiscard."[101] The death of his half-brother Humphrey (1057) cleared the way for Robert's succession as count of Apulia and for him to utilize its resources to dominate what remained of Byzantine Calabria. It is significant that with Robert's newfound wealth and power came, according to Amatus, a newfound humility and contrition for his past behavior.

> After taking control of Apulia and Calabria, Robert's honor grew continually. The hand of God aided him in all things. Duke Robert wept for the sins that he had committed in the past and guarded against sinning in either the present or the future. He began to love the church of God and to have reverence for its priests. Now that he was rich, he made amends and satisfaction for those things that he had done while he was poor.[102]

By ascribing such a change of attitude to Robert, Amatus was able to "write off" to the constraints of poverty the less than exemplary behavior that Robert had displayed as a Calabrian castellan. Once he knew where his next meal was coming from, Amatus's Robert felt awful for his previous actions and made amends. In particular Amatus's Robert made up for his shoddy treatment of Peter of Bisignano by "making him richer that he had been before" his abduction.[103] Amatus went on to observe, in a wonderfully ambiguous theological aside:

> For everything that a man who is in mortal sin does is dead; that is, despite the good that he might do in the world, he will not pass on to eternal life. . . . [But] for every good thing that man does while in a state of mortal sin, God gives him grace so that he can escape that sin, as he does for Duke Robert Guiscard: either God gives him prosperity in temporal matters, or he delivers him from the pain of hell.[104]

Once Robert had repented of his former life, he could do nothing that would compromise Amatus's high opinion of him. Thus Amatus interpreted Robert's repudiation of Alberada on the grounds of consanguinuity as a sign of his newfound respect for the church, despite the obvious political advantages that Robert stood to gain by marrying Sichelgaita, the daughter of the late Guaimar V of Salerno.[105] From Amatus's perspective, the marriage joined a man who was "the richest of the rich, the humblest of the humble, and the strongest of knights," to a woman "noble in ancestry, comely in body, and wise in mind."[106]

In short Robert, like Richard, was transformed into a paradigm of secular lordship, as seen from a monastic perspective. He was "adorned with the dignity of every virtue," in particular, that of humility. "He was so humble that when he was among his people he did not seem like a lord but rather appeared to be one of the knights." He listened to any of his subjects no matter how poor or hungry they were, "observing well these words: 'You will be the greater the more you humble yourself to all.'"[107] He exercised justice firmly but with proper doses of pity. Most important-ly, he was respectful of the church: "he honored the leaders of the church and directed and preserved their possessions, giving from his own. He held the bishop and abbot in reverence and feared Christ in those who were his members. He did not desire to receive service from these prelates as from some prince, but he inclined himself to serve them." Yet, all of the humility and deference to the church aside, Robert remained a formidable military force: "The machinations of the emperor did not frighten him. The counsel of his rivals did not disturb him. Fortified castles and arms did not move him. He instilled fear in every man. And his prosperity and good fortune was disturbed by no man."[108] Most importantly, he had Christ on his side, assuring him of victory.

Two visions bore witness to the role of providence in Robert's career. A monk at Benevento dreamt that he saw two fields, one with a small number of people in it, representing the nations that "the majesty of God had already subjected to Robert Guiscard" and another with a great many, representing those that he was still destined to conquer.[109] On another occasion, a priest envisioned a tall tree with the Virgin Mary sitting amidst its branches and Robert on the ground underneath it, the two working together to resist the floodwaters, representing the armies that would unsuccessfully try to overwhelm him.[110]

The key to Amatus's transformation of Robert the brigand into Robert the divinely-favored duke of Apulia was not his relationship to Montecassino, which at this early stage was practically non-existent. Nor was it a function of Robert's relationship with the papacy, which was tem-pestuous to say the least. More than anything else, it was a product of his role in the conquest of Muslim Sicily, a military venture that allowed Robert to exercise his natural "robustness" and indomitability in a way that contributed to the extension of Christendom. Whether or not Robert was attracted by, or for that matter was even aware of, the spiritual benefits that he could accrue by extending his conquests across the Straits of Messina, his biographer made the most of them. According to Amatus, the idea first came to Robert after his successful siege of Troia in 1060. He began to "consider in his heart how he might be able to offend the Saracens, who had so violently killed Christians. But, because nothing can be done without the will of God, he waited for some sign by which he would be able to determine God's will."[111] That sign finally came in the form of a disaffected emir from Palermo who offered to ally himself to "the most Christian Duke Robert" if he should undertake an invasion of Sicily. According to Amatus, Robert delegated the command of the expedition to Geoffrey Ridel and sent his younger brother Roger along with him "to chase away the Saracens who had removed the island from Christian control."[112]

The first tentative foray into Sicily almost ended in disaster when bad weather prevented the Normans from returning to Reggio. But with the help of God, the storm subsided, allowing the Normans to disembark. Back in Reggio they acknowledged the divine assistance by using the booty they had won to pay for the restoration of a church.[113] According to Amatus, Robert decided to intervene personally in the Sicilian campaign once he had learned that eleven Christians from Reggio had been killed in a skirmish with the "pagans" of Sicily.[114] He invited his knights to take Sicily, telling them: "I would like to deliver the Christians and Catholics who are bound in servitude to the Saracens…and avenge the injury to God."[115] When Messina fell in 1061, Robert, who was still on the Calabrian side of the straits,

> gave thanks to God Omnipotent, from whom come all victory and triumph. And although his heart was so joyful and happy, he always kept in mind his celestial benefits. And he attributed all of the power and the victory that he had to have come from God, not from his own power. He commanded all of the Normans to go and bear witness that this battle came from God, who had given the power to be victorious and had surrendered the city to this small band of knights that Robert had sent, so as to upset all of the pagans."[116]

After overseeing the fortification of Messina, Robert—"who," as Amatus was fond of reiterating, "always put his trust more in God than in the number of his men"—set out to conquer more of the island.[117] "Due to the fame of this great lord, the inhabitants of the cities fled before his face, melting like ice before a fire."[118] The subsequent battle between the Normans and the superior forces of the emir of Castrogiovanni at Cerami (1063) was depicted by Amatus as a holy war. Robert's address to his men prior to the battle is illustrative:

> We have placed our hope more firmly in God than in any great number of soldiers. Do not be afraid. We have with us Jesus Christ, who said: "If you have the faith of a mustard seed and you tell a mountain to move, it will move." The firmness of our faith enjoys the warmth of the Holy Spirit so that in the name of the Holy Trinity, we will attack this "mountain," not a mountain of rock born of the earth but a mountain of the filth of heresy and hidden perversity. Therefore let us purge our sins through confession and penance, receive the body and the blood of Christ, and take up our arms. God is the source of the power of this small, faithful band, and he will give us victory over the multitude of the infidel.[119]

Robert's men made the sign of the cross and attacked. "God fought for the Christian Normans: he protected them and confounded the infidel."[120] The "pagans" were put to flight, suffering countless casualties while the Christians lost not a single man.[121]

Throughout Amatus's description of the Sicilian campaign, we find Robert motivated by concerns that had never disturbed him before. Like the Norman pilgrims at Salerno, Robert is troubled by the simple fact of political domination of Christians by Saracens, and sets out to do something about it. He is presented as a Christian leader who is aware, in a way that even the Norman pilgrims were not, that the Saracens posed something of a religious challenge to Christianity; that they represented a heresy that needed to be extirpated by a holy campaign of Christian soldiers fortified with the body and blood of Christ.

Despite this auspicious beginning, the conquest of Sicily dragged on for thirty years and was for the most part conducted by small Norman forces led, not by Robert, but by his younger brother Roger.[122] Robert did join forces with his brother to besiege Palermo, forcing it to surrender in 1072.[123] But that was it for the duke's participation in the Sicilian conquest, there being many more pressing concerns on the mainland to keep his attention. This was not a problem for Amatus. He simply made the conquest of Sicily coterminous with Robert's participation in it, depicting the siege of Palermo as its culmination. Not only did Amatus ignore

Roger's subsequent twenty-year solo effort to subdue the rest of the island, but by recounting the miracles that graced the reconsecration of the cathedral in Palermo, he left the impression that Robert had succeeded—at least from a divine perspective—in restoring the island to Christian rule.[124]

Amatus went on to contrast Duke Robert's success in Sicily with the failures of the German and Greek emperors who had taken on the Saracens in the past. Despite the awesome resources at his disposal, Otto II

> was not able to dominate or beat down the malice of the Saracens. The pagans came against him from the other side of the sea and they captured the emperor and destroyed him, him and his company, and all of his knights, and they put the best of his men in prison and did great damage to them.[125]

Likewise the Byzantine emperor had "fought for a long time against the Saracens of Sicily and spent his treasure," but his conquest of Sicily proved ephemeral. "But the duke Robert, who was glorious in all his deeds, conquered Palermo in five months." What accounted for Robert's success? His humility and the favor that he found in God's eyes. Given this achievement, it seemed only fair to Amatus "that the name and the power of 'emperor' could be attributed to [Robert]."[126]

If Robert had been able to spend more of his time in Sicily fighting the Saracens, Amatus's job as a historian would have been considerably easier. But given his choice of protagonists, Amatus had no alternative but to follow Robert back to Italy where the political realities did not lend themselves to such straightforward casting of "good guys" and "bad guys." In particular Amatus was faced with the task of recounting a rebellion against Robert led by none other than Richard of Capua (1073), a situation that once again forced him to tip-toe on the fence dividing his allegiances. In this case, Amatus favored Robert. The duke remained at the siege of Palermo even after he got word about the rebellion because he knew that the conquest of Palermo mattered more to God.[127] When he finally made his way back to Apulia and suppressed the rebellion, Robert "knew that this victory had come from Almighty God,"[128] and Richard, to his credit, "recognized that the power of God was against him."[129]

Still, there is some ambiguity in Amatus's sympathies. When Amatus recounted how Richard's forces managed to capture Gerard of Buonalber-

ga, Robert's longtime ally, he wrote that "the prince [Richard] was over-
joyed with the victory that his knights had won against the duke and gave
thanks to St. Benedict and the brothers who lived in his monastery."
Even Amatus had to comment on the irony that "the one lord as well as
the other believed he had won victory by the merit of St. Benedict and by
the prayers of his monks!"[130]

Robert's perennial antagonism toward Gregory VII posed another
potential difficulty. It is indicative of the endless friction between the two
that Amatus was only able to find one expression of warmth on Gregory's
part toward the duke and that this should have been a letter of condolence
to Sichelgaita upon hearing a rumor of Robert's death. "A great, incurable
pain has come to the church of Rome, the pain caused by the death of that
most dear son of the holy church, Duke Robert."[131] For his part Amatus'
Robert, touched by the pope's sympathy, wrote back to correct him,
thanking him for the kind words and promising "to serve him faithfully."

Amatus was not complimentary in his treatment of Gregory's futile
efforts to form a coalition against Robert. He made fun of the pope's
reliance on Beatrice and Mathilda: "since he could find no men to help
him, he sought the aid of women."[132] Amatus's Gregory, like his Frederick of Lorraine at Civitate, vastly underestimated Robert's military aptitude, boasting that even a fraction of the forces pledged by his patronesses
would prevail over "that little, most vile Norman...should it please
God."[133] Like the Normans who faced Leo IX, Amatus's Robert was too
humble and deferent to relish the thought of fighting the pope.[134] He
(and Amatus) were spared this difficulty when Gregory's coalition self-
destructed and Desiderius managed to work out a truce between the two
principal Norman rulers.[135] It is interesting that Amatus, who authored at
least two works dedicated to Gregory VII, should have been less sympathetic with his efforts to subvert Robert than he was with Leo IX's efforts
at Civitate.

Despite the ongoing conflict between Robert and Gregory, Amatus
did his best to present Robert's relations with the church in positive
terms. When, at the outset of Henry IV's breach with the papacy, the king
sent an embassy to Robert offering imperial recognition of his conquests,
Robert's response made him appear to be a dutiful papal vassal:

> I have taken this land from the dominion of the Greeks with great
> loss of blood and after suffering great need, poverty, hunger and mis-

ery. And many times Normans have conspired against me trying to persecute and capture me. I withstood the pride of the Saracens as well as hunger and great tribulation on the other side of the sea. So that I might have the assistance of God and so that my lords St. Peter and St. Paul—to whom all the kingdoms on earth are subject— would pray for me, I submitted myself to their vicar, the pope, along with all the land that I had conquered. And I received them back from the hands of the pope so that, through the power of God, he would be able to protect me from the malice of the Saracens and vanquish the pride of foreigners. We know that, from ancient times up to our own, the pride of the Greeks ruled Apulia and Calabria and that all of Sicily was constrained and subjugated by the error of the Saracens. Now Almighty God has glorified me in this victory and has subjected the land, which had been subjugated by cruel power, to me and has made me greater than anyone else from among my people. Because I desired to be subject to God, I was able to conquer it through His grace. I hold from Him the land which you say you want to give to me. Because the hand of my lord the King is just and generous, he gives me of his own beyond the little that I have and possess, and I will be subject to him, always and forever preserving the fidelity of the church.[136]

Robert's response to the German overture summarizes nicely all of the narrative elements that Amatus employed to elevate the Normans. Robert's conquests had been won through a tireless and taxing personal effort. He had wisely enlisted divine assistance against his enemies by becoming a papal vassal and, with God's help, had overcome both the Greeks and the Saracens, rightfully taking from them the lands that they had ruled for so long. According to Amatus, the imperial messengers returned to Germany convinced that they had met "the greatest lord in the world."[137]

The only thing that Robert lacked, from the point of view of a Casinese historian, was a close relationship with Montecassino. This was remedied in the second half of 1076 by Robert's successful siege of Salerno. This conquest was, from Amatus's perspective in the late 1070s, the culmination of Robert's career. From a narrative standpoint, it could be thought of as the final chapter in the forty year process by which Salerno was displaced by the Norman principality that it had helped to foster.

From Amatus's perspective, the story had begun the moment the Norman pilgrims relieved Salerno from the Saracen attack and Guaimar IV began to encourage Norman immigration. Guaimar V helped the process along by arranging marriage alliances between his family and the successive dukes of Apulia,[138] thus lending nobility and local roots to the parvenu sons of Tancred. Humphrey played a decisive role in securing Gisulf's succession after the assassination of Guaimar. But in the end, Gisulf himself would have to step aside for Robert Guiscard. Like the ruling dynasty of Capua that had yielded to Richard, Robert's "rise to greatness" was predicated on the "fall" of a Lombard ruler.[139]

In order to account for Robert's takeover of Salerno without making the Normans appear ungrateful for the indispensible assistance offered by the Guaimar during the early years of the Norman settlement, Amatus had to cast Gisulf II in an entirely different role from the one played by Guaimar V. Guaimar had played the part of the benevolent and powerful blue-blooded lord who recognized the value of the parvenu Normans as a fighting force. His principal role had been to dispense legitimacy to the sons of Tancred. After the Normans of Melfi elected William as their count (1042),

> They went to the court of Guaimar, prince of Salerno, and he received them as if they were his sons and bestowed upon them the greatest of gifts. And so as to honor William, the new count, above all others, he gave him the daughter of his brother Guido to take as his wife. The Normans were very happy with the gifts they received and also with their count who now had such noble family ties. From that hour on Guaimar called William "prince" and referred to himself as "rector." He invited William to share his land, both that which had already been acquired as well as that which would be acquired.[140]

For their part the Normans of Melfi—in particular Drogo—served Guaimar faithfully.[141] Amatus described his death as a dark day, heralded by portents.[142]

In stark contrast to this glowing portrait of Guaimar is the decadent image that Amatus paints of Gisulf. For one thing Amatus downplayed the biological connection between Gisulf and his father Guaimar, preferring to see him as the son of his mother, Gemma of Teano. Casinese relations with the counts of Teano were often strained, making it easy to appreciate Amatus's disgust when he identified Gisulf as one "born of a viper-like people."[143]   Whereas Guaimar had managed to remain on the best of terms with the various Norman principalities, Gisulf succeeded only in alienating them, beginning with his lack of gratitude for the services rendered by the Normans in securing his succession and his general failure to recognize his feudal obligations.[144]

But Gisulf's crimes went much further than this and Amatus felt compelled to take a long detour to lay them out for the edification of his readers. Gisulf was, from Amatus's perspective, the personification of "envy, deception, arrogance, pride, covetousness, gluttony, avarice, murder, perfidy, sacrilege, the repaying of good with evil, discord, and false chastity."[145] Amatus proceeded to give examples of how Gisulf personified each of these vices. He was envious towards his brother-in-law Robert and was always trying to do him harm, despite the fact that "'there is no counsel or wisdom against the power of God'[146] and no one is able to condemn him whom God glorifies. He was a worthless thing pestering a most powerful lion; he will become the lion's food."[147]   According to Amatus, Gisulf feigned a pilgrimage to Jerusalem so that he could meet with the emperor in Constantinople to enlist his aid against Robert.[148] He demonstrated his covetousness by trying to falsify his currency.[149] He was such a glutton that "it is not possible to say how much food was needed to fill his insatiable stomach."[150]   He tortured to death a doctor and a woman.[151]   He repaid the support that he had received from his uncle Guido by giving him only one small fortress in return.[152] "That rapacious wolf Gisulf, master of all malice," also "persecuted the members of Christ," specifically struggling with one Gauferius over the limits of secular and ecclesiastical jurisdiction[153] and sowing discord between Desiderius and Hildebrand.[154] Finally, according to Amatus, Gisulf spurned his wife on the grounds of a "false vow of chastity."[155]

Visions foretold the imminent end of Gisulf's rule. A monk named Jocundus prophesied: "During the lordship of the son of Guaimar, prince of Salerno, the lordship of the Lombards will end and it will be conceded to a great man from another people, through whom the city will be exalted."[156] As the end for Gisulf approached, his iniquity grew: he gave vent to an "insatiable rage that seemed to surpass the cruelty of Nero and Maximian."[157]   In particular, he authorized piracy against the merchant ships of Amalfi (which, ever since the death of Guaimar, had been reasserting its independence from Salerno), confiscating their goods and ransoming their crews. Amatus was particularly scandalized by—and therefore described in the greatest detail—the tortures that Gisulf inflicted on his prisoners by depriving them of their eyesight and of various bodily members.[158] Amatus described the treatment of one Mauro, whose father was a prominent Amalfitan, in particular detail, going so far as to call him a martyr after he was tortured to death.[159] Gisulf committed similar crimes against Pisan and Genoese shipping in his perverse effort to "exceed the wealth of the emperor."[160] His increased wealth nurtured overblown pride: "he did not appear to himself to be a mortal man, but one of the gods."[161]

Gisulf's close ties to Gregory VII put Amatus in another one of those difficult positions. Having just described Gisulf as a monster, he found himself having to explain why it was that the pope would not accept the offer that the people of Amalfi made to place their city under his protection. "The pope, who loved Gisulf above all other lords because Gisulf loved the pope so much and was so obedient to him that he would make no other alliance with any other lord or have friendship with it without the permission of the pope, did not want to accept Amalfi," and encouraged it to acknowledge Gisulf as their lord.[162] On the other hand, the ties between the two may have provided Amatus (as a spokesman for Desiderius) with a safe way of indirectly criticizing Gregory by holding up his ally Gisulf for reproach.

This is where Robert Guiscard entered the picture, that is, as Amalfi's second choice in its search for an outside protector. Gisulf, blinded by his pride, refused to negotiate despite the formidability of his opponent. Gregory, Desiderius, and Sichelgaita (Gisulf's sister) all tried unsuccessfully to dissuade him from attacking Amalfi. Encouraged by the false prophecy of a monk named Leo,[163] Gisulf boastfully responded to his sister's entreaties with a promise to dress her in widow's black.[164] After Robert had surrounded Salerno, Gisulf only added to his crimes by forcing the people of Salerno to endure a long and difficult siege. Amatus described their suffering in great detail.[165] "As a result of the great weakness that came with the famine, old people died like beasts without the blessing of priests, the young died suddenly, and infants, unable to receive baptism, died as pagans."[166] To top it all off, Gisulf ordered that a dog, who had been begging bread from the besiegers each night and delivering it to a priest in the city each morning in an effort to relieve the famine, be killed.[167] For his part, the dog's clerical accomplice was imprisoned, as was another priest named Gratian, who became a "martyr of God."[168] Even after Gisulf had been captured, he remained singularly unregenerate. When Robert asked for the teeth of St. Matthew, whose body was the chief relic of Salerno, Gisulf delivered to him the teeth of a Jew instead. Only when Robert threatened to replace the teeth with Gisulf's if they proved to be fake did the deposed prince comply with the duke's request.[169]

Throughout his extended description of Gisulf, Amatus treated him as the antithesis of Robert Guiscard. Whereas Robert was always concerned about exercising his authority in a manner supportive of the church, Gisulf dedicated himself to the subversion of peace and justice. And if Robert came to rival the emperor in wealth and power through the exercise of legitimate power, Gisulf's imperial pretensions were fueled by piracy. The contrast that Amatus drew not only served to justify Robert's takeover of Salerno, but clarified to the reader what it was that made Robert's rise to power in the region so remarkable, given the fact that he could have tried, like Gisulf, to achieve a similar result through unscrupulous means.

It was in the course of the siege that Robert, in the company of his new ally Richard, came to Montecassino. At first he refused to accept the gifts that Desiderius offered him on the noble grounds that "he had come not to take things from the monastery but to add to them."[170] But "the abbot went to him and asked that Robert not refuse the gifts of the brothers, who wanted to pray to God on his behalf." Then came a procession "to receive the duke with great honor." Robert took the opportunity to pass among the brothers in the chapel to speak with them and "humbly and peacefully give them gifts so that they would pray to God to pardon his sins." "And like a father to the brothers, he went through the monastery and visited the sick and administered in abundance to them all whatever they needed, asking each to pray to God for him." When Robert sat down to eat, he asked for the salt and rewarded the monk who brought it to him with a gift of 100 besants.[171] Armed with the power of prayer, Robert returned to the siege and Salerno fell shortly thereafter, "God having conceded the victory to [the duke]."[172]

The most significant aspect of Robert's takeover of Salerno for Amatus's purposes is that it brought him into the sphere of Montecassino, allowing him to be recognized as protector just as Richard had been so many years before. From a narrative (as well as a strategic) standpoint, Robert needed Desiderius's support, because once he had secured his hold

over Salerno and returned the favor to Richard by assisting in his conquest of Naples, Robert turned on Benevento, which lay under papal protection.[173] "And the pope, for this reason and others, assembled his
ministers and excommunicated the duke and all of his followers."[174] But
from Amatus's Casinese perspective, this low point in Robert's relations
with the pope in no way diminished the new ties that he had forged with
Desiderius. Despite the excommunication, Amatus felt comfortable sup-
plementing his eulogy for Richard with an encomium for Robert.

> It is proper, now, as I said at the beginning of this work, to recount
> briefly the good that these two lords did for our monastery. Because
> after Richard had become prince of Capua, he tried to make happy
> our church which his predecessors had disturbed, and to oppress,
> with the strong hand of his defense, those who persecuted and threat-
> ened it and to destroy those who destroyed the possessions of the
> monastery. He took the monastery's fortresses from the hands of the
> tyrants who held them and he devoutly handed over many other
> fortresses of his to the monastery so that the brothers would continu-
> ally pray to God on his behalf. When they fasted he consoled them
> with fish.

As for Robert:

> The duke so loved Abbot Desiderius that he held him in reverence
> like St. Benedict, and did not want to be absent from him. The abbot
> was no less loved by the duchess [Sichelgaita] and although she was
> not related to him, he always treated her like a daughter. The [duke
> and duchess] had concern for their "father" as well as for the protec-
> tion and well-being of their souls. And if there was a day in which the
> abbot did not go to the court, they sent to him by means of a letter or
> message, requesting his presence. And when he came they gave him
> many things; for the honor of the church, they gave him various
> *pailles* and sent many pieces of gold and silver. And each day they sent
> many *besants* and *tarin* for the food and clothing of the brothers. And
> on the solemn feast, they honored the refector with a vessel of gold or
> silver. And, either by mule or by a Saracen servant, they enriched the
> entire monastery. And, to tell the truth, as a result of their benefice,
> the entire monastery was illumined. Through the merit of St. Bene-

dict, may God, the father and remunerator of every good, grant these two lords eternal life.

Richard's path to respectability as a Norman ruler was shorter and more direct than Robert's. The proximity of Capua to Montecassino assured that when Richard took it over in 1058 he would be incorporated by Desiderius as the monastery's protector. Robert did not have this advantage, but he was able to reap the symbolic benefits of overseeing the conquest of Muslim Sicily. His active role in extending Christian territory allowed Amatus to overlook his singularly antagonistic relations with Gregory VII despite the fact that Amatus was something of a devotee of the pope. And once Robert had assumed control of Salerno and Richard had died, Robert's relationship with Montecassino assumed much greater significance than it had had in Robert's early years. Given the fact that Amatus was writing in the wake of Richard's death, when the balance of power that he had established in the region was shattered, it is likely that the positive image of Robert Guiscard that emerges from the *Historia Normannorum* represented as much Amatus's hope for the future as his understanding of the past.

Notes

1. Hermann a. 1053, p. 132.
2. CMCas 3.35, p. 411. Anselmo Lentini, "Il poema di Amato su S. Pietro Apostolo," *Misc. Cassinese* 30 (1958–59).
3. Bartholomaeis, in Amatus, pp. xxiii, lxxxi–lxxxv.
4. Bartholomaeis, in Amatus, p. xxvi.
5. Cowdrey, *Age of Abbot Desiderius*, p. xx; CMCas 3.35, p. 411 n. 18; Bartholomaeis in Amatus, pp. xxviiff, assumes that he had to have been bishop after he dedicated the *Historia Normannorum* to Desiderius, where he identified himself as a monk.
6. Amatus 8.33, pp. 372–73.
7. Bartholomaeis, in Amatus, p. lxviii, interpreted Amatus's account as presupposing the end of the rift between Robert Guiscard and Gregory VII, though there is no particular reason why this has to have been the case. He also saw reference to Balkan campaigns in the vision of peoples conquered by Robert "on this side of the sea as well as the other" (Amatus 5.3, p. 223). But this is more likely a reference to Italy and Sicily than to Italy and the Balkans. See Mathieu in William, p. 9 n.3.
8. For scholarly attempts to evaluate the translation, see W. Schmidt, "Die

'Historia Normannorum' von Amatus. Eine Hauptquelle für die Geschichte der süditalischen Politik Papst Gregors VII," *Studi Gregoriani* 3 (1948), pp. 172–231; and F. Torraca, "Amato di Montecassino e il suo traduttore." *Casinensia* 1 (1929), pp. 161ff.

9. Bartholomaeis, in Amatus, p. xcvi.

10. For more on this matter, see Bartholomaeis, in Amatus, pp. civ–cviii.

11. Amatus, Dedication, pp. 3–4.

12. Amatus, Dedication, p. 3; Isaiah 45:1–3.

13. 2 Chronicles 36:22; Ezra 1:1–4.

14. The term "Norman," noted Amatus, came from "Nore," the name of the island that was their ancestral home. This was a widely accepted etymology at the time Amatus wrote. See: Bartholomaeis, in Amatus, p. 10, n. 1.

15. Amatus 1.1–2, pp. 9–11.

16. Amatus is the only Latin source that identifies the leader of the expedition by name. The Cordoban historian Ibn Haiyan identified him only as the "commander of the cavalry of Rome." Reinhart Dozy identified him as William of Montreuil, who, as Amatus himself tells us, served as a papal vassal and carried the papal banner. But Bartholomaeis contests this: Amatus p. 13 n. 3, p. 14 nn. 1, 2.

17. Amatus 1.3, pp. 11–12.

18. Amatus 1.5, p. 13.

19. Amatus 1.5, pp. 13–14.

20. Amatus 1.7, p. 15.

21. Amatus 1.9, p.17. Amatus went on to describe how Roussel, "a man of great courage and a formidable warrior," conquered Armenia but was ultimately undone by the Greeks who treacherously sided with the Turks against him: Amatus 1.14–15, pp. 19–20.

22. Amatus 1.17, pp. 21–22.

23. Amatus 1.17, p. 22.

24. Amatus 1.18, p. 23.

25. As Boehm ("*Nomen Gentis Normannorum*," p. 649) points out, Guaimar's supposed invitation to prospective Norman immigrants also served to cast the Norman influx as a product of local Lombard initiative.

26. Amatus 1.19, p. 24.

27. Amatus 1.20, p. 25.

28. Amatus 1.21, p. 27

29. Amatus 1.20, p. 26.

30. Amatus 1.22, p. 29.

31. Amatus 1.33, p. 49; Deuteronomy 32:30.

32. Where did the Saracens fit into all this? Only when Amatus, describing the results of Henry II's intervention into southern politics in 1022, referred in passing to the establishment of some Norman garrison "to defend the faith and challenge the Saracens." Amatus 1.31, p. 42.

33. A common device used by "barbaric" Latins to deprecate "civilized" Greeks. Décarreaux, *Normands, papes, et moines*, p. 22.

34. It is interesting that Amatus did not push the Rome vs. Constantinople

ecclesiastical jurisdiction issue, which seems to have been a key motivating factor, at least from a papal perspective, behind the Treaty of Melfi. Décarreaux, *Normands, papes, et moines*, pp. 83– 84.

35. Amatus 2.8, p. 67.

36. Amatus 2.10, pp. 68–69.

37. Amatus 2.14, pp. 72–73.

38. Amatus 2.16, pp. 74–75; There was a long tradition of Lombard hostility toward the Greeks, as evidenced by Erchempert's observation: *Archivi, ut habitudinis similes sunt, ita animo aequales sunt bestiis, vocabulo christiani, set moribus tristiores Agarenis*. Erchempert, *Historia Langobardorum Beneventanorum*, MGH *Scriptores rerum Langobardicarum et Italicarum* 81:264.

39. Amatus 2.17, pp. 75–76.

40. Amatus 2.19, pp. 77–78.

41. Amatus 2.20, p. 79.

42. Amatus 2.21, pp. 79–80.

43. Amatus 2.21, p. 80.

44. Amatus 2.22, p. 83.

45. Amatus 2.23, pp. 85–86.

46. Amatus 2.26, p. 90.

47. Amatus 4.1, p. 181.

48. Amatus 1.35, p. 46. Psalm 1:1.

49. Amatus 1.35, 37, pp. 47, 50.

50. Amatus 1.35, pp. 47–48.

51. Amatus 1.35, p. 48.

52. Amatus 1.38, p. 50.

53. Amatus 1.38–39, pp. 51–52.

54. Amatus 1.40, p. 52. Cf. Desiderius's account of Pandulf's abuses in *Dialogues* 1.9, p. 1123.

55. Amatus 1.23, pp. 31–32.

56. Amatus 1.44–5, pp. 55–56.

57. Amatus 2.3, p. 60.

58. Amatus 2.5–6, pp. 62–65.

59. Amatus 2.7, p. 65.

60. Amatus 2.34, pp. 99–101.

61. Amatus 2.35, pp. 101–2.

62. Amatus 2.37, p. 104.

63. Amatus 2.38, p. 106.

64. Amatus 2.42, p. 108.

65. Amatus 2.43, p. 109; cf. Desiderius, *Dialogues* 2.22, pp. 1138–39; CMCas 2.71, pp. 309–12.

66. Amatus 3.15, pp. 129–30; 3.21, pp. 134–35; 3.42, p. 158.

67. Amatus 3.16, pp. 130–31.

68. Amatus 3.17–18, pp. 132–33.

69. Amatus 3.18, p. 133.

70. Amatus 3.20, p. 134.

71. Amatus 3.23, p. 138.

72. Amatus 3.23, p. 139.

73. Amatus 3.24, pp. 139–40.

74. Amatus 3.24, p. 140.

75. Amatus 3.30, pp. 146–47.

76. Amatus 3.25, pp. 140–41. Deuteronomy 32:30 and 1 Samuel 18:7.

77. Amatus 3.38, pp. 151–52.

78. Amatus 3.39, p. 153.

79. Amatus 3.39, p. 154.

80. Luke 6:1. Amatus 3.40, p. 154.

81. Amatus 3.41, pp. 157–58.

82. Amatus 3.47, p. 163.

83. Amatus 3.48, p. 163.

84. Amatus 3.49–50, pp. 165–66.

85. Amatus 3.50, pp. 166–67.

86. Amatus 3.51, p. 167.

87. Amatus 3.52, p. 170.

88. Amatus 6.9–10, pp. 270–72.

89. Amatus 4.11, p. 189.

90. Amatus 4.13, pp. 191–92.

91. Amatus 4.30, p. 205. David distinguished himself from Saul precisely by placing his trust in God rather than in his own military strength. See, for instance, 1 Samuel 17:45–47.

92. Amatus 4.31, p. 205.

93. Amatus 6.1, p. 258.

94. Amatus 6.24, p. 287.

95. Amatus 6.25, pp. 287–88.

96. Amatus 3.8, p. 121.

97. Amatus 3.8, pp. 121–22.

98. Amatus 3.9, p. 122.

99. Amatus 3.10, pp. 122–23.

100. Amatus 4.1, p. 181.

101. Amatus 3.11, pp. 125–26.

102. Amatus 4.17, p. 194.

103. Amatus 4.17, p. 194.

104. Amatus 4.18, p. 194.

105. Amatus 4.18, p. 194.

106. Amatus 4.18, p. 195.

107. Luke 22:26.

108. Amatus 5.1, pp. 222–23.

109. Amatus 5.2, p. 223.

110. Amatus 5.3, p. 223.

111. Amatus 5.7, p. 229.

112. Amatus 5.9, p. 231.

113. Amatus 4.10, p. 233.

114. Amatus 5.11, p. 234. Note how the Christians and Saracens of Reggio unite against Saracen attacks from Sicily.

115. Amatus 5.12, p. 234.

116. Amatus 5.18, p. 237.

117. Amatus 5.20, p. 238.

118. Amatus 5.22, pp. 239–40.

119. Amatus 5.22, pp. 241–42.

120. Amatus 5.22, p. 242.

121. Amatus 5.22, p. 242.

122. Amatus apparently intended to write a separate history dedicated to Roger's conquests: Amatus 6.23, p. 286.

123. Amatus 6.13–19, pp. 275–82.

124. Amatus 6.20, p. 283.

125. A reference to the imperial defeat under Otto II at the battle of Stilo in 982.

126. Amatus 6.22, p. 284.

127. Amatus 7.2, p. 293

128. Amatus 7.3, p. 295.

129. Amatus 7.4, p. 295.

130. Amatus 7.22, p. 314.

131. Amatus 7.8, p. 298.

132. Cowdrey, *Age of Abbot Desiderius*, p. 127.

133. Amatus 7.12, pp. 303–4.

134. Amatus 7.14, p. 306.

135. Amatus 7.16, 7.29, pp. 308, 322.

136. Amatus 7.27, p. 321.

137. Amatus 7.27, p. 321.

138. Guaimar gave a niece to William, a sister to Humphrey, a daughter to Drogo, and another daughter to Robert.

139. Amatus 3.1, p. 181.

140. Amatus 2.29, p. 94.

141. Amatus 2.37, 2.39, 3.12, 3.17, pp. 104, 106, 127, 132.

142. Amatus 3.26–27, pp. 141–42.

143. Amatus 3.44, p. 159.

144. Amatus 3.44–46, 4.15–16, pp. 159–63, 193–94.

145. Amatus 4.34, p. 207.

146. Proverbs 21:30.

147. Amatus 4.35, p. 207.

148. Amatus 4.36–9, pp. 207–11.

149. Amatus 4.39, pp. 211–12.

150. Amatus 4.40, p. 212.

151. Amatus 4.41, pp. 212–13.

152. Amatus 4.42, pp. 213–14.

153. Amatus 4.43, pp. 215–16.

154. Amatus 4.48, p. 219.

155. Amatus 4.49, pp. 219–20.
156. Amatus 8.1, p. 339.
157. Amatus 8.2, p. 339.
158. Amatus 8.2, pp. 340–41.
159. Amatus 8.3, pp. 341–46.
160. Amatus 8.4, pp. 346–47.
161. Amatus 8.5, p. 347.
162. Amatus 8.7, p. 348.
163. Amatus 8.9, p. 350.
164. Amatus 8.13, p.353.
165. Amatus 8.16–20, pp. 359–60.
166. Amatus 8.19, p.359.
167. Amatus 8.20, pp. 359–60.
168. Amatus 8.20, pp. 360–61.
169. Amatus 8.29, p. 370.
170. Amatus 8.22, pp. 361–362.
171. Amatus 8.22, pp. 361–62.
172. Amatus 8.24, p. 365.
173. Amatus 8.32, p. 372.
174. Amatus 8.33, pp. 372–73.

5. William of Apulia and the Normans

While Robert Guiscard figures prominently in the *Historia Normannorum*, it is really Richard of Capua, as the protector of Montecassino from 1058 to 1078, who serves as the focal point of Amatus's work. And although—as we will see in the next chapter—Robert played an important role in the *De rebus gestis Rogerii et Roberti* of Geoffrey Malaterra, the principal protagonist of the work is his younger brother Roger. William of Apulia's *Gesta Roberti Wiscardi* enjoys, therefore, the distinction of being the only one of this first generation of histories of the Normans in Italy to give its full attention to Robert Guiscard. It recounts in detail his exploits in Calabria, Apulia, Sicily, Campania, and the Balkans, incorporating other Norman leaders only in so far as their careers intersected that of the duke of Apulia.

Textual references allow us to locate the writing of the *Gesta Roberti Wiscardi* sometime in the last two or three years of the 1090s. When recounting the attacks made by the Seldjuk Turks in Anatolia, William claimed that the empire would have lost that province if the Latin forces "had not been incited by divine will to deliver it by overcoming the enemy" and "to open the holy routes to the Sepulchre that had been closed long before."[1] That William should draw his reader's attention to the "deliverance" of Anatolia and the opening of the pilgrimage route but not to the actual conquest of Jerusalem that was to follow suggests that he composed this part of the *Gesta* sometime between the summer of 1097, when the Frankish armies were marching through Anatolia, and the summer of 1099, when Jerusalem fell.[2] This dating of the *Gesta* also fits William's characterization of Richard of Capua's grandson Richard (II) as an "adolescent,"[3] for we know from Geoffrey Malaterra[4] that Richard II rebelled as a *pusillus* in 1090 on his father Jordan's death and finally arrived *ad intelligibilem aetatem* in 1098.[5] It would seem that William did not actually finish the work until after Urban II's death on July 29, 1099, however, for while the prologue acknowledges both Urban II[6] and Roger as patrons of the work, the epilogue refers only to Roger.[7]

William's identity must be reconstructed entirely from what little can be gleaned from his history.[8] The incipit of the *Gesta Roberti Wiscardi* refers to the author as Guillermus Apuliensis, indicating that he was either a native or a resident of the province that served as the principal venue for the events he described. One serious attempt has been made to identify him with one Willelmus Apulus, a cleric in Bordeaux, but the references to this William place him in France at the time that he should have been writing the *Gesta Roberti Wiscardi* in Italy.[9]

William would seem to have been a member of Roger Borsa's court. This would explain the *Gesta's* close attention to Robert Guiscard's designation of Roger as his heir on the eve of the first Balkan campaign, not to mention the confidence with which William pronounced Roger duke of Apulia after his father's death in 1085.[10]   Indeed it is quite possible that Roger commissioned the *Gesta* with the intention of solidifying his claim to Apulia in the face of the ever-present challenge posed by his half-brother Bohemund.

It is conceivable that William was a layman. That would help explain the relative paucity of religious motifs in the *Gesta*.[11]   Once in a great while William punctuated his account with some formulaic reference to divine involvement—*Deo nolente*[12] or *spirante Deo*[13]—but this was not typical. He acknowledged the role of providence behind the rise of the Normans, but rarely did William identify its workings as the Norman destiny unfolded.[14] One of the few occasions was at Civitate where the Germans thought they would win easily, but "victory in war is not a function of numbers, or horses, or people, or arms; but to whom it is given by God."[15]   Another occurred during the siege of Durazzo where Robert, again facing formidable odds, uncharacteristically rejected a clever plan on the grounds that victory under such circumstances could only come from on high.[16]   In this same vein, there are only two recorded portents in the *Gesta*: a deep freeze that William connected to the arrival of the Normans in Italy[17] and the landing of a huge fish in Apulia which preceeded the conquest of Palermo.[18]

Nor did William try to shape Robert into a paradigmatic defender of the church as Amatus had done. At one point in the course of his description of Robert's conquest of Calabria, it seemed as if William might be moving in this direction: "Wanting to take control of the region, [Robert] extended his love to everyone. There was never a lord more affable or humble than he." But then William continued: "The Calabrians were terrified at the arrival of the duke, filled as he was with such ferocity. Supported by no small band of soldiers, Robert ordered that the land be plundered and burned everywhere. He wished it to be despoiled so as to strike fear in the inhabitants."[19] Apparently the love and humility that Robert expressed was directed toward the men he led, not toward the peoples unfortunate enough to inhabit the regions he conquered.

The only real exception to William's secular tone orientation was his account of the Norman campaigns in Sicily. Even William recognized that fighting Muslims meant something different than fighting Christians. A war fought to defend Christendom from non-Christian assailants required a different type of narrative. Thus the Sicilian Muslims were identified as a *perversa gens*[20] or an *iniquus populus*[21] that could not possibly expect to withstand armies comprised of *cultores Christi*.[22] At the siege of Palermo, William's Duke Robert addressed his men, who had fortified themselves by partaking of the eucharist,[23] with the words of a holy warrior: "This is a city inimical to God, ignorant of the divine cult, subject to demons, bereft of its ancient vigor. . . . This city, so difficult to capture, will be opened, with Christ's mercy, for he makes all difficult undertakings easy."[24] Once the city had fallen, Robert "destroyed the entire edifice of their iniquitous temple and where the mosque had been he built a church dedicated to the Virgin Mother. And what had been a seat of demons he transformed into a seat of God, and it became a door to heaven for the worthy."[25] But when the duke returned to Apulia, he left the trappings of holy war behind him in Sicily, resuming the role of the militarily adept warlord operating entirely within the secular sphere. It is significant in this regard that, although William had little to say about Roger's career, he felt obliged to admit that "none of his brothers, however excellent, entered into such a noble war. For he always fought against the Sicilians, enemies of the divine name, seeking to exalt the holy faith."[26]

If William was oblivious—with the exception of the Palermo campaign—to God's role in the rise of the Normans, he was keenly aware of the importance of military factors. Thus he described in intimate detail the battle of Civitate,[27] Robert's extended siege of Bari,[28] the conquest of Palermo,[29] and the struggle for Durazzo,[30] with particular attention to the composition of the forces, to the siege machines employed, and above all to the particular strategy pursued. William criticized the Italian contingent at Civitate for not knowing "how to prepare their battlelines in the proper order"; they were, he observed, *omnes conglomerati*.[31] In contrast, the Normans prevailed at Durazzo after their initial setback precisely because Robert knew enough to reconfigure his forces *in media res*.[32] William's fascination with the martial aptitudes of the various peoples who figured in his account is equally telling in this regard.[33] His detailed evaluation of the Swabian contingent at Civitate—the one group that posed a serious challenge to Humphrey—is indicative:

> These courageous people have fierce spirits, but they are not careful when they manage their horses. They are more capable at administering blows with swords than with lances, for they do not control their horses well with their hands. They do not give strong blows with their lances, but excel with their swords. Their swords are especially long and sharp. They are in the habit of striking on the head and splitting the body in two. They stand firmly after they are unhorsed. They would rather die fighting than turn in flight. They are to be feared more when they are on the ground than when they are on horseback, so great is the boldness of this people.[34]

It is this passionate consideration of the art of war—in conjunction with the paucity of religious motifs—that suggests lay authorship for the *Gesta Roberti Wiscardi*. But it is certainly not inconceivable, despite these stylistic tendencies, that William was, like Amatus and Geoffrey Malaterra, a monk. If he was, then the differences in tone are better understood as a function of the expectations of William's courtly audience.

William's name in and of itself would suggest Norman ancestry, but his conspicuously complimentary treatment of the Lombards in the *Gesta* leads one to believe that William had more local roots.[35] We might have expected him to be positively disposed toward the Lombards of Salerno given the fact that Roger Borsa was the son of Guaimar V's daughter Sichelgaita.[36] But William's admiration for Melo, Harduin, and Argyro indicates that his sympathies were more generally Lombard than specifically Salernitan. Thus William described Melo as a *tutor prudens* for his role in sponsoring the earliest Norman immigrants.[37] He depicted Harduin as the one responsible for rousing the Normans to return to Apulia after their defeat at Cannae.[38] Later he criticized the Normans at length for replacing Harduin with Atenulf as their leader.[39] Moreover

Melo's son Argyro, whom the Normans chose to be their leader after Atenulf, is treated with similar warmth: "Though poor, Argyro was bold and generous. He claimed that he could not be the lord of such a people because he was unable to offer them anything in the way of silver or gold. But [the Normans] claimed to love not gold, but him, whose father [Melo] had treated them kindly."[40]

It is interesting to note, in this regard, that William was one of the very few commentators on the Battle of Civitate who did not fault the Italians as a people for the defeat of Leo's forces. William's criticism was directed more specifically at the people of the March: "Leo placed his trust in that most unworthy people, the dregs of Italy, the people of the March, rightly condemned by upright Latins. While a great many Italians redound with great bravery, these ones are naturally fearful, panicky, and dissolute."[41]

Such sympathetic treatments of the Lombards, especially in light of the negative images of them that pervade the histories of Amatus and Geoffrey Malaterra, strongly suggest that William had Lombard blood in his veins. If this was indeed the case, then the *Gesta Roberti Wiscardi*, like the *Historia Normannorum*, should be regarded as a history written "from the other side," that is, as a history written from the perspective of a group that, although initially hostile to the Normans, ultimately came to terms with their dominion. For Amatus, as a Casinese monk, this meant transforming Norman aggression into the kind of defensive military activity one would expect from "protectors" whose task it was to promote the security of Montecassino and indeed Christendom as a whole. For William, as a Lombard in Roger's court, this meant finding a place for the Normans within a Lombard historiographical tradition that stretched back to the *Historia Langobardorum* of Paul the Deacon in the late eighth century.

William set out to do just that by placing special emphasis on the ties that were forged between the parvenu Normans and the long-standing Lombard powers in Italy. The Normans came to Italy, observed William, as a people without roots: *vagi, instabiles, iam per loca multa vagantes*.[42] Almost immediately they were enlisted by Lombards like Melo in their efforts to throw off the yoke of the Greeks in Apulia. But from William's perspective, the key factor in the transition from *vagi* to *stabiles* was the conclusion of a series of marriage alliances that linked the sons of Tancred with Guaimar of Salerno. William treated this as a real step up for the

Normans. He made much of the social distance that separated Robert from Sichelgaita, the Lombard princess whom he sought as his second wife. "At first Gisulf spurned Robert's request, not that he would have been able to find any man more powerful or noble to marry his sister, but because the Gauls [Normans] seemed to him to be a crude, barbarous, and cruel people of inhuman spirit."[43] The image conveyed here is one of a sophisticated, well-established dynasty reluctant to admit into its privileged circles someone of Robert's background no matter how impressive his military credentials might be. But in the end Gisulf relented and Robert's reputation benefited enormously. Not only was the "noble name of Robert elevated" by this marriage, but he came to enjoy a newfound legitimacy as a force in southern Italy. For "the people who had formerly served him because they had been forced to do so, gave to him the obedience which they properly owed to their forebears, because the Lombard people knew that his wife's ancestors had subjected Italy."[44] Thus William explicitly linked the rise of the Normans in Italy to their incorporation into the pre-existing Lombard power structure.

Having done so, the door was open for William to treat the deeds of Robert Guiscard as something of a continuation of the deeds of the Lombard princes of southern Italy. In particular William portrayed the Norman occupation of Apulia and Calabria as the culmination of five centuries of Lombard struggles to remove Italy from imperial rule. This allowed William to avoid the whole potentially fractious issue of the Norman displacement of the Lombards. From the perspective of the *Gesta*, the Normans were not competing with the Lombards; they were working with them—or at least with their "blessing"—to bring to a successful conclusion the anti-imperial campaign that the Lombards had initiated in the sixth century.[45]

William's decision to reduce the complicated history of the establishment of Norman hegemony in southern Italy to a simple linear narrative about the Norman displacement of the Greeks influenced (or was influenced by) his decision to package the deeds of Robert in the form of an epic poem.[46] He justified his choice of genre this way: "The ancient poets sang of the deeds of ancient leaders. I, a modern poet, am setting out to proclaim the deeds of modern leaders."[47] In other words, if the accomplishments of the Normans in Italy rivaled those of the conquerors of old, then the Normans deserved their own epic, one which would rival those produced by the poets of old. Hence William, in his epilogue, referred to Roger Borsa as a "leader more worthy than the Roman leader Octavian," and hoped that he might see fit to reward his literary efforts, which paralleled those of Octavian's court poet Virgil.[48]

It was not simply the magnitude of the Norman achievement that made such epic trappings seem appropriate. At least as important in this regard was the fact that the Normans had achieved their success in Italy at the expense of the Greeks who, conveniently enough, could be considered not only the heirs to the Roman empire but the descendents of the heroes of the Homeric epics. From William's perspective, the Greeks who retreated before Robert's army lost more than their Italian foothold. They also forfeited their epic stature. Conversely, the Norman conquest of Apulia entitled them to the services of the Muses that had for so long sung for the Greeks and Romans.

The very fact that the Greeks let Italy slip through their fingers proved, from William's perspective anyway, that they no longer measured up to the epic proportions of their heroic past. William's Harduin would upbraid the Normans for not taking Apulia from "the feminine Greeks, a lazy race that participates in drunkenness and surrenders itself to debauchery," a people who were not only cowards, but who "dressed in a disagreeable fashion, and were inept in their use of arms."[49] Such negative characterizations recur throughout William's work. The Greeks were effeminate,[50] cowardly,[51] immoral,[52] avaricious,[53] cruel,[54] and they dressed funny.[55]

According to William, the Greeks themselves were painfully aware of their own loss of stature. On the eve of the first decisive Greek defeat at the hands of the Normans at Montepeloso, William had the Greek commander rebuke his men for their cowardice in the face of battle, for "placing [their] trust in [their] feet." He went on to enumerate the accomplishments of the outstanding Greeks of the past:

> Be mindful of your ancestors, by whose vigor the entire world was subdued. The arms of Achilles killed mighty Hector. Troy fell, burned with the fire of Mycenean fury. India knew the magnitude of Philip's vigor. Did not his son, Alexander, subject the strongest kingdoms to the Greeks? In the western regions the fame of the Greeks used to be the terror of the entire world. What people, hearing the name of the Greeks, would dare to stand before them on the

battlefield when they could scarcely secure their towns, fortresses, and cities from the power of their armies? Stand strong, I beseech you. Be mindful of your ancestral courage.[56]

This summary of Greek military history not only served to remind the reader of the epic tradition that extolled the accomplishments of the ancient Greeks, but underscored the decadence of their modern heirs. The battle that followed was a rout: the Greeks, who had "experienced no battle more harsh," were routed.[57]

That the Muses were part of the spoils won by William of Apulia's Normans at Montepeloso is apparent in the many epic touches found within the *Gesta Roberti Wiscardi*. The most obvious is William's use of classical names for the peoples and places figuring in his account.[58] He often referred to the Normans as *Galli*, linking them to the Gauls made famous in their struggle with Julius Caesar.[59] The Byzantine Greeks appear in a variety of classical guises: Argives (*Argi*), Danaens (*Danai*), Achaeans (*Achivi*), and Pelasgians (*Pelasgii*). The Italians are referred to as Samnites (*Samnites*), Ausonians (*Ausonii*), or simply the people of *Latium*. The Seldjuk Turks who threatened Anatolia are called Persians and the Swabians at Civitate are identified as *Suevi*.[60]

William also peppered his narrative with epic similes. The Norman army that defeated Michael Doukeianos's forces at the river Olivento was like a falcon that, although accustomed to preying on smaller birds, happened to kill a swan and thus realized just how powerful it was.[61] Count William, who tried to get Maniakes to leave Taranto and engage him in battle, was like a snake charmer using every means possible to get the serpent to leave its hole.[62] The Italian contingent at Civitate, when attacked by Richard of Aversa, scattered like a flock of doves in the presence of a falcon.[63] At the same battle, Robert worked himself into a frenzy as if he were a lion among cattle.[64] The defenders of Bari conducted themselves like a badly wounded boar that refused to submit to its fate.[65] And Roger Borsa, who was trapped for a time by a rebellion in Ascoli, reacted to his liberation like a tigress that, while appearing calm enough in the cage, vented its fury with particular violence upon its release.[66]

There is also something of an epic quality to the way in which William depicted the Normans as decided underdogs, who in the early stages of their conquest of Apulia were extremely tentative and uncertain in the face of what seemed to be formidable opposition. William wrote that the "Teutons" at Civitate, "famed for their hair, the beauty of their form, and the size of their bodies, ridiculed the Norman physique—for they appeared to be shorter—and disdained their petitions as from a people inferior in both number and power."[67] William's Normans were the first to admit their own weakness. "After the death of Melo, whom the Normans had hoped to assist, they lost all hope and returned sadly to the region of Campania. They had no secure place to set up their camp. Their diminished numbers terrified them, as they were surrounded by a very numerous and powerful enemy. No place seemed secure."[68] As we have already seen, they had to be upbraided by a Lombard before daring to return to Apulia to fight the Greeks again.[69] Even as late as the Battle of Civitate, "the Normans, although famous for their brilliant warfare, were afraid to go out to meet the enemy when they saw how large their armies were."[70] They would have fled if they had had the opportunity.[71]

Thus William's Normans were surprised yet heartened by each of their early successes on the battlefield. "This powerful victory increased the courage of the Normans, having proved the Greeks to be of little valor, more accustomed to flight than to boldness."[72] "Thus the discord of Latium brought back to the Gauls the hope that had been extirpated before."[73] "The victory increased the strength of the Gauls in their minds and they no longer feared making war against the Danaeans."[74] "The Normans grew in courage; their fortunate success in arms added to it even more."[75] Even as late as the sieges of Bari and Palermo, the successes of the Norman navy provided welcome boosts in Norman confidence.[76]

Against this backdrop of general Norman uncertainty, Robert Guiscard stood out as a confident and formidable warrior with all the trappings of an epic hero. At Civitate, Robert

audaciously rushed with great courage into the very midst of the enemy. He pierced them with his lance, he butchered them with his sword, he struck terrible blows with his strong hands. He fought with both arms, neither his lance nor his sword remaining bloodless, no matter where he directed them. Three times he was knocked off his horse, three times he gathered his strength and returned to the fighting more effectively than before. His furor spurred him on. When a lion, gnashing its teeth and fiercely attacking weaker animals, finds something in his path, it becomes enraged and its kindled anger rouses it against beasts greater in number and size so that it permits none to pass by unhurt, dragging down one, eating another, and scattering those that it is unable to eat, thus afflicting every beast to the point of death. So too Robert did not cease to lay low the Swabians that he met with various forms of slaughter.

William went on to describe the physical effects of Robert's zeal on the battlefield in language as graphic—if not quite as poetic—as any in the *Iliad*.

He severed the feet of some, the hands of others; he decapitated one body, and cut open the stomach of another all the way up to the chest; he impaled one opponent through the ribs after cutting off his head; and he rendered large bodies equal in magnitude to smaller ones by cutting them down to size. With his bravery he showed that the palm of victory can be won not only by big men but by small ones as well. In the wake of the battle it was clear that no one there, whether among the victors or the vanquished, had dealt out such great blows.[77]

But Robert was not simply another Achilles, for in addition to his prodigious strength and courage, he was crafty. As William explained, "his cognomen was 'Guiscard' [wily], for he was no less shrewd [*callidus*] than Cicero and no less clever [*versutus*] than Ulysses."[78] From his earliest exploits in Calabria, Robert had been forced to rely on both his strength and his shrewdness to survive. "Whether he obtained the palm of victory for himself by craft or through the exercise of arms, Robert regarded it as the same, because what he was not always able to bring about through violence, he accomplished by means of the craftiness of his mind."[79] And again this quality lent itself to legendary accretions. When Robert was unable to overcome a Calabrian fortress by force, he had one of his men pretend to be dead, and then requested that he be buried in the monastery within the fortress walls. In the midst of the funeral, the Normans who had carried the body inside the walls suddenly armed themselves with the swords that they had hidden under the "body" and took control of the fortress.[80]

William also bestowed predictably heroic trappings on the character of Sichelgaita. As Robert lay dying in Cephalonia, his wife mourned him and lamented her own fate:

> When she realized that Robert, in whom she as his wife had placed all her hope, was suffering from a fever, she wept, rent her garments, and quickly made her way to him. Seeing that her husband was wasting away and that he had come to the end of his life, she scratched her cheeks with her nails and tore at her disheveled hair, shouting, "O what pain is in store for me, wretched one that I am; where shall I, who am so unfortunate, go? Will not the Pelasgians, having learned of your death, now attack me, your son, and your people, whose only glory, hope, and strength was you, your presence protecting us even when far from home? With you present, no one of your people feared the threats of your enemy, no one feared their attacks. Your encouragement made them safe, no matter how great the number of troops in the opposing battle line. They were unafraid to wage war, having already seen that no earthly power couldly resist you. Behold your son, your wife, and your people, allowed to be seized by wolves, never being safe without you. You were the courage of our people and without you our people cannot be brave."[81]

The spirit and indeed much of the language of this lament brings to mind Andromache who feared that she, her son, and Troy would suffer a similar fate at the hands of the Achaeans without the protection offered by her husband Hector.[82]

William's decision to model the *Gesta Roberti Wiscardi* on the ancient epic tradition influenced its content in other less apparent ways. For one thing, as we have already noted, it encouraged William to concentrate on the struggle between the Normans and the Greeks to the exclusion of the other political challenges that Robert faced in Italy. As a result, the *Gesta* contains much more information about the Greeks than either the *Historia Normannorum* or the *De rebus gestis Rogerii et Roberti*. Large sections of the *Gesta* are devoted to the political history of Byzantium, sometimes even when it does not directly impinge on the Normans, as in the case of William's account of the career of the emperor Romanus Diogenes (1068–71). William described at some length his campaigns against the Turks, his capture at Manzikert, his negotiations and treaty with Alp Arslan, his release, his subsequent death in civil war, new Turkish attacks, and the punishment meted out to Romanus's killers. All this without mentioning the Normans, except for a brief reference to Jocelyn's involvement in the conspiracy against the emperor and a passing reference to the crusade, which William described as a "Gallic" expedition.[83]

Likewise books four and five of the *Gesta Roberti Wiscardi* are dominated by Alexius Comnenus, whom William seems to have regarded as the epic foil for Robert. As such Alexius had to be portrayed as a worthy opponent. "Thriving with astute reason and strenuous in arms, he was illustrious in his valor, and born of excellent parents. By the first flower of his adolescence, he had already passed many years of his life in arms. He did not hesitate to undertake anything, no matter how difficult, if the empire required it."[84] And elsewhere: "Energetic yet cautious, victorious Alexius overcame many enemies of the empire by the use of arms as well as artifice."[85]   He was, in other words, another Robert Guiscard, willing to do whatever it took to overcome his enemies.

William's effort to "foreground" the conflict between the Normans and the Greeks meant that he tended to ignore or relegate to the status of sideshows other challenges to Norman rule in Italy. William had little to say, for instance, about the struggle between Henry's and Robert's forces for control of Rome. He simply noted that Henry fled: "the audacity of the duke terrified him."[86]   That was, however, enough for William to give Robert credit for two impressive victories in a single year: "Thus the two lords of the world, that is the king of Germany and the great leader of the Roman empire, were defeated at the same time. One, rushing to arms, was defeated in battle, while the other retreated after having learned of the formidabilty of the Normans."[87]

William also overlooked Robert's tense relationship with the papacy. Indeed if the *Gesta* were the only source we had for Norman-papal relations in this period, the Apulian Normans would have been remembered as dutiful sons of the church. William's version of the Battle of Civitate is a case in point. Neither the Normans nor the pope seemed to have a clear idea as to why they were fighting. Leo was simply responding to complaints—which William is quick to point out were based on partially inaccurate information—from the Apulian Greeks about the Normans.[88] Argyro had "beseeched [the pope] to liberate Italy, which had been deprived of its freedom, and to compel this iniquitous people, whose oppressive yoke was ruining the region of Apulia, to withdraw."[89]   The Normans, awed by the size of Leo's army, immediately sued for peace,

offering to become papal vassals and hold their lands as papal fiefs.[90] But
the Germans refused to consider the petition of such an apparently weak
people and convinced Leo, against his better judgement, to reject their
offer.[91] The shortage of supplies finally forced the issue, the Normans preferring to die in battle than from hunger.[92] Afterward the victorious Normans approached Leo at Civitate and "venerated him on bent knee,
begging his pardon. The pope kindly received them as they bowed before
him and kissed his feet. With pious words he admonished and then
blessed them. Lamenting greatly that their envoy who had offered terms
of peace had been spurned, he wept as he prayed for the dead brothers."[93]

In short, William treats the battle of Civitate as one big misunderstanding between two powers that, under normal circumstances, would
have been expected to work together. Neither the pope nor the Normans
was to blame for the unfortunate incident. If anyone was at fault, it was
the Germans who would not let Leo negotiate when he had the chance.
Six years later, when Nicholas II came to Melfi, he and the Normans
arrived at an agreement very similar to the one that Leo had been forced,
by the "pride of the Germans" to reject. "At the end of the synod, Pope
Nicholas, in response to the requests of many, bestowed ducal honor
upon Robert. He alone of the counts was officially granted the title of
duke, and he became a vassal of the pope by swearing an oath. As a result,
Calabria and all of Apulia was granted to him along with the lordship of
the people of the land in Latium."[94] From the perspective of the *Gesta*, if
the Normans and Leo IX had been left alone to work out their own agreement before the battle, there would have been no need for Nicholas II to
negotiate the treaty of Melfi six years later.

Though historically the treaty proved to be dead letter even after it
was revived at Ceprano in 1080, William treated it as if it were emblematic
of Robert's devotion to the holy see. As a result, despite the fact that Gregory VII's conflict with Robert was every bit as heated as the pope's more
famous struggle with Henry IV, William completely ignored it. He
described the duke's acquisition of Salerno without ever mentioning Gregory's outspoken support of Gisulf, though William admitted that Gisulf
was well-received by the pope in his exile.[95] William *did* report that
Robert's siege of Benevento in late 1077 irritated Gregory. But there is
nothing in the *Gesta* to suggest that Robert's actions regularly rubbed the
pope the wrong way or even that he was even aware that his actions had
any effect on the pontiff. Instead, when Robert became aware of Grego-

ry's disapproval, he "hastened to the city of the pope so that he might receive indulgence for the offense. He beseeched the pope and kissed the feet of the holy father."[96]   It was Civitate all over again. Gregory, like Nicholas, accepted the Normans as vassals and Robert swore to be faithful in his service of the holy church. To underscore the respect that Robert enjoyed in Rome, William reported a rumor that the pope had gone so far as to "promise Robert the crown of the Roman kingdom" at that time.[97]

It is Henry IV who emerges from the pages of the *Gesta* as the real *hostis Gregorii*.[98] The subsequent litany of his crimes against the church— simony, incest, adultery, sacrilege, and debauchery—only added to the impression that Robert was a comparatively dutiful son of the church.[99] In William's eyes, Robert and Gregory belonged on the same side. When Henry sent to Robert in hopes of forging an alliance with him, the duke declined and, according to William, dutifully reported everything to Gregory. Even when Robert ignored papal appeals as Henry pushed south into Italy, William minimized its effect on Robert's relationship with the papacy. Robert, who always "favored [the pope] with a pure heart," assured him that he would never have undertaken a campaign to the Balkans if he had known that the pope would need his help in Italy, but that he could certainly not back out now.[100]   Before crossing the Adriatic, the duke ordered Robert of Loritello and Gerard of Buonalbergo—the guardians of Roger Borsa—not to withhold any aid that they might be able to offer the pope.[101]   There is no indication in the *Gesta* that Gregory was disappointed in Robert. On the contrary, William reported that Robert attacked Alexius's army near Durazzo "trusting in the standard which he had received from the pope in honor of Peter the supreme shepherd, and in the merits of St. Matthew, whose church he had built [in Salerno]."[102]   Predictably William made much of Robert's last minute decision to suspend his Balkan campaign so that he could return to Italy and free the pope, who had been confined to Castel Sant'Angelo by Henry's "barbarian troops." At the same time, he downplayed the destruction that Robert's forces inflicted on the city of Rome: "Having burned a few buildings," Robert escorted Gregory to Salerno with great honor.[103]

Finally Gregory's death elicited from William the most elaborate eulogy outside of the one he reserved for Robert himself.[104]   "Hearing of the death of such a man, the duke was unable to contain his grief. The death of a father would not have prompted more tears, nor the sight of a son or a wife in the last moments of life. His sorrow over this death was as great as it was because of the great love that had connected the two while they were alive." For, the *Gesta* would have us believe, Robert "never receded from Gregory's love, once they both had signed their peace treaty."[105]

One final epic motif that William introduced was that of the tragic flaw. For all their many strengths as a people, the Normans, William conceded, suffered from greed. We first see this side of the Normans when William describes the early, mercenary phase of Norman involvement in Italy, when the newly arrived knights were selling their services to the highest bidder. "Because the souls of the mundane mind are prone to avarice, and because money conquers all, [the Normans] disdained one [lord] after another, always attaching themselves to the one who offered them the most."[106] William also speculated that greed was at the root of the Normans' ultimate rejection of Harduin as their leader: "Perhaps [Atenulf], by giving them gold or silver, compelled them to break the vow of their previous pact. Is there nothing that the desire for gold will not compel one to undertake? Indeed it is capable of overturning the senses of the sane and dissolving the rigid bonds of sworn faith."[107] Elsewhere William told how the emperor Constantine IX Monomachus, despairing of his chances to expel the Normans from Apulia by force, tried to buy them off: "He heard that the people of the Normans were always prone to avarice; that the more one offered them, the more he was loved by them."[108] To their credit, the Normans turned down the offer, choosing to remain in Apulia until someone came along who was strong enough to force them out. William apparently meant this to be something of a turning point in Norman history.

Once the Normans had begun to settle down in Italy, their characteristic avarice manifested itself on a grander scale as a "lust for domination [that] resulted in great wars being fought amongst them, each one wanting to be the most powerful and struggling to subject the other to his dominion."[109] Robert Guiscard, who from William's perspective represented the highest form that "Norman-ness" could achieve, was not entirely immune from the effects of this vice. The *Gesta* tells us that on the eve of Robert's first invasion of the Balkans, his men were hesitant about taking their anti-imperial struggle abroad. "The expedition seemed to many to be unusual and impetuous, especially to those who had women and dear children at home: they did not want to take part in such a war."[110] William underscored the idea that Robert's invasion was uncalled for by reporting that Alexius went out of his way to treat Robert's daughter—who had been confined to a nunnery after the fall of Michael Ducas—respectfully in an attempt to appease the duke.[111] "But the arduous mind of the duke did not know how to back away from his plans."[112] William also made it clear that Robert knew that the self-identified emperor who turned up in his camp was a fraud, yet the duke stubbornly pressed on with his ill-advised campaign. Again "he did not know how to turn back from what he had begun."[113] Presumably William's motive for unmasking this darker side of Robert's "lust for domination" was to prepare the reader for the only real setback that the duke would ever suffer in his long and distinguished career as a conqueror. By linking this motivation to the "greed" of the early Norman mercenaries, William also effected a rather smooth narrative transition from the Normans as antagonists to the Normans as protagonists.

It is important to note in conclusion that the epic elements that have been the principal focus of this analysis are not evenly distributed throughout the *Gesta Roberti Wiscardi*. Much of what William recorded about Robert's life could, in fact, be described as "straight" prose history disguised as epic by the simple superimposition of metrical structure. This is true especially of the later books. The detailed descriptions of the Balkan campaigns, which dominate books four and five, and of the periodic revolts in Apulia[114] are punctuated only infrequently, if at all, by the types of epic motifs that regularly infuse the earlier books. Much of this narrative imbalance can be explained in terms of the amount of data that William had at his disposal: he simply had too much information to convey about the later years of Robert's life to be able to package it every step of the way in epic language. Moreover, having pushed his choice of framework hard at the beginning of his account, William could afford to let up at the midway point and allow its inertia to carry it through to the end.

Notes

1. William 3.100–105, pp. 168–70.
2. Mathieu, in William, p. 12.
3. William 1.179, p. 108.
4. William 4.26, p. 206.
5. For other less precise references to contemporary events, see Mathieu, in William, pp. 11–13.

6. Urban II spent three years (1090–93) in Norman Italy while Rome lay in the hands of the imperially–supported anti–pope, Clement III. Kelly, *Dictionary of Popes*, p. 159.

7. William 5.410, p. 258.

8. For a recapitulation of the debates, see Michele Fuiano, "Guglielmo di Puglia," *Studi de storiografia mediovale ed umanistica*, 2nd ed. (Naples: Giannini, 1975), p. 3, n. 4.

9. Mathieu, in William, pp. 24–25.

10. William 4.186–92, 5.345–51, pp. 214, 254. Note the complimentary treatment of Roger Borsa in his suppression of the Apulian revolt during Robert Guiscard's first Balkan campaign and in his participation in Robert's second. William 4.189–92, 4.512–24, 5.155–98, pp. 214, 232, 244.

11. Though William located the initial meeting between Melo and the Normans at the shrine of St. Michael at Monte Gargano, he made nothing of the pilgrim status of the Normans, saying only that they had come to "fulfill a vow." William 1.15–17, p. 100. The Greeks who perished in the Olivento river were not, as they were in Amatus's account, the victims of any miraculous swelling of the river. They simply drowned. William 1.280–84, p. 114.

12. William 1.402, p. 120.

13. William 3.104, p. 168.

14. "When it pleased the King—who has the power to change times and reigns—that the Apulian region, long held by the Greeks, should no longer be inhabited by them, the people of the Normans, famous for the ferocity of their knights, entered and, after expelling the Achaeans, dominated Latium." William 1.1–5, p. 98. It is worth noting, however, that unlike the *Aeneid*, where the fates are invoked at every juncture in Aeneas's conquest of Latium, the *Gesta* leaves them in the background, leaving Robert considerably more control over his own destiny.

15. William 2.146–47, p. 140.

16. William 4.348–54, p. 222.

17. William 1.47–53, pp. 100–102; cf. Lupus a. 1009, p. 57.

18. William 3.167–184, pp. 172–74. The Greek general Maniakes used sorcery to calm the Adriatic so that he could escape Apulia but was subsequently killed by imperial forces. William 1.568–75, p. 130. William also related the story about the dog who begged food from the Normans to relieve the plight of the starving people of Salerno. William 3.432–40, pp. 186–88.

19. William 2.320–29, pp. 148–50.

20. William 3.270, p. 178.

21. William 3.261–62, p. 178.

22. William 3.218, p. 176.

23. William 3.235–37, p. 176.

24. William 3.286–87, 3.292–93, pp. 178, 180. Compare this address to the one delivered at Durazzo in which Robert simply appeals to the desperateness of the Norman position, claiming that their only hope of survival lay in an unlikely victory. On the other hand, William explains the subsequent Norman victory by pointing to their faith in St. Matthew and the fact that they carried a papal banner.

William 4.402–11, p. 226.

25. William 3.332–36, p. 182.

26. William 3.196–203, p. 174.

27. William 2.122–256, p. 138.

28. William 2.480–573; 3.112–62, pp. 158, 170–72.

29. William 3.204–339, pp. 174–82.

30. William 4.235–452, pp. 216–28.

31. William 2.193–95, p. 142.

32. William 4.398–400, p. 226.

33. For instance, Venetian naval prowess: William 4.277–78, 4.284–85, pp. 218–20.

34. William 2.153–63, p. 140.

35. When offering his etymology of the word "Norman," William explained that the second syllable "is for them (*apud hos*) what for us (*apud nos*) is called *homo*." It is possible, as many have suggested, that William was using "them" and "us" in an ethnic way, indicating that he was not himself of Norman descent. But I think it just as likely that he was simply referring to the linguistic differences that separated the language of the word "Norman" from the language (Latin) in which he was writing.

36. When Sichelgaita is wounded by a projectile during the battle at Duraz-zo, she pulls through because "God did not want such a noble and venerable matron to be mourned." William 4.430–31, p. 226.

37. William 1.33, p. 100. When Melo died in Germany, where he was seeking support for another uprising in Apulia, Henry II "buried him in the manner of a king." William 1.101, p. 104.

38. William 1.223–30, p. 110.

39. William 1.318–327, p. 116.

40. William 1.422–26, pp. 120–22. Later Argyro was recalled to Constantino-ple where the emperor received him "with great honor." William 2.19, p. 132. Note also the courage of Lombard Bari and the fidelity of Lombard Giovinazzo: William 2.495–507, 3.39, pp. 158–60, 166.

41. William 2.108–11, p. 138. See Mathieu, in William, p. 22, n. 2, for specula-tion as to why William singled out this people for reproach. William did report that the Lombards and Calabrians were frightened as the Greek army approached Durazzo, but he went on to point out that even Robert's knights were intimidated on the eve of that battle. William 4.375–76, p. 224.

42. William 1.115–19, p. 104.

43. William 2.424–28, p. 154.

44. William 2.436–41, p. 156.

45. Lombard historians like Paul the Deacon and Erchempert were fond of casting the Greeks as interlopers in Italy. See Kreutz, *Before the Normans*, p. 99.

46. This placed William among the pioneers of the late eleventh-century revival of epic poetry as a genre in the Latin west, alongside the authors of the *Carmen de Hastingae proelio* 1066, the *Carmen de bello saxonico* 1075–76 and the *Carmen de victoria Pisanorum* 1088. Mathieu, in William, p. 57. For a detailed dis-

cussion of William's sources, see Mathieu, in *William*, pp. 26–56.

47. *William*, prologue i–v, p. 98.

48. *William* 5.413–14, p. 258. It should be noted that although William explicitly referred to himself as another Virgil, he did not model his work specifically on the *Aeneid*. Although there are a number of phrases that reveal Virgilian influence (see Mathieu, *William*, pp. 61–62, n. 4, for a full list), William's work is a more direct reflection of medieval epic literature which, as a genre, borrowed heavily from Virgil as well as Ovid, Lucan, and others. A. Pagano, *Il Poema Gesta Roberti Wiscardi di Guglielmo Pugliese* (Naples, 1909), pp. 111–18.

49. *William* 1.223–28, p. 110.

50. *William* 1.212, 1.225, p. 110.

51. *William* 1.77–79. 1.227, 1.282, p. 102, 110, 114.

52. *William* 1.226–27, p. 110.

53. *William* 1.210–11, p. 110.

54. *William* 1.20, 1.452, pp. 100, 122.

55. *William* 1.14–16, 1.228, pp. 100, 110.

56. *William* 1.351–72, p. 118. The Greeks were equally incapable of defending their territory in the east. If it had not been for the *gens Gallorum* at Manzikert, Romania would have been lost to the Turks: *William* 3.99–105, p. 168.

57. *William* 1.390–92, p. 120.

58. Dudo of St. Quentin was the first to do this with the Normans. But William probably got the idea from the Lombard histories. See, for instance, Paul the Deacon, *Historia Langobardorum* 4.44, 4.46, 6.2, etc; Kreutz, *Before the Normans*, p. 10.

59. This also allowed William to connect the Normans with the participants in the First Crusade. *William* 3.100–105, p. 168.

60. *William* 2.152, p. 140. The Straits of Messina remained the haunt of Scylla and Charybdis (*William* 3.192, p. 174) and Rainulf, the first Norman ruler of Aversa, was described as a consul (*William* 1.170, p. 108).

61. *William* 1.292–96, p. 114.

62. *William* 1.547–51, p. 128.

63. *William* 2.202–9, p. 142.

64. *William* 2.228–35, p. 144.

65. *William* 2.508–17, p. 160.

66. *William* 4.518–23, p. 232.

67. *William* 2.93–97, p. 136.

68. *William* 1.104–11, p. 104.

69. *William* 1.223–30, p. 110.

70. *William* 2.85–86, p. 136.

71. *William* 2.180–81, p. 142.

72. *William* 1.77, p. 102.

73. *William* 1.162–64, pp. 106–8.

74. *William* 1.290–91, p. 114.

75. *William* 1.307, p. 114; 2.284, p. 146.

76. *William* 3.137–38, 3.255, pp. 170, 178.

77. William 2.221–43, p. 144.

78. William 2.129–30, p. 138.

79. William 2.302–4, p. 148. See also 2.460–77, 3.567–73, 3.686–87, 4.502–3, 5.241–54, pp. 156, 194, 202, 230, 248–50. Note how Argyro—Robert Guiscard's competitor for control of Apulia—is unable to dislodge the Normans whether by force or by craft William 2.269–71, p. 146.

80. William 2.334–54, p. 150. This is, as Mathieu (in William, pp. 46–52) has pointed out, a common Norman motif.

81. William 5.295–315, p. 252.

82. *Iliad* 6.407ff and 24.725ff.

83. William 3.1–110, pp. 164–70.

84. William 4.82–85, p. 208.

85. William 4.120–21, p. 210. See also: 4.92–93, p. 208.

86. William 4.549–50, p. 234.

87. William 4.566–70, p. 234.

88. William 2.69–70, p. 134.

89. William 2.72–74, p. 136.

90. William 2.85–92, p. 136.

91. William 2.93–114, pp. 136–38.

92. William 2.115–21, 2.137–41, p. 138.

93. William 2.261–66, p. 146.

94. William 2.400–405, p. 154.

95. William 3.462–64, p. 188.

96. William 4.19–21, p. 206.

97. William 4.31–33, p. 206.

98. William 4.537, p. 232.

99. William 4.32–41, pp. 204–6.

100. William 4.179–84, p. 214.

101. William 4.198–99, p. 214.

102. William 4.408–12, p. 226.

103. William 4.557, p. 234.

104. William 5.255–67, p. 250.

105. William 5.268–75, p. 250.

106. William 1.138–55, p. 106. William makes the point again with regard to Normans who supported Rainulf. William 1.182–87, p. 108.

107. William 1.318–27, p. 116.

108. William 2.44–45, p. 134.

109. William 1.138–55, p. 106.

110. William 4.128–31, p. 210.

111. William 4.142–70, p. 212.

112. William 4.158–59, p. 212.

113. William 4.230–31, p. 216.

114. Especially those of 1078–80. William 3.509–687, pp. 192–202.

6. Geoffrey Malaterra and the Normans

At one point in the *Historia Normannorum*, Amatus of Montecassino expressed his intention to write a separate history of the Norman conquest of Sicily. The anonymous French translator of the original Latin text paraphrased Amatus on this matter: ". . . the monk who compiled this history . . . says that he wanted to record the battles waged by Count Roger against the Saracens, and that it would be most appropriate to write a separate book [about them], one that would be a very large volume indeed."[1] If Amatus ever got around to writing such a work, it has not survived in any form. The only full and contemporary account of the conquest that we have is one sponsored by Roger himself: the so-called *De rebus gestis Rogerii Calabriae et Siciliae comitis et Roberti Guiscardi ducis fratris eius*.[2]

We know little more about the author of the *De rebus gestis Rogerii et Roberti* than we do about Amatus of Montecassino or William of Apulia. In a dedicatory letter to Bishop Angerius of Catania, he identified himself as a monk named Geoffrey, "who bears the cognomen Malaterra from his ancestors."[3] The letter also makes it clear that Geoffrey had recently returned to the cloister after having served in some secular clerical capacity, but it tells us neither what prompted him to leave the "felicity of the peace of Mary" for the "worldly condition of Martha" in the first place nor what led him to return.

Modern historians have assumed that Geoffrey was born in Normandy even though the documentary evidence is not specific about this. In the letter Geoffrey attempts to forestall potential criticism of his historical project by pointing out that he was not actually present when most of the events he described took place: "You are well aware that I come from a region on the other side of the mountains, having only recently become an Apulian and indeed a Sicilian." The mountains he is referring to are no doubt the Alps, and Normandy *does* lie on the other side of them from a Sicilian perspective. But so do many other regions in Europe. Pontieri, the most recent editor of the *De rebus gestis Rogerii et Roberti*, managed to convince himself that "senza dubbio egli fu di stirpe normanna" on the basis of the "senso di orgoglio" that pervades Geoffrey's account, but, as we have seen in the cases of Amatus and William, pride in the Norman achievement was not limited to people of Norman birth.[4] Pontieri went even further, confidently placing Geoffrey—before his emigration to Italy—in the Norman monastery of Saint-Evroul, the institution that Robert of Grandmesnil abandoned before coming to Calabria and founding St. Eufemia in 1062.[5] White[6] followed Pontieri's lead, as did Chibnall,[7] both locating the young Geoffrey in St. Evroul without citing any authority other than Pontieri himself.

Given the patterns of migration that developed early on between Normandy and southern Italy, Normandy would have to be considered the most likely candidate for Geoffrey's homeland "on the other side of the mountains." On the other hand, Count Roger's efforts to reconstitute the church in Sicily in the wake of his conquests involved the recruitment of ecclesiastics from various parts of France, including Savoy (Gerland) and Brittany (Angerius), as well as Rouen (Stephen).[8] Less specific is a charter issued by Roger from Mileto in about the year 1085. It states that the count had persuaded a group of *viros religiosos clericos* "who had recently come from transalpine regions for the sake of going to the Holy Sepulchre of Jerusalem" to remain "in these parts," supplying them with everything they needed to "live according to the holy regimen that they had sworn to uphold."[9] The parallelism between this reference to transalpine Europe and Geoffrey's mention of "regions on the other side of the mountains," suggests that Geoffrey might well have been one of these co-opted pilgrims. But the problem of identifying these "transalpine regions" remains unresolved. Again the pilgrims could have been Norman, or they could have come from some other part of France or indeed from somewhere else in northern Europe.

No matter where Geoffrey was born, there is little doubt that he came to Sicily as one the many ecclesiastical recruits enlisted by Roger in his effort to reestablish the Latin church in newly conquered Sicily. Though reticent about his own relocation, Geoffrey did elaborate on the circumstances that brought Angerius to the island. According to Geoffrey, Roger visited St. Eufemia, where Angerius was a monk, second in command only to the abbot, and offered him the episcopacy of Catania.[10] In December 1091 Roger endowed the monastery of St. Agatha—which would be officially recognized as a bishopric in March 1092—with no less than the entire city of Catania.[11] Geoffrey's own arrival in Catania would seem to have post-dated that of Angerius. For Geoffrey noted that the count, "finding the church [of Catania] in disarray, uprooted, as it had been, by the jaws of an unbelieving people," at first concentrated solely on the installation of secular clergy in the region. Only later did Roger direct his attention to monastic concerns, "gathering to himself no small crowd of monks."[12] Presumably Geoffrey was among this group, being placed in the monastery of St. Agatha—the first Latin monastery in Sicily.[13] That Geoffrey came to Sicily after 1091 accords well with his disclaimer that he had "only recently become an Apulian and indeed a Sicilian" and therefore not being "present" when some of Roger's deeds were performed.

Geoffrey regarded Roger as a patron whose "beneficence toward me has been so great" that he did not feel he could refuse when asked to "commit to writing [Count Roger's] laborious and perilous victories, specifically how he first subjugated Calabria and then Sicily." According to Geoffrey, Roger specifically asked him to write his account "in plain and simple words so that it would be understandable; so that it could be told, revealed and narrated to everyone with ease." Roger had in mind a particular kind of narrative, one that resembled the "ancient histories" which were regularly recited in his court.[14] Geoffrey explained that

> In the tradition of the ancient philosophers it became customary to transmit for posterity the deeds of valiant men, recording them with honor, so that the things remembered along with [the names of] those by whom they were done, would not be lost to silence, but rather, committed to letters, would be read and made known to future generations, in a way that might make those who accomplished such deeds come to life through such memorials.[15]

To support his point, Geoffrey went on to quote the opening lines of Sallust's *Bellum Catilinae*: "it befits all men who seek to place themselves above the animals to strive with the greatest effort not to pass through life in silence, like cattle, fashioned by nature to be stooped over in obedience to their stomachs."[16] Geoffrey's readers, who would have been well-versed in Sallust, given the popularity of his works at the time, understood the point of the passage: that men worthy of being remembered took pains to exercise their minds rather than simply satisfying their bodies, and that others, also worthy of some praise, commit the deeds of such as these to writing.[17] By recording the deeds of Roger, Geoffrey was self-consciously following in the footsteps of the Roman historians, preserving from oblivion the impressive deeds of an admirable man.

That Geoffrey intended his work to be entertaining is apparent not only from the inclusion of such "light" episodes as Robert Guiscard's duplicitous capture of the governor of Bisignano, but from the occasional aside on some matter entirely incidental to the main storyline. After recounting the successful suppression of a rebellion led by one Gualterius, Geoffrey added that the rebel's sister "is said to have been so beautiful that, whenever she came to the sea to bathe, or if she put her legs in some fish-filled river to test the water, the fish, lured by the whiteness of her skin, would swim so close to her that they could be caught with one's bare hands."[18] Elsewhere, after detailing the capture of Messina, Geoffrey told of a Muslim who was so concerned about the possibility of his sister falling into Norman hands, that he killed her with his own hands, "preferring to become his sister's murderer and to lament her death rather than have her become a prevaricator of their law and be raped by someone who would not permit her to observe their law."[19] Geoffrey also paused to educate his readers about the Muslim use of homing pigeons[20] as well as to describe the tarantulas that contributed to the failure of the first Norman siege of Palermo.[21]

It is interesting to note that Geoffrey began the *De rebus gestis Rogerii et Roberti* in verse, as if to add grandeur to his subject by giving it an epic touch. After a few laborious lines, however, Geoffrey abruptly and rather unceremoniously abandoned the effort: "Let the meter cease; let prose be spoken for what follows."[22] From time to time, especially toward the end of his account, Geoffrey reverted to poetry as if to demonstrate to the reader that he could have rendered the entire account in verse had he chosen to. But the metrical diversions never lasted for long. The vast bulk of Geoffrey's opus is a work of prose.

The *De rebus gestis Rogerii et Roberti* covers Italo-Norman history up to 1098, ending with a transcription of Urban II's bull of July 5, 1098, in which the pope named Roger and his heirs legates of the Roman church.[23] The absence of any formal ending may indicate that Geoffrey intended to push his history a bit further into Roger's reign. Be that as it may, it appears that Geoffrey wrote the last portion of the work as we have it shortly after Urban issued his bull. The fact that late in the fourth and final book Geoffrey recounted Bohemond's departure on the Crusade without ever reporting the fall of Jerusalem (in July 1099) or, for that matter, Bohemond's conquest of Antioch (June 1098), supports this time frame.[24]

By medieval standards, Roger was an old man—in his later sixties—when Geoffrey was writing. It is quite possible that the count, aware that his days were numbered, commissioned Geoffrey to write a history with an eye to solidifying the memory of his own role in the conquest of Calabria and Sicily. It is important to remember in this regard that these conquests were a joint enterprise, combining the efforts and resources of Roger and his older brother Robert Guiscard. While it is clear that Roger devoted more time and energy to the conquests—in particular to that of Sicily—than his brother did, it was Robert who supplied the bulk of the forces and materials needed to take the strategic strongholds of Reggio, Messina, and Palermo. In fact, even the territory that Roger won without his brother's help was secured in his capacity as Robert's vassal. Under such circumstances it may have been important to the future claims of Roger's minor sons and heirs—Simon and Roger (II)—to have an account of the conquest that emphasized the central role played by their father, all the more so given the relative political strength of Robert Guiscard's son and heir Roger Borsa, duke of Apulia.

We can only hypothesize about the extent to which these considerations were factors in Roger's decision to sponsor such a history. If they were, it might explain Geoffrey's repeated and caustic references to unnamed detractors whom he thought likely to "gnaw" at his best historiographical efforts with "hostile teeth."[25] Geoffrey, in other words, might have been aware that there were other ways of telling the story of the conquest of Sicily that were not as favorable to Roger. Indeed Amatus of Montecassino and William of Apulia had themselves effectively diminished Roger's role in the conquest simply by restricting their attention to those pivotal campaigns in which Robert participated.

Geoffrey's depiction of the rivalry between the two brothers, in which more often than not Roger appears as a victim of Robert's reluctance to share his wealth and power, is consistent with this interpretation. Shortly after his arrival in Italy, Roger found himself financially hard-pressed in Calabria and turned to his brother for support. "But Guiscard, although generous with the rest of his men, began to be more stingy with Roger than was his custom, resorting to the counsel of depraved men against him." The reason for this stinginess? Robert was jealous, having observed "that young knights all over Apulia adhered more closely to

Roger than to himself on account of Roger's vigor."

> As a result he wanted to force Roger, in his poverty, to be content
> with only a few men, so that Guiscard would have no reason to fear
> him becoming haughty against him. But when Roger, a man of great
> spirit, realized that he was being dragged down in this way by his
> brother as if he were ignoble or unworthy, when in fact he had
> climbed to the top with fortune favoring him, he left his brother in
> anger and withdrew to Apulia.[26]

Geoffrey went on to recount how the two brothers patched things up and
worked together for a time, only to have Robert fail yet again to remuner-
ate Roger appropriately for the services he had rendered. Roger was fed
up—"as if he knew Sallust's proverb innately without ever having read
it:[27] It is useless to strive, earning nothing but reproach with such exhaust-
ing efforts; in the end it is the height of folly, because it is essential that
one also be well served by good fortune"[28]—and broke the truce. In the
end Roger was able to force Robert to divide Calabria with him.[29] But
this reconciliation was itself short-lived, and Roger, as Geoffrey saw it,
had continually to exert pressure on Robert to live up to his agreements.
In each instance, Geoffrey portrayed Roger as a dutiful vassal, always
most reluctant to take up arms against his brother and feudal lord[30] and
going out of his way to avoid inflicting injury on Robert's person.[31] At
one point, in the midst of one of their most heated quarrels, when Robert
found himself trapped by the angry citizens of Gerace, it was Roger who
saved him by threatening to annihilate the city if they did not release his
brother.[32]

The first of the four books of Geoffrey's history is dedicated to the
deeds accomplished by the Normans in Italy prior to 1060, the year in
which Roger first directed his gaze from the pacification of Calabria to the
conquest of Sicily. In order to explain how the Normans came to Italy in
the first place, Geoffrey backtracked to the turn of the tenth century when
Rollo, that *dux fortissimus* from Norway, first came to France and "devastated Frisia and certain coastal regions to the west." These raids ultimately gave way to conquest when Rollo discovered along the banks of the
Seine a particularly attractive region—the future Normandy—the inhabitants of which he "began to subject to his rule."

Geoffrey's description of this process of territorial domination is more sexual than it is military. Normandy is depicted as a beautiful, defenseless woman, passively waiting to be ravished by the virile, war-like Normans. "Penetrating the interior parts of France by river with his great fleet, [Rollo] took note of the pleasantness of these regions and chose to embrace with his love this one [the future Normandy] over the others through which he had passed." The land was not only attractive but fecund: "For [Normandy] is most abundant in rivers filled with fish and forest replete with game; it is also most suitable for falconry. It is fertile with wheat and other types of grain, abundant in sheep, and a nourisher of cattle."[33] Geoffrey's language here is reminiscent of the so-called barbarian histories of late antiquity. Their authors sometimes resorted to just this sort of poetic "dressing up" of the initial act of aggression against part of the Roman empire. Personifying the territory in question and depicting "her" freely bestowing the fruits of her fertility on her conquerors helped in some sense to legitimate barbarian conquest. Isidore's famous prologue to his *History of the Kings of the Goths* is a case in point: the manly Visigoths simply take *mater Spania*, the most beautiful and fertile region on earth, from her effete Roman "husband."[34]

To complete the picture, Geoffrey's Normans are described as the quintessential warriors, the very paradigms of manliness, of the desire to dominate:

> They [the Normans] are a very shrewd people, indeed, quick to avenge injury, scorning the fields of their homeland in hopes of acquiring something more, avid for profit and domination, ready to feign or conceal anything, achieving a certain balance between largess and avarice. In their love for good fame, their princes are most liberal in their giving. This people knows how to flatter: they are in fact so devoted to the study of eloquence that you would do well to give heed to their sons as if they were rhetors. Unless checked by the yoke of justice they can be most unrestrained. They are ready to endure great effort, hunger, and cold when fortune requires it. They devote themselves to hunting and falconry. They delight in luxury when it comes to horses and to the rest of the tools and costumes of war.[35]

Again, this is quite consistent with the barbarian histories which tended to depict the invaders as strong, militarily adept men against whom the decadent, weak Romans did not stand a chance. According to Geoffrey, one Norman family in particular—that of Tancred of Hauteville—epitomized this aggressiveness, this drive to subject others to its dominion. Geoffrey observed that "this custom was naturally inborn [*mos insitus*] in the sons of Tancred: they were always avid for domination [*dominationis avidi*]. When their strength sufficed, they suffered no one to have lands or possessions near their own without emulation, so that they would immediately subject them and be served by them. Indeed these same ones gained mastery over everything within their power."[36]

The first book of the *De rebus gestis Rogerii et Roberti* appears to have been written precisely to illustrate how this *mos insitus* manifested itself in the actions of the sons of Tancred in southern Italy. It tells how the sons of Tancred, afraid that any further division of their Norman patrimony would render the resulting portions too small to support them, left their homeland, "seeking their fortune through the exercise of arms."[37] It was precisely their reputation on the battlefield that led to Tancred's oldest son, William, being enlisted to fight for the Lombard princes of Capua and Salerno and later for the Byzantine governor of Apulia.[38] But deprived of his share of the booty during an Greek-led expedition to Sicily, William began working for himself, carving out his own sphere of influence in Apulia at the expense of the Greeks and Lombards. Though few in number, the ferocity of William's Norman followers terrified their opponents. A Byzantine envoy, sent to the Norman castle at Melfi, was unnerved when a Norman knocked his horse out from under him with a single blow of his fist.[39] Later during the decisive battle for control of Apulia, William, though weakened by a fever, seized his weapons and, "raging like a lion" [*quasi leo furibundus*], went straight for the commander of the Greek army, whom he killed "as if he were an ox" [*quasi bove*].[40] Geoffrey proudly contrasted the Norman proficiency in the art of war with the relative weakness of both the Greeks, who were "by habit given more to luxuries and pleasures than to the exertions of war,"[41] and the Pisans, who were "by custom devoted to commercial profits rather than military efforts."[42]

Geoffrey's Normans in Italy were also survivors, willing to do and suffer anything to further their domination of the region. Geoffrey savored the tale about how Robert, hard pressed to make ends meet in Calabria, tricked Peter, the Greek governor of Bisignano, into leaving behind his body guard during one of their occasional, friendly meetings.

"Having conversed for quite a while, they rose about to depart from one another, when Guiscard, noting the enormity and bulk of Peter's body...seized Peter at his waist and began to carry him on his shoulder in the direction of his own men." The ransom that he received in exchange for his prisoner allowed Robert to "reward his men abundantly, thus strengthening their fidelity to him."[43] As Geoffrey observed, this was typical of Robert: "He was always most confident [*praesumptuosus*] and audaciously ready to attempt even the most difficult tasks." Such *calliditas* was as characteristic of the sons of Tancred as their indomitability in battle. That incident, according to Geoffrey, prompted the Calabrians to observe that "while there were more powerful men [than Robert], there was no one who could be compared to him in the exercise of either arms or wits."[44]

Roger, who received his brother's tenuous position in Calabria as something of a "hand-me-down" upon his arrival in Italy in the mid-1050s, was himself depicted as a personification of the Norman *mos insitus*. Geoffrey described him as "a most handsome youth, tall in stature, graceful in body, most eloquent in speech, shrewd in counsel, intelligent in planning the execution of things, pleasant and affable to everyone, physically strong, and fierce in battle."[45] Like the young King David, he one day "killed, laying him low with his strong spear, a certain very powerful man with an enormous body who had been offending the army of the Normans with many insults, a man whom everyone feared as if he were a giant."[46] Calabria's relative poverty forced Roger to do whatever was necessary to procure sufficient plunder or tribute. At one point, Geoffrey reported, Roger was so impoverished that he was "sustained in large part by the larceny of his squires" who, among other things, stole horses from the Norman castle at Melfi. Geoffrey added: "We say this not to shame him . . . but so that it might be made clear to all how laboriously and with what great anguish he managed, from the depths of such poverty, to reach the highest summit of riches and honor."[47]

To say that the Norman conquests were motivated by a *mos insitus* which led them to dominate southern Italy was not to say that they accomplished what they did entirely through their own efforts. For one thing, the concept of fortune played a significant part in Geoffrey's narrative. Fortune as a force in history was commonplace among the Roman historians. According to Sallust, "she makes all events famous or obscure according to her caprice rather than in accordance with truth."[48] The popularity of Sallust as well as Boethius's *Consolation of Philosophy* guaranteed that the "fickle goddess" would appear repeatedly in medieval historical narratives, particularly those of the late eleventh and twelfth centuries.[49] The *De rebus gestis Rogerii et Roberti*, in fact, turns out to be a particularly rich source for this motif. After a successful early raid in Calabria, Robert Guiscard's men congratulated themselves on their good luck, but cautioned their intrepid leader to be more careful, "lest perchance fortune, which was now smiling upon him, later, if tempted, bestow a less favorable outcome."[50] Later Robert, trapped in Gerace, would advise its hostile citizens not to be "carried away falsely by overabundant joy lest the wheel of fortune, which is presently smiling on you and against me, foretell with its very smile, some adverse judgement against you in the future."[51] Elsewhere, after recounting a thwarted Saracen raid against Mazara, Geoffrey observed: "Thus wheel-like fortune at first plays with men, granting them victories, but then laughs at those deceived ones who are allured by the expectations stemming from earlier success."[52] It is important, however, not to overestimate the role of fortune as a narrative device in the *De rebus gestis Rogerii et Roberti*. The steady, unabated rise of the Normans as a force in Italy did not lend itself particularly well to the traditional capriciousness of fortune. As a result its role was limited to explaining away the occasional setback and to cautioning the perennially victorious Normans against indulging in over-confidence.[53]

Alongside fortune, Geoffrey acknowledged the role of providence in the rise of the Normans to dominance in Italy. In fact he seems to have regarded the consistant good fortune that the Normans enjoyed as a symptom of divine favor.[54] The very success of the sons of Tancred—which Geoffrey's fifty years of hindsight permitted him to appreciate—proved that they had somehow succeeded in finding favor in God's eyes. This same perspective allowed Geoffrey to identify hints of Norman greatness in their humble beginnings. Thus the "high" in Hauteville—Tancred's family estate—became more than a topographical reference. It was an "omen of the noble and prosperous achievements of its future heirs, who, with the help of God and through their own effort, would gradually climb to the summit of honor."[55] It was as if, Geoffrey continued, the Normans had been the beneficiaries of a new covenant of Abraham, "growing into a great nation and extending their dominion through the exercise of arms, subjecting to themselves the necks of many other peoples."[56] As it turns out, this was as far as Geoffrey would take the "religious" interpretation of the Norman conquest of southern Italy. Like William of Apulia, Geoffrey set up a loose providential framework only to leave it behind, proceeding to describe how the Normans fought and plundered their way to the successful domination of southern Italy. At this early stage in the Norman conquests, God, like fortune, took a back seat to *aviditas dominationis* as the driving force behind the success of the Normans.[57]

Beginning with the second book, the *De rebus gestis Rogerii et Roberti* turns to the main story line: Roger's conquest of Sicily. "Now," wrote Geoffrey, "that we have recounted, . . . if not everything that is worth remembering, at least a few of the things which have come to our attention because of their fame, let us turn to those deeds which were performed in infidel Sicily [*incredula Sicilia*]."[58] For our purposes we will be particularly interested in the effect that this change of venue from Christian Italy to Muslim Sicily had on Geoffrey's portrayal of Roger and his conquests.

Geoffrey explained at the beginning of the second book that Roger first conceived of conquering Sicily when he and his brother had pushed their conquest of Calabria all the way to Reggio.

> Hearing about infidel Sicily, and observing it on the other side of that very narrow strip of water, Roger, who was always avid for domination, was seized by ambition to acquire it, thinking that it would be of benefit both to his soul and indeed to his body if he could restore that land, which had been surrendered to idols, to divine worship and dispose of it in service to God, and take temporal possession of the fruit and produce of the land which that people, disagreeable to God, had usurped for themselves.[59]

This paragraph is a fitting introduction to the ensuing account of the Sicilian conquest. For just as Geoffrey considered the benefits to Roger's soul within the context of his undiminished *aviditas dominationis*, so he treated the conquest of Sicily as a manifestation of the same *mos insitus* that had brought the Normans to Italy in the first place, only now with religious implications that the acquisition of Apulia and Calabria never had.

Geoffrey's description of the campaigns leading up to the conquest of Messina in the spring of 1061 illustrates how this new religious ingredient could be introduced without fundamentally altering the thrust of the narrative. The campaign began with a quick raid on Messina during which Roger, *semper astutissimus et militia callens*, managed to put the Messinan army to flight by first feigning retreat and then suddenly turning to confront his pursuers.[60] Back on the mainland, Roger wintered with Robert in Apulia and planned a new Sicilian expedition.[61] Returning to Reggio, he met with "Betumen," who sought his assistance against a rival Sicilian emir.[62] "Greatly pleased, the count received him with honor."[63] Together they organized a joint nocturnal raid on Milazzo, near Messina, where they engaged a small force and won some booty.[64] Their passage back to Reggio was hindered, however, by uncooperative weather that left them stranded on the Sicilian side of the straits, exposed to the Messinan militia. In response to this dilemma, "the count, making use of wise council, offered to give all of the booty which he had won to St. Andronius for rebuilding the church dedicated to him near Reggio. As a result of the kindness of this saint, as we believe, the wind began to blow more favorably and the calm sea became navigable, permitting them to cross safely."[65]

Back in Calabria, Roger began preparing immediately for another Sicilian expedition. This time his brother Robert came with ships and men to assist him. But "although our navy was very great, theirs was bigger, with a greater abundance of strong ships,"[66] and the Normans could not get out of their harbor.

> Seeing that their crossing would be hindered, the duke took counsel with the count and the wisest men of the army and decided to invoke divine assistance. He ordered everyone in the army to confess to the priests, receive penance, and take communion. He, with his brother, vowed to be more devoted to God in the future if, with divine help, the land should be given to them, taking to heart, with firm faith, that which is written: "In all your dealings God will assist you and you shall be successful."[67]

Roger then came up with a plan. While Robert waited in Reggio with the bulk of the Norman army, Roger secretly crossed the straits further south, surprised the Messinans, and took the city.[68] "What difference does it make," interjected Geoffrey, "whether the palm of victory is attained by means of arms or trickery?"

There is much in this account of the conquest of Messina that is parallel to Geoffrey's description of the previous campaigns on the mainland. Roger is as brave, crafty, tenacious, resourceful, and piratical as he and his older brothers had been in Apulia and Calabria. In the interests of securing a strategic foothold in Sicily, Roger is perfectly willing to ally himself with a Saracen ruler. There are two occasions on which the exercise of Roger's inherent "Normanness" is supplemented with requests for heavenly assistance. But in neither case is the granting of the request predicated on any modification of Norman behavior. God and his saints seem willing to intervene when asked, but otherwise are perfectly content to allow the Norman *mos insitus* to unfold without their interference.

This account of the Messina campaign, with its occasional superimposition of divine intervention onto the more consistent operation of the Norman *aviditas dominationis*, is typical of Geoffrey's re-creation of the Sicilian conquest as a whole. There are, in other words, very few instances where he introduced holy war motifs at the expense of the dominant story line. Geoffrey's description of the events leading up to the fall of Syracuse (1085) is one of only two examples in the entire account. The emir of the city had been harassing the Calabrian coast with his navy.

> Coming to Reggio, he and his men depopulated a church dedicated to St. Nicholas not far from the city and another church dedicated to St. George, tearing down and trampling underfoot its holy images and carrying off the sacred vestments and vases used there. From there they proceeded to a certain nunnery near Squillace consecrated to honor of the Virgin Mary, Mother of God, called Rocca Asini, and destroyed it. With foul senselessness, they violated the nuns that they had abducted.[69]

Roger, "divinely inspired with anger to a greater degree than usual, rose up to avenge this injury inflicted on God." Participating in a barefoot procession, he committed the success of the expedition to God. Arriving at Syracuse by sea, Roger and his men prepared for the naval encounter by confessing their sins. When the emir, *instinctu diaboli*, finally attacked he was promptly knocked into the water and sank under the weight of his armor, punished by the God whom he had so deeply offended.

The only other example of the *aviditas dominationis* pattern yielding entirely to a holy war narrative is Geoffrey's description of the Battle of Cerami (1063). As in the Messina episode, the Normans prepared themselves for battle by confessing their sins and receiving penance.[70] When, in a preliminary skirmish, Roger's nephew put a larger Muslim force to flight, Geoffrey interpreted it as a sign from God that he would be the *fautor* of the Normans that day. The exhortation that Geoffrey put into Roger's mouth immediately prior to the main battle gave biblical stature to the confrontation:

> Arouse your souls, O valiant young Christian knights [*christianae militiae*]. We are all marked with the name of Christ [*Christi titulo insigniti*]. He will not forsake his sign [*signaculum*] unless he is offended. Our God, the God of gods, is omnipotent. . . . All the kingdoms of the world belong to Him and he imparts them to whomever he will. This people is in rebellion against God, and those who are not ruled by God will be quickly exhausted. They glory in their own power, but we are secure in the protection of God. For it cannot be doubted and indeed is certain that with God preceding us, nothing can withstand us. Gideon, who had no doubts about God's assistance, destroyed many thousands of the enemy with but a few men.

When Roger finished there suddenly appeared "a knight, splendidly armed, mounted on a white horse, with a white banner tied to the top of his lance bearing a wonderful cross." No sooner had the Normans identified the apparition as St. George when they noticed that the same cross had also appeared on Roger's standard, "placed there by none other than God." So fortified, the Normans put the "pagan enemy" to flight and collected their booty. From the spoils Roger sent gifts, including four camels, to Alexander II, "having recognized how this victory had been attained for him due to the patronage of God and St. Peter." The pope in turn,

> Happier with the victory that God had given them over the pagans than he was with the gifts delivered to him, sent his apostolic blessing and granted absolution from their offenses . . . to the count and to any others who might assist him in acquiring Sicily from the pagans and keeping it perpetually for the faith of Christ. He also sent a banner, with the sign of apostolic authority, from the Roman see, with

which prize, trusting in the protection of blessed Peter, they might safely wage war upon the Saracens.[71]

In his rendition of the Battle of Cerami, as in his reconstruction of the events leading up to the fall of Syracuse, Geoffrey completely suspended the *mos insitus* narrative, replacing it with the language and images of holy war. As a result, the Roger fighting at Cerami and Syracuse is a different kind of warrior than the one found on most of the pages of the *De rebus gestis Rogerii et Roberti*. Instead of revelling in his self-reliance and priding himself on his strength and wits, he turns to God. In fact Geoffrey goes so far in these two instances as to criticize the Saracens precisely for their singularly Norman-like reliance on their own power. Far from being driven by the desire to dominate, Roger is on these two occasions solely concerned with the well-being of the church.

But the cases of Cerami and Syracuse are the exceptions rather than the rule. In Geoffrey's account of the first full-scale battle between Christian and Muslim forces near Castrogiovanni in 1061 there is no mention whatsoever of God or of the extension of Christendom; the "Saracens" are, in fact, deprived of their religious identity altogether, being described simply as "Sicilians" and "Africans." The only notable aspect of the battle from Geoffrey's perspective was the unusually large quantity of booty that it netted for the Normans.[72] This was true of most of the individual campaigns that made up the thirty-year conquest of Sicily. They were depicted as if the Normans had never left Italy: seasonal plundering raids and occasional sieges conducted by armies that were too small to undertake anything more decisive. Geoffrey did not bat an eye at the alliances Roger formed in the course of his campaigns with Sicilian and Tunisian emirs.[73] Nor was he surprised when Roger treated his rebellious son leniently so as to keep him from joining forces with the local Muslim leaders against him.[74] Geoffrey had no problem with the fact that most of the cities that Roger "conquered" actually capitulated under terms that allowed the Muslims to stay and live according to their own law.[75] Nor was he ever critical of Roger's use of Muslim troops to supplement his own meager forces.[76] Finally Geoffrey never upbraided Roger for allowing his attention to be so easily diverted from the "holy" conquest of Sicily to the more mundane fraternal squabbles on the mainland.[77]

Geoffrey was quite capable, in fact, of forgetting all about the religious considerations that he had attributed to Roger on the eve of the conquest of Messina.

> Count Roger was intent on acquiring Sicily and impatient with any inactivity. Wandering everywhere, he struck terror with his frequent incursions. He was by custom so constant in his efforts that neither the most troublesome weather nor the blindness of a dark night could discourage him. Passing from place to place, attending to everything personally, the enemy trembled more at his presence than anything else. And they were so terrified by his speed that he was never thought to be absent.[78]

And elsewhere:

> [Count Roger] never held himself back for the sake of any pleasure or permitted himself to be far from the enemy. Nothing deterred him from what he had undertaken: whether it be deprivation, the difficulty of the task, enemy threats, the imminence of battle, lack of sleep, or bitter weather. Rather, the more he was shaken by adversity, the more ardent was his determination, motivated as he was by the innate desire for domination in his soul, to conquer rather than be conquered.[79]

Again, the most consistent narrative element is the irrepressibility of the *mos insitus* that Roger had inherited from his father.

When the language of holy war *did* enter into the account of a particular battle or siege, it normally did so, as in the case of Messina, without displacing the more mundane images of the Norman *aviditas dominationis*. This often led to some interesting and seemingly incongruous narrative hybrids, as in the case of Roger's address to his men delivered before the battle at Misilmeri in 1068:

> Hail most noble of nobles! Fortune, favoring us, is bringing us the booty that we have been seeking for a long time, thus sparing us the effort, lest we be exhausted in its pursuit. Behold the booty that has been granted to us by God! Take it from those who do not deserve it! Let us use it, dividing it in an apostolic manner, as necessary. Do not be afraid of those whom you previously defeated. They may have

changed their commander, but they are of the same nation, quality, and religion. Our God is immutable and if the integrity of our faithful hope does not change, neither will He change the triumphal outcome.[80]

Here we see Geoffrey introducing God into the narrative but only to reinforce the insatiable Norman appetite for plunder.

The same curious mixing is apparent in Geoffrey's account of the rebellion at Troina, a town that had remained predominately (Greek) Christian despite Muslim rule. After its capitulation to Roger, the Normans set up a garrison in the city. But when the local Christians, whose homes were used for billeting the Normans, became "fearful for their wives and daughters," they rebelled, trapping Roger and his wife in the city. There the count and countess remained without sufficient supplies ("between the count and the countess they had only one cape, which they took turns wearing depending on which of the two needed it more") for four months with the local Saracens offering their assistance to the rebels. As Geoffrey put it, Roger "was liberated only by means of his valor and the help of God." A miraculously unseasonable snow and hail storm forced the rebellious Troinans to find warmth in alcohol and their subsequent inebriation allowed Roger, who was "never found deficient in the face of any challenge," to escape and retake the city.[81] In assisting Roger's escape, Geoffrey's God seems to have been oblivious to the unseemly behavior of the Norman soldiers that led to the rebellion in the first place.

The same is true of Geoffrey's account of the "fall" of Palermo in 1071. Roger, with the help of Robert, had managed to breach the outer walls of the city but in their apparent haste to be done with the siege, the brothers made do with a negotiated settlement. The surrender terms, which, Geoffrey notes, the Muslims swore on the Koran to uphold, allowed them to remain in Palermo and guaranteed "that their law would not be violated." Despite this rather anti-climactic end to the siege and the decision to respect the religion of the citizens of Palermo, Geoffrey picked this moment to adopt the language of holy war:

Having obtained [the city], the faithful became imitators of that passage of scripture: "Seek first the kingdom of God and the rest will follow." They reconciled the church of the Most Holy Mother of God, Mary—which had been an archbishopric in ancient times but had subsequently been violated by the impious Saracens and transformed into a temple of their superstition—to the Catholic church with great devotion and furnished it lavishly with ecclesiastical ornaments.[82]

Not only does the anti-Islamic rhetoric seem a bit out of place given the circumstances of the settlement, but the reader of Geoffrey's history is left to balance this deprecatory treatment of Islam with a number of other images of Saracens that range from benign to downright sentimental. Particularly noteworthy is the tale—referred to above—of the young Muslim who, imagining the fate of his sister at the hands of the Normans beseiging his city, decided to take matters into his own hands and killed her.[83] The romance of the image presumably appealed to the sensibilities of a courtly audience despite the fact that it reflected badly on the integrity of the Normans and their mission.

Consider Geoffrey's description of the abortive siege of Amalfi undertaken in 1096 by the combined armies of Roger and Robert's sons and heirs Roger Borsa and Bohemond:

> In that same year there was a very fervent expedition to Jerusalem as a result of an edict by Pope Urban. But Bohemond, who some time before had invaded Romania with his father Robert Guiscard and who always wanted to subjugate it to himself, seeing the great multitude hastening through Apulia without a leader, sought to make himself prince of the army by associating them to himself and affixed the symbol of this expedition, that is a cross, to his garment. When the youthful warriors of the armies of the duke [Roger Borsa] and the count [Roger] saw Bohemond's cross, they, with a taste for novelty typical of the young, quickly rushed off and placed themselves under his command. Thus, having taken up the cross, they were obliged by their oath immediately to attack the territory of the pagans, not that of Christians. The duke and the count, seeing that they now lacked the greater part of their army, sadly gave up on the siege. Thus the city, which had been distressed to the very point of surrender, was liberated by this misfortune.[84]

Though acknowledging the religious fervency of the crusade, Geoffrey forced it to fit into his principal narrative by depicting it primarily as a source of conflicting Norman *aviditates*: that of Bohemond for the empire and that of the two Rogers for Amalfi.

And finally there is the account of Roger's campaign against Malta.

> Having thus wisely disposed all of Sicily as he saw fit, the count, accustomed to military exercises, impatient with activity, hungry for some task, looking longingly for profit, would not allow his body to become unaccustomed to its usual exercises; instead he pondered in his mind, with a heart intent on domination, which overseas kingdoms he would subject to himself.

Setting his sights on Malta, Roger was able to force its emir to become his tributary and to release all Christian prisoners that he held in captivity. "Seeing the captive Christians proceeding from the city, overflowing with tears from the depths of their hearts in joy over their unanticipated liberation, carrying in their right hands crosses made of branches or reeds, whatever they found at hand, shouting out 'Kyrie Eleison,' and bowing down at the count's feet, our men were covered with tears as a result of the emotion of such a pitiful sight." The count feared that the number of liberated Christians would be too great for the ships to bear in their return to Sicily. "But the [assistance of the] hand of God, as we believe, was evident in this event. Bearing the ships through the waves, he lifted them one cubit higher on the sea so that the weight [of the cargo] burdened the ships [on their return] less than it had when they were sailing to the island."[85]

In each of these cases Geoffrey was able to introduce the language of holy war without feeling obliged to temper his portrait of the Norman *mos insitus* because his idea of holy war relied far less on the motives or methods of the participants than on the results of their actions.[86] Geoffrey's Roger was first and foremost a son of Tancred and thus an heir to the family's innate *aviditas dominationis*. He fought anyone he had to in order to extend his power and increase his fortune. He was a holy warrior only by circumstance, that is, when he happened to be exercising his desire for domination in Muslim Sicily. Under these circumstances, his actions assumed an additional level of significance—that is, they became holy—simply because they served to extend the boundaries of the church. Geoffrey did not feel compelled by the incidental holiness of the conquest of Sicily to recast Roger as a holy warrior. He simply treated the spiritual benefits as yet another type of booty that Roger could expect to acquire through the exercise of the *mos insitus* that was his birthright as a son of Tancred.

Geoffrey's insertion of holy war motifs into a narrative built around the Norman *aviditas dominationis* stands in rather marked contrast to Amatus of Montecassino's careful subordination of Norman aggression to the interests of the church. Amatus, as we have seen, found it difficult to find anything positive to say about the earliest Norman immigrants and their treatment of the church in general and Montecassino in particular. He dealt with this problem by directing his readers' attention to the later careers of Richard of Capua and Robert Guiscard, portraying them as paradigms of secular lordship who worked for rather than against the church. In other words Amatus created, historiographically speaking, a watershed in Norman history—one which corresponded chronologically with Richard's conquest of Capua in 1058—after which the unruly and predatory Norman mercenaries gave way to counts and dukes whose military campaigns were henceforth to be seen as the legitimate acts of monastic protectors and defenders of Christendom.

Geoffrey, on the other hand, embraced the Normans as a whole, not attempting to make any qualitative distinctions between the actions and motives of the earliest mercenaries and those of the subsequent dukes and counts. The *aviditas dominationis* that had propelled the first Norman émigrés was the same that infused the deeds of Robert and Roger. In fact the sons of Tancred embodied this attribute even more than the others; hence their unparalleled success as conquerors. There is therefore no watershed to be found in Geoffrey's account; no "before and after" pictures. In so far as the Normans of the *De rebus gestis Rogerii et Roberti* had a relationship with the church, it was a perennially positive one: Robert and Roger were dutiful papal vassals.[87] Even the hostilities at Civitate were properly understood as a colossal misunderstanding perpetrated by the treacherous Apulians.[88] But Robert's and Roger's relationship to the church is at best a leitmotif of Geoffrey's history. The central story is the consistent actualization of the Norman *aviditas dominationis*. Sometimes this process had explicit ecclesiastic implications. Most of the time it did not.

It is much easier to see the hand of a monk behind Amatus's *Historia Normannorum* than behind Geoffrey's *De rebus gestis Rogerii et Roberti*. Rarely did Geoffrey make his ecclesiastical orientation obvious. On one occasion he made much of Tancred's wisdom in deciding to marry a second time after the death of his first wife: "Since he was a decent man who abhorred indecent sexual relations, he married a second time, preferring to be content with one legitimate woman than to be stained with the foul embrace of concubines, mindful as he was of the saying of the apostle: 'Let one take a wife so as to avoid fornicating'; and that which follows: 'God will judge fornicators and adulterers.'"[89] In the same vein, Geoffrey applauded Robert's decision to repudiate Alberada on the grounds of consanguinuity.[90]

Later, after recounting Roger's promise to St. Andronius that he would use the booty he had acquired at Messina to rebuild a Calabrian church dedicated to the saint, Geoffrey felt compelled to offer an *apologia* because the scriptures clearly state that "sacrificing a victim taken by means of rapine or from the possessions of a pauper, is, in the eyes of God, like sacrificing one's own son." Geoffrey justified Roger's actions on the grounds that the booty was taken from those "who confess God neither with their mouths nor their hearts. Thus it seems by no means absurd that they should offer to God what was taken, for by so doing they put to good use that which has been taken from those who are displeasing [to God], from those who do not recognize God as the giver."[91]

On two occasions Geoffrey seemed to take a page from Amatus, blaming the Normans for contributing to the instability of eleventh-century Italian life. "In the year 1058 there was a great disaster, a heaven-sent scourge from an angry God, made necessary—or so we believe—by our sins." Uncharacteristically Geoffrey identified the "Norman sword," which had "spared virtually no one," along with hunger and disease, as the three mortal dangers that the scourge brought to Italy. But having done so, Geoffrey stopped short of taking the Normans to task for their actions, since their violence was, like the famine and pestilence that accompanied it, simply one of the ways that God chose to vent his unexplained wrath. It should also be noted that the chapter devoted to this three-part scourge was, in fact, dominated by descriptions of the famine and the extremes to which the people went to alleviate its effects, inviting disease in the process. The specific effects of the Norman "sword" were not enumerated.[92] Elsewhere Geoffrey described how, when Roger's son-in-law Hugo was killed in an ambush, the count

set out for the province of Noto seeking fuller vengeance, and he so exterminated everything that they were unable even to take in their crops—the time for threshing being at hand—because he had burned them all so completely. Doing the same here and there in various other regions of Sicily, he afflicted the island with the greatest of famines that same year.[93]

Geoffrey aphoristically observed: "Thus hunger is born because vengeance has taken away the bread."[94]

It is tempting to interpret the subordination of religious elements in the *De rebus gestis Rogerii et Roberti* to the influence that Roger, as patron, must have exercised over the shape of the account. The emphasis on vigor, fortitude, audacity, and unrestrained desire as the keys to Norman success was one that presumably would have appealed to someone of the warrior class in his day. Working under the constraints of such expectations, it would have made perfect sense for Geoffrey to give supernatural forces an ancillary role, either by placing every event within a loose and therefore practically invisible providential framework, or by introducing God and his saints in a way that would supplement, rather than supplant, the strengths inherent within the Normans as a people. But this is, I think, only part of the story. For while Roger might have found Geoffrey's depiction of his "deeds" to be positive and complimentary, anyone versed in the types of Latin histories that monks like Geoffrey read would have found the *De rebus gestis Rogerii et Roberti* to be a rather more ambiguous eulogy of the Norman achievement.

For as a matter of fact it is no easy task to find a "history of the ancients" that treats *aviditas dominantionis* as a reputable force in history. The Romans in particular held such base motives in low regard.[95] Sallust, whose *Bellum Catilinae* was much admired and quoted by Geoffrey, was no exception. In this work, Sallust specifically criticized the Athenians and Spartans of Thucydides's time for their unabashed subjection of other peoples. As Sallust put it, they made "the lust for domination [*libidinem dominandi*] a pretext for war, to consider the greatest empire the greatest glory."[96] Roman historians like Sallust invariably treated the *libido dominandi* pejoratively, identifying it as the motivating factor most often associated with tyranny. They contrasted it sharply with the noble quest for fame and honor characteristic of the leaders of the Roman republic in its heyday.[97]

Is it possible, then, that the *De rebus gestis Rogerii et Roberti* was written equivocally: as a work of praise doubling as a subtle critique of the

Norman "accomplishment"? Is it possible, in other words, that Geoffrey, far from silencing his "monastic voice," simply disguised it? Textual evidence—specifically, Geoffrey's adaptation of particular passages in Sallust—strongly suggests that it is.

Let us consider again the verbal portraits of "Norman character" that Geoffrey painted for his readers in the *De rebus gestis Rogerii et Roberti*. He described the Normans as a whole as

> a very shrewd people, indeed, quick to avenge injury, scorning the fields of their homeland in hope of acquiring something more, avid for profit and domination, ready to feign or conceal anything, achieving a certain balance between largess and avarice. In their love for good fame, their princes are most liberal in their giving. This people knows how to flatter: they are in fact so devoted to the study of eloquence that you would do well to give heed to their sons as if they were rhetors. Unless checked by the yoke of justice they can be most unrestrained. They are ready to endure great effort, hunger, and cold when fortune requires it. They devote themselves to hunting and falconry. They delight in luxury when it comes to horses and to the rest of the tools and costumes of war.[98]

Later, he applied many of the same attributes specifically to Roger:

> Count Roger was intent on acquiring Sicily and impatient with any inactivity. Wandering everywhere, he struck terror with his frequent incursions. He was by custom so constant in his efforts that neither the most troublesome weather nor the blindness of a dark night could discourage him. Passing from place to place, attending to everything personally, the enemy trembled more at his presence than anything else. And they were so terrified by his speed that he was never thought to be absent.[99]

And elsewhere:

> [Count Roger] never held himself back for the sake of any pleasure or permitted himself to be far from the enemy. Nothing deterred him from what he had undertaken: whether it be deprivation, the

difficulty of the task, enemy threats, the imminence of battle, lack of sleep, or bitter weather. Rather, the more he was shaken by adversity, the more ardent was his determination, motivated as he was by the innate desire for domination in his soul, to conquer rather than be conquered.[100]

Now consider two of Sallust's character sketches from his *Bellum Catilinae*, first a positive one nostalgically depicting the Roman army during the "golden age" of the Republic:

> As soon as the young men were able to withstand the hardships of war, they learned a soldier's duties in camp by means of hard work. They took more pleasure in handsome arms and war horses than in women and revelry. As a result, to such men as these no labor was unfamiliar, no place too rough or steep, no armed foe dreadful; their virtue overcame all. Their greatest struggle was with one another and it was for glory; each hastened to strike an enemy, to scale a wall, and to be seen by everyone while doing such a deed. They considered this to be riches, this good fame and high nobility. Avid for praise, they were generous with their money. They sought unbounded glory through honorably gained riches.[101]

Some of the attributes that Geoffrey ascribed to the Normans in general and to Roger in particular match this description of the Roman army closely: the Norman delight in horses and the other trappings of war, their liberality in their quest for fame, and their willingness to endure any hardship to accomplish their goals. Others do not match up well at all. The Romans are concerned first and foremost with fame and honor and their achievement through the execution of brave deeds. Moreover, the riches that they seek, being part and parcel of their quest for fame, are not to be secured by dishonorable means.

Now consider the following negative characterization of the "tyrant" Catiline offered by Sallust in his *Bellum Catilinae*:

> Lucius Catilina, scion of a noble family, was powerful in both mind and body, but with inborn evil and depravity. From adolescence he delighted in intestine war, murder, rapine, and civil discord, and among these he passed his youth. His body could withstand hunger,

cold, and lack of sleep to a degree beyond belief. His mind was audacious, subtle, variable, capable of feigning or concealing anything.
Hungering for the possessions of others, he was prodigal with his
own. He was ardent in his passions. He was quite eloquent, but short
on wisdom. His devastated mind always craved the immoderate, the
unbelievable, the unreachable.[102]

The similarities between this passage and Geoffrey's initial description of
the Normans as a people are striking. Both Catiline and the Normans are
described as strong, audacious, crafty, eloquent, jealous of the property of
others, always ready to undertake seemingly impossible tasks. Moreover
both Roger and Catiline are described as ardent. Even the ability to
endure physical hardship—a trait that a moment ago the Normans
seemed to share with the Republican army—turns out to be perfectly
amenable to a tyrannical character as well. The only real difference
between the description of Catiline and that of the Normans is the use to
which Sallust and Geoffrey put them. Sallust held up Catiline's characteristics as morally reprehensible, as the attributes of a deviant, power-hun-
gry Roman. Geoffrey recast them as the basis for a superficial eulogy of
people whose saliant attribute was their military indomitability.

But Geoffrey's application of *aviditas dominationis* as a motivating
force was more complex than Sallust's use of *libido dominandi*. For Geoffrey and his monastic peers were well aware what Augustine—another
devotee of Sallust—had done with the concept of *libido dominandi*. In the
De Civitate Dei, Augustine elaborated at great length the idea that every
terrestrial political entity, past and present, was properly understood as
the product of the misdirected love of man after the Fall, the manifestation of his principal post-lapsarian shortcoming: his *libido dominandi*. In
short he took Sallust's definition of tyranny and applied it to every political structure that had ever appeared on the face of the earth. Because
empires were built and directed by men, they naturally suffered from the
same moral misdirection, the same confusion about the proper object of
love, that individual humans have suffered from since the expulsion from
Eden.

An understanding of Augustine's Christian adaptation of the Roman
libido dominandi is, I suggest, very important for appreciating the purpose
behind the *De rebus gestis Rogerii et Roberti*. For if Geoffrey were simply
adapting Sallust, his Catiline-like description of the Normans could be

interpreted as a specific criticism of Roger and Robert as eleventh-century versions of an ideal Roman tyrant. Augustine's universalization of the concept of *libido dominandi* allowed Geoffrey to criticize Norman "state-craft" in a more generic, less personal way. Compared to other peoples in history, the Normans were no less guilty—and at the same time no less innocent—of the excesses that were part and parcel of every human effort to govern. Augustine's version of the *libido dominandi*, in other words, allowed Geoffrey to focus on this aspect of the Norman rise to power without running the risk of offending his patron.

Geoffrey's familiarity with and apparent admiration for Sallust's *Bellum Catilinae* make it hard to believe that his treatment of a Roman vice as a Norman "virtue" was not a deliberate move on his part. At face value, he offered the *De rebus gestis Rogerii et Roberti* to Roger as a positive history of reputable Norman deeds, one that placed the Norman campaigns on the same level as those of other great empire-builders in the past. However, just below the surface is an implicit critique of the Norman achievement. In so far as the driving force behind their accomplishment is identified as their *aviditas dominationis*, Geoffrey encouraged the well-read monastic reader to see a Sallustian and an Augustinian counter-interpretation at work. Looked at through lens of the *Bellum Catilinae*, the *De rebus gestis Rogerii et Roberti* becomes a story of the perversion of the once noble craft of empire building into a frenzied pursuit of political domination. Considered in light of the *De Civitate Dei*, it becomes another chapter in a long, post-lapsarian history of misguided commitments to the "earthly city."

Notes

1. Amatus 6.23, p. 286.
2. It is often simply referred to as the *Historica Sicula*, a name given the work by one of its earliest editors, L. A. Muratori. Geoffrey, p. vii.
3. Geoffrey, p. 5.
4. Pontieri, in Geoffrey, p. iv.
5. In Pontieri's words, Geoffrey "fu iniziato alla vita del chiostro e ricevette gli ordini presbiterali nel monastero di Saint'Evroul." Pontieri, in Geoffrey, p.iv.
6. Lynn T. White, Jr., *Latin Monasticism in Norman Sicily*, (Cambridge, MA: Harvard University Press, 1938), p. 109.
7. Ord. Vit. 2:xxii.
8. Geoffrey 4.7, p. 89.

9. K. Kehr, *Die Urkunden der Normannisch-Sicilischen Könige. Eine Diploma-tische Untersuchungen*, Innsbruck 1902, p. 411, quoted by Pontieri, in Geoffrey, p. v, n. 2.

10. Geoffrey 4.7, p. 89.

11. White, *Latin Monasticism*, pp. 106, 117.

12. Geoffrey 4.7, p. 90.

13. White, *Latin Monasticism*, p. 53.

14. For other references to the recitation of such tales in Norman courts, see Capitani, "Specific Motivations," pp. 18–19. See also A. Nitschke, "Beobachtungen zur normannischen Erziehung im 11. Jahrhundert" in *Archiv für Kulturgeschichte* 43 (1961), pp. 265–98.

15. Geoffrey, prologue, p. 4.

16. Sallust, *Bellum Catilinae* 1, tr. J. C. Rolfe (Loeb edition) (London: Heine-mann, 1921), p. 3.

17. Sallust, *Bellum Catilinae* 3, p. 7.

18. Geoffrey 1.33, p. 23.

19. Geoffrey 2.11, pp. 32–33.

20. Geoffrey 2.42, p. 50.

21. Geoffrey 2.36, p. 46.

22. Geoffrey p. 5.

23. Geoffrey 4.29, p. 108.

24. Geoffrey 4.24, p. 102.

25. He uses the same image when describing Lombard efforts to discredit the Normans in front of Guaimar. Geoffrey 1.6, p. 10.

26. Geoffrey 1.23, p. 20.

27. Adapted from Sallust's *Bellum Jugurthinum* 3.

28. Geoffrey 1.26, p. 20.

29. Geoffrey 1.29, p. 22.

30. Geoffrey 2.21, p. 36.

31. Geoffrey 2.23, p. 36.

32. Geoffrey 2.24–27, pp. 37–39.

33. Geoffrey 1.1, p. 7.

34. Wolf, *Conquerors and Chroniclers*, p. 20.

35. Geoffrey 1.3, p. 8.

36. Geoffrey 2.38, p. 48. Capitani ("Specific Motivations," p. 9) and Oldoni ("Mentalità," pp. 165–66) place more emphasis on the concept of *strenuitas*. Boehm ("*Nomen Gentis Normannorum*," p. 676) considers *dominationis libido* to be one of the four "virtues" ascribed by Norman historians in general (along with craftiness, *strenuitas*, and persistence).

37. Geoffrey 1.5, p. 9.

38. Geoffrey 1.6–7, pp. 10–11.

39. Geoffrey 1.9, p. 12.

40. Geoffrey 1.10, p. 13.

41. Geoffrey 3.13, p. 64.

42. Geoffrey 2.34, p. 45. The Lombards and the Calabrians are also singled

out as cowards (1.14, 1.17, pp. 15, 17); the Muslims are not (2.6, 2.15, pp. 31, 33).

43. Geoffrey 1.17, p. 18.

44. Geoffrey 1.17, p. 18.

45. Geoffrey 1.19, pp. 18–19.

46. Geoffrey 1.34, p. 23.

47. Geoffrey 1.25, p. 20.

48. Sallust, *Bellum Catilinae* 8, p. 15.

49. Beryl Smalley, *Historians in the Middle Ages* (London: Thames and Hudson, 1974), p. 46; see Jerold C. Frakes, *The Fate of Fortune in the Early Middle Ages: the Boethian Tradition* (Leiden: E. J. Brill, 1988).

50. Geoffrey 1.16, p. 17.

51. Geoffrey 2.24, p. 45. The wheel itself was not all that commonly used as a metaphor for fortune in the early Middle Ages. Capitani, "Specific Motivations," p. 14.

52. Geoffrey 3.9, p. 61.

53. See Capitani, "Specific Motivations, pp. 8–15, for more about the concept of fortune.

54. A good example of divine favor and fortune intertwined: the successful evasion of Saracen pirates by a ship carrying Roger's envoy, Bishop Henry of Nicastro. Geoffrey 4.25, p. 104.

55. Geoffrey 1.3, pp. 8–9.

56. When a plot against Robert or Roger failed, Geoffrey thought it appropriate to quote Proverbs 21:30: "There is no prudence, wisdom, or counsel against the Lord." Geoffrey 3.15, p. 66.

57. See Capitani, "Specific Motivations," pp. 9–11, for more on the role of providence among the Norman historians.

58. Geoffrey 1.40, p. 25.

59. Geoffrey 2.1, p. 29.

60. Geoffrey 2.1, p. 30.

61. Geoffrey 2.2, p. 30.

62. Geoffrey 2.3, p. 30.

63. Geoffrey 2.4, p. 30.

64. Geoffrey 2.4, pp. 30–31.

65. Geoffrey 2.6, p. 31.

66. Geoffrey 2.8, p. 32.

67. Geoffrey 2.9, p. 32.

68. Geoffrey 2.10, p. 32.

69. Geoffrey 4.1, p. 85.

70. Geoffrey 2.33, p. 42.

71. Geoffrey 2.33, p. 45.

72. Geoffrey 2.17, p. 34.

73. Geoffrey 2.3–4, 2.18, 2.20, 2.22, pp. 30–31, 34, 35, 36; cf. 4.3, p. 87.

74. Geoffrey 3.36, p. 78.

75. Geoffrey 2.13, 2.45, 4.16, pp. 33, 53, 95.

76. Geoffrey 3.18, 3.20, 3.30, 4.22, pp. 67, 69, 75–76, 100.

77. Geoffrey 2.21–27, pp. 35–39.

78. Geoffrey 2.38, pp. 47–48.

79. Geoffrey 3.7, p. 60.

80. Geoffrey 2.41, p. 50.

81. Geoffrey 2.29–30, pp. 39–41.

82. Geoffrey 2.45, p. 53.

83. Geoffrey 2.11, pp. 32–33.

84. Geoffrey 4.24, p. 102.

85. Geoffrey 4.16, p. 95.

86. Boehm ("*Nomen Gentis Normannorum*," p. 686) also commented on the apparent dissonance between the religious motifs of the *De rebus gestis Rogerii et Roberti* and the secular goals of its Norman protagonists, but explained it away as "eine eigenwüchsige Synthese aus unverbogenem germanischem Heldenethos, religiösem Instinkt und nationalen Politik."

87. Geoffrey 3.37, 4.29, pp. 79–80, 106–7.

88. Geoffrey 1.14, p. 15.

89. Geoffrey 1.4, p. 9.

90. Geoffrey 1.30, p. 22.

91. Geoffrey 2.7, p. 31. The concept of "Egyptian gold," made popular by Augustine in his *De doctrina Christiana* 2.40. See also Geoffrey 2.1, p. 29.

92. Geoffrey 1.27, p. 21.

93. Geoffrey 3.10, p. 62.

94. In general, raiding was treated very matter–of–factly by Geoffrey. Consider Geoffrey 2.35, 2.36, pp. 45–47.

95. Not to mention the Roman distaste for lawlessness (Geoffrey 1.16, pp. 16–17) and the selling of loyalty for cash (Geoffrey 1.6, 1.7, 1.8, pp. 10–12).

96. Sallust, *Bellum Catilinae* 2, p. 5.

97. There are a few examples of this motivation in the *De rebus gestis Rogerii et Roberti*: Hugo of Gircé longs "to carry out some noble deed for which he would merit military praise." Geoffrey 3.10, p. 62.

98. Geoffrey 1.3, p. 8.

99. Geoffrey 2.38, pp. 47–48.

100. Geoffrey 3.7, p. 60.

101. Sallust, *Bellum Catilinae* 7, p. 15.

102. Sallust, *Bellum Catilinae* 5, p. 8.

Conclusion

Amatus of Montecassino, William of Apulia, and Geoffrey Malaterra were the first historians to write accounts of the Norman conquest of southern Italy and Sicily that were sympathetic to the Normans. Because each wrote his history in ignorance of the efforts of the other two, the three of them share the distinction of being pioneers in the making of Norman history, creating narratives that transformed an outside aggressor into a legitimate authority. The fact that the three chose very different means of effecting this transformation adds to the value of this particular body of historical texts as a sampling of the historiographical options available to Latin authors of the time.

The first and most obvious difference between the three treatments of the Norman conquests is the scope of their coverage. Amatus opted for a broad approach, interweaving the complicated histories of both of the principal Norman enclaves in the south. In contrast William and Geoffrey produced more focused treatments of the careers of Robert Guiscard and Roger of Sicily respectively. Regardless of which subset of the Norman past the individual historian selected, however, all three felt compelled to say something about what brought the Normans to Italy in the first place and how they went about securing places for themselves on the political checkerboard that they encountered.

Beyond considerations of historical scope and focus, each the three historians also had to select a narrative pattern that would allow him to transform the data available to him into a story depicting the inevitable rise of the upstart Normans to a position of power and respectability in the region. For his part Amatus chose to build on the familiar concept of the monastic protector. After Richard of Aversa's takeover of Capua in 1058 and his subsequent enlistment by Desiderius as the protector of Montecassino, it was easy for Amatus to describe Norman activities in the region as extensions of Richard's ecclesiastically-sanctioned role as peacemaker. The fact that Robert Guiscard and the Normans of Apulia were too far away—at least until their absorption of Salerno in 1076—to serve this same function vis-à-vis Montecassino did not matter because Robert's campaigns against the Muslims of Sicily made him a different kind of protector, not of any one monastery, but of all of Christendom.

William of Apulia emphasized Norman ties not to Montecassino, nor to any ecclesiastical institution for that matter, but to the Lombard dynasties that dominated Campania when the first of the Normans arrived. Extrapolating from the series of marriage alliances that joined the sons of Tancred to the ruling family of Salerno, William effectively grafted Norman history onto the already centuries-old Lombard historiographical tradition. By so doing, he was able to present the Norman conquests as a continuation of Lombard efforts dating back to the sixth century to wrest the peninsula from the hands of the Greeks. Thus the Norman struggle with the Greeks, first on one side of the Adriatic and then on the other, occupied center stage in William's *Gesta Roberti Wiscardi*, a struggle quite literally elevated to epic proportions by William's use of verse and classical imagery and motifs.

Geoffrey Malaterra's narrative grew out of the idea that the Normans were driven, even before they came to Italy, by a distinctive "avidity for domination," an innate motivation that would render them irresistible in their efforts to carve out territory in Italy and Sicily. Even though Geoffrey's principal focus was the conquest of Muslim Sicily, a subject which lent itself to a liberal use of holy war motifs, he never did so to the exclusion of the dominant *aviditas dominationis* pattern. Considering what Sallust and especially Augustine had to say about the role of such motivations in the world of politics, it would seem that Geoffrey's *De rebus gestis Rogerii et Roberti* represents something of a cross between a specific glorification of the Norman achievement and a generic Augustinian critique of any and all state-building endeavors.

In our approach to each of the three histories, we have assumed that the author's choice of material as well as his decisions—whether or not they were entirely conscious ones—about the shape of his narrative framework must in some way reflect the identity of the author. Thus it seems natural to us that the *Historia Normannorum*, written by a monk at Montecassino in the wake of the death of the monastery's protector, should glorify the twenty-year relationship between Richard and Desiderius. It also makes sense that it would downplay not only the problems that other earlier Norman powers had posed for the monastery but the longstanding difficulties between the papacy and the Normans of Capua and Apulia. Likewise we feel comfortable in deducing, primarily on the basis of William of Apulia's complimentary treatment of Roger Borsa and his effort to see the Normans as the logical allies and heirs of the Lombards against the Greeks, that the author of the *Gesta Roberti Wiscardi* was a high-ranking Lombard with close connections to the ducal court. Finally Geoffrey Malaterra, a monk recruited by Roger to assist in the ecclesiastical restructuring of Sicily, produced an account of the careers of Roger and Robert that effectively placed their admirable achievements within an Augustinian framework that allowed Geoffrey simutaneously to express his gratitude to Roger and his disdain for the things of the world that he left behind when he entered the cloister.

The content and style of each of the three histories would also have had to reflect in some way the expectations of its audience, or more accurately the author's sense of those expectations. The problem is that we cannot be certain who the intended audience for these histories was, outside of the individual or individuals specifically identified in the dedications. We know only that Amatus wrote in accordance with the wishes of his abbot Desiderius, that William dedicated his work to both Roger Borsa and Urban II, and that Geoffrey was asked to write his history by Count Roger.

It may be, however, that we do not need to look further than the patrons themselves in our attempts to reconstruct the audiences of these histories. For there is no evidence that any of these texts existed in more than a single manuscript version for decades or even centuries after the original composition.[1] If this is an accurate assessment of the number of original manuscripts, it seems unlikely that either the patrons or the authors actually expected these works to have any appreciable effect on how their contemporaries viewed Norman history.

As curious as it may sound, it may be anachronistic to treat these histories as if they were even intended to be read at all. The symbolic importance of simply *having* a history, and thereby joining the ranks of great peoples and rulers of the past who had their own histories, may have been enough from the perspective of the patrons. We see this most clearly in the case of Roger of Sicily, at least in Geoffrey's characterization of his motives for sponsoring the *De rebus gestis Rogerii et Roberti*. "That most famous prince Roger, familiar with many authors, having had the histories of the ancients recited to him, decided, on the advice of his men, to commit [to writing] for the sake of posterity his laborious and perilous victories."[2] By commissioning such a work, Roger was implicitly associating himself with Alexander, Julius Caesar, Charlemagne, and the other protagonists of the many other *de rebus gestis* accounts that were, in oral as well as written form, such standard features of courtly entertainment at the time. Even if it was less likely that Geoffrey's work would actually be recited in his court alongside the accounts of the semi-legendary heroes of antiquity, Roger could take some satisfaction from the simple fact that his exploits, like those of his heroes, had been preserved in writing.

Without elaborating to the extent that Geoffrey did on his patron's motives for sponsoring the project, William of Apulia nonetheless made it clear from the outset of the *Gesta Roberti Wiscardi* that the idea to compose a poem about the exploits of the Normans that would put them on a par with the great military figures of antiquity came from Roger Borsa.[3] Even Amatus, who was writing at the request of his abbot rather than of any Norman ruler, regarded his history as a modified *de rebus gestis* of Richard and Robert, one which would immortalize their deeds at the same time as it would present them as the deeds of God "done through these men."[4]

In short, the symbolic import of simply having a history of this sort may have been more important to Roger of Sicily or Roger Borsa than the actual influence that the contents of such a work might have had on their contemporaries. Just as a successful medieval ruler might build churches, mint coins, or issue legal codes, so he might commission a history, all with an eye to "decorating" his reign with the trappings of legitimacy.

None of this, of course, diminishes the value of the histories themselves as important sources of data for the history of mentalité. Even if no one at the time actually sat down and read them, their authors wrote them as if their patrons intended to do just that. And in their attempts to write histories that would satisfy their sponsors, they inadvertently produced for us textual artifacts that not only tell us something about what happened in southern Italy and Sicily in the eleventh century, but how an educated person at that time might have gone about making sense of it all.

Notes

1. As we have seen, there are no extant copies of the original Latin version of Amatus's *Historia Normannorum* although Leo Marsicanus came across one—per-

haps the original kept in Montecassino's library—while composing his *Chronica monasterii Casinensis*. The two earliest known redactions of the *Gesta Roberti Wiscardi* have come down to us from the late twelfth century while the oldest versions of Geoffrey Malaterra's history date from the fourteenth. Mathieu, in William, pp. 70–74; Pontieri, in Geoffrey, pp. li–lvii.

2. Geoffrey, p. 4.

3. William, p. 99.

4. Amatus, Dedication, pp. 3–4; 1.1–2, pp. 9–11.

Select Bibliography

Amari, Michele. *Storia dei musulmani di Sicilia*. 2nd ed. 3 vol. Annotated by C. A. Nallino. Catania: R. Prampolini, 1933–39.

Atti del congresso internazionale di studi sulla Sicilia normanna, Palermo, 1972. Palermo: S. Sciascia, 1973.

Bartholomaeis, Vincenzo de. *Storia de' Normanni di Amato di Montecassino volgarizzata in antico francese*. Rome: Istituto storico italiano per il medio evo, 1935

Aubé, Pierre. *Les empires normands d'Orient, XIe–XIIIe siècle*. Paris: Tallandier, 1983.

Aziz, Ahmad. *A History of Islamic Sicily*. Edinburgh: Edinburgh University Press, 1975.

Béraud-Villars, Jean. *Les Normands en Méditerranée*. Paris: Michel, 1951.

Bloch, Herbert. *Monte Cassino and the Middle Ages*. 3 vols. Cambridge, MA: Harvard University Press, 1986.

Boehm, Laetitia. "*Nomen gentis Normannorum*. Der Aufstieg der Normannen im Spiegel der normannischen Historiographie." *I Normanni e la loro espansione in Europa nell'alto medioevo*, pp. 634–39, 647–50.

Capitani, Ovidio. "Specific Motivations and Continuing Themes in the Norman Chronicles of Southern Italy in the Eleventh and Twelfth Centuries." *The Normans in Sicily and Southern Italy*, pp. 1–46.

Chalandon, Ferdinand. *Histoire de la domination Normande en Italie et en Sicile*. 2 vols. Paris: Librairie Picard et fils, 1907; reprint New York: Burt Franklin, 1969.

Chibnall, Marjorie. *The World of Orderic Vitalis*. Oxford: Clarendon Press, 1984.

Cilento, Nicola. *Italia meridionale Longobarda*. 2nd ed. Milan: Ricciardi, 1971.

————. "La storiografia nell'Italia meridionale." *La storiografia altomedievale*. Settimane di studio 17 (1969). 2 vols. Spoleto: Centro italiano di studi sull'alto medioevo, 1970: 2:521–56.

Citarella, Armand O. "The Relations of Amalfi with the Arab World before the Crusades." *Speculum* 42 (1967): 299–312.

Cochrane, Eric W. *Historians and Historiography in the Italian Renaissance*. Chicago: University of Chicago Press, 1981.

Comnena, Anna. *The Alexiad of Anna Comnena*. Tr. E. R. A Sewter. Baltimore: Penguin Books, 1969.

Courcelle, Pierre. *Histoire littéraire des grandes invasions germaniques*. 3rd ed. Paris: Études augustiniennes, 1964 [originally published: 1948].

Cowdrey, H. E. J. *The Age of Abbot Desiderius: Montecassino, the Papacy, and the*

Normans in the Eleventh and Early Twelfth Centuries. Oxford: Clarendon Press, 1983.

————. "Pope Gregory VII's 'Crusading' Plans of 1074." *Outremer: Studies in the History of the Crusading Kingdom of Jerusalem Presented to Joshua Prawer*, ed. Benjamin Z. Kedar et al. Jerusalem: Yad Izhak Ben-Zvi Institute, 1982, pp. 27–40.

Curtis, Edmund. *Roger of Sicily and the Normans of Lower Italy, 1016–1154.* New York: G. P. Putnam's Sons, 1912.

D'Alessandro, Vincenzo. "Roberto il Guiscardo nella storiografia medievale." *Roberto il Guiscardo tra Europa, Oriente e Mezzogiorno*, pp. 181–96.

————. *Storiographia e politica nell'Italia normanna.* Naples: Liguori, 1978.

Davis, R. H. C. *The Normans and Their Myth.* London: Thames and Hudson, 1976.

Décarreaux, Jean. *Normands, papes, et moines: Cinquante ans de conquêtes et de politique religieuse en Italie méridionale et en Sicile (milieu de XIe siècle-debut du XIIe).* Paris: A. J. Picard, 1974.

Deér, Josef. *Papsttum und Normannen: Untersuchungen zu ihren Lehnrechtlichen und kirchenpolitischen Beziehungen.* Cologne: Böhlau, 1972.

Delarc, Odon. *Les Normands en Italie depuis les premières invasions jusqu'a l'avenement de S. Grégoire VII (859–862; 1016–1073).* Paris: E. Leroux, 1883.

Delogu, Paolo. *I Normanni in Italia: cronache della conquista e del regno.* Naples: Liguori, 1984.

De Pasquale, Giuseppe. *L'Islam in Sicilia.* Palermo: S. F. Flaccovio, 1980.

Erdmann, Carl. *The Origin of the Idea of Crusade.* Tr. Marshall W. Baldwin and Walter Goffart. Princeton, NJ: Princeton University Press, 1977.

Frakes, Jerold C. *The Fate of Fortune in the Early Middle Ages: The Boethian Tradition.* Leiden: E. J. Brill, 1988.

Fuiano, Michele. "Guglielmo di Puglia." *Studi de storiografia mediovale ed umanistica.* 2nd ed. Naples: Giannini, 1975, pp. 1–103.

Gabrieli, Francesco and Umberto Scerrato. *Gli Arabi in Italia: cultura, contatti, e tradizioni.* Milan: Libri Scheiwiller, 1979.

Galasso, G. "Social and Political Developments in the Eleventh and Twelfth Centuries." *The Normans in Sicily and Southern Italy*, pp. 47–63

Gay, Jules. *L'Italia meridionale e l'impero bizantino dall'avvento di Basilio I alla resa di Bari ai Normanni, 867–1071.* Florence: Libreria della voce, 1917.

Goffart, Walter. *The Narrators of Barbarian History (A.D. 550–800).* Princeton, NJ: Princeton University Press, 1988.

Guillou, André. "Grecs d'Italie du sud et de Sicile au Moyen Age: les moines." *Mélanges d'archéologie et d'histoire* 75 (1963): 79–110.

Hirsch, Ferdinand. *Amatus von Monte Cassino und seine Geschichte der Normannen.* Göttingen: Berlag der Dieterichschen Buchhandlung, 1868.

Hoffmann, Hartmut. "Die Anfänge der Normannen in Süditalien." *Quellen und Forschungen aus italiensichen Archiven und Bibliotheken* 49 (1969): 95–144.

Houben, Hubert. "Roberto il Guiscardo e il monachesimo." *Benedictina* 32 (1985): 495–520.

Jahn, Wolfgang. *Untersuchungen zur normannischen Herrshaft in Suditalien (1040–1100)*. Frankfurt am Main/New York: P. Lang, 1989.

Jameson, Evelyn. "The Norman Administration of Apulia and Capua." *Papers of the British School at Rome* 6 (1913): 211–481.

Joranson, Einar. "The Inception of the Career of the Normans in Italy: Legend and History." *Speculum* 23 (1948): 353–96.

Kelly, J.N.D. *The Oxford Dictionary of Popes*. Oxford: Oxford University Press, 1986.

Kreutz, Barbara M. *Before the Normans: Southern Italy in the Ninth and Tenth Centuries*. Philadelphia: University of Pennsylvania Press, 1991.

Lentini, Anselmo. "Gregorio VII nelle opere di Amato." *Roberto il Guiscardo tra Europe, Oriente e Mezzogiorno*, pp. 197–208.

————. "Le Odi di Alfaro ai principi Gisulfo e Guido di Salerno." *Aevum* 31 (1957): 230–40.

Lopez, Robert S. "The Norman Conquest of Sicily." *A History of the Crusades*. ed. Kenneth M. Setton. vol. 1. Philadelphia: University of Pennsylvania Press, 1955, pp. 55–67.

Loud, G. A. *Church and Society in the Norman Principality of Capua, 1058–1197*. Oxford: Clarendon Press, 1985.

————. "How 'Norman' was the Norman conquest of Southern Italy?" *Nottingham Medieval Studies* 25 (1981): 13–34.

Lyngby Jepsen, Hnas. "The Normans in the South—as Seen by Contemporary Sources." *Souvenir normand* (1988): 30–39.

Martin, Jean-Marie and Ghislane Noyé. "La Conquête normande de l'Italie: pouvoir et habitat." *État et colonisation au MoyenÂge et à la Renaissance*. Reims, 1987. Lyons: La Manufacture, 1989, pp. 347–64.

Mathieu, Marguerite. Tr. Guillaume de Pouille, *La Geste de Robert Guiscard*. Istituto Siciliano di studi bizantini e neoellenici. Testi e monumenti. Vol 4. Palermo: 1961.

Matthew, Donald. *The Norman Kingdom of Sicily*. Cambridge: Cambridge University Press, 1992.

McQueen, William B. "Relations Between the Normans and Byzantium, 1071–1112." *Byzantion* 56 (1986): 427–76.

Ménager, Léon-Robert. *Recueil des actes des ducs normands d'Italie (1046–1127)*, I: *Les prémiers ducs (1046–1087)*. Società di storia patria per la Puglia, documenti e monografie, 45. Bari: Grafica Bigiemme, 1981.

I Normanni e la loro espansione in Europa nell'alto medioevo. Settimane di studio 16 (1968). Spoleto: Centro italiano di studi sull'alto medioevo, 1969.

The Normans in Sicily and Southern Italy. Lincei Lectures, 1974. Oxford: Oxford University Press, 1977.

Norwich, John Julius. *The Normans in the South, 1016–1130*. London: A. Longmans, 1967.

Oldoni, Massimo. "Mentalità ed evoluzione della storiografia normanna fra l'XI e il XII secolo in Italia." *Ruggero il gran conte e l'inizio dello stato normanno*, pp. 139–174.

Palumbo, Pier Fausto. "L'età normanna nelle fonti e nella letteratura storica." *Rivista storica del mezzogiorno* 6,1–4 (1971): 36–84.

Peri, Illuminato. *Uomini, città, e campagne in Sicilia dall'XI al XIII secolo*. Rome: Laterza, 1978.

Petrucci, Enzo. *Ecclesiologia e politica di Leone IX*. Rome: Elia, 1977.

Pontieri, Ernesto, ed. *De rebus gestis Rogerii Calabriae et Siciliae comitis et Roberti Guiscardi ducis fratris eius auctore Gaufredo Malaterra*. Rerum Italicarum Scriptores. 2nd ed. Vol. 5, Pt. 1. Bologna: Nicola Zanichelli, 1925–28.

_____. *I Normanni nell'Italia meridionale*. 2nd ed. Naples: Libreria scientifica editrice, 1964.

Poupardin, René. *Etude sur les institutions politiques e administratives des principautés lombardes de l'Italie méridionale*. Paris: H. Champion, 1907.

Resta, Gianvito. "Per il testo di Malaterra e di altre cronache meridionale." *Studi per il CL anno del Liceo-Ginnasio*, ed. T. Campanella. Reggio: n.d.: 3–60.

Reynolds, Susan. "Medieval *Origines Gentium* and the Community of the Realm." *History* 68 (1983): 375–90.

Rizzitano, Umberto. "Ruggero il gran conte e gli arabi di Sicilia." *Ruggero il Gran Conte e l'inizio dello stato Normanno*, pp. 189–212.

_____. *Storia e cultura nella Sicilia saracena*. Palermo: Flaccovio, 1975.

Roberto il Guiscardo e il suo tempo: relazioni e comunicazioni nelle prime giornate normanno-sveve. Bari, 1973. Fonte e studi del Corpus membranarum Italicarum, 11. Rome: Il Centro di ricerca, 1975.

Roberto il Guiscardo tra Europa, Oriente, e Mezzogiorno. Potenza-Melfi-Venosa, 1985. Galatina: 1990.

Rotter, Ekkehart. *Abendland und Sarazenen: Das okzidentale Araberbild und seine Enstehung im Frühmittelalter*. Berlin and New York: De Gruyter, 1986.

Ruggero il gran conte e l'inizio dello stato normanno. Bari, 1975. Fonti e studi del corpus membranarum italicarum, 12. Rome: Il Centro di ricerca, 1977.

Samarrai, Alauddin. "Medieval Commerce and Diplomacy: Islam and Europe, A.D. 850–1300." *Canadian Journal of History* 14 (1980): 1–21.

Schmidt, W. "Die 'Historia Normannorum' von Amatus. Eine Hauptquelle für die Geschichte der süditalischen Politik Papst Gregors VII." *Studi Gregoriani* 3. Rome, 1948, pp. 172–231.

Searle, Eleanor. "Fact and Pattern in Heroic History: Dudo of St. Quentin." *Viator* 15 (1984): 119–37.

Torraca, F. "Amato di Montecassino e il suo traduttore." *Casinensia* 1 (1929): 161ff.

Tabacco, Giovanni. *The Struggle for Power in Medieval Italy: Structures of Political Rule, 400–1400*. Tr. Rosalind Brown Jenson. Cambridge: Cambridge University Press, 1990

Taviani-Carozzi, Huguette. *La Principauté Lombarde de Salerne (IXe–XIe siècle): pouvoir et société en Italie Lombarde méridionale*. 2 vols. Rome: École Française de Rome, 1991.

Tramontana, Salvatore. "Sovrani normanni nella coeva cronachistica méridionale." *L'Historiographie médiévale en Europe*, ed. Jean-Philippe Geret. Paris: Éditions du CNRS, 1991, pp. 141–48.

————. *I Normanni in Italia: Linee di ricerca sui primi insediamenti*. Vol 1: *Aspetti politici e militari*. Messina: Peloritana, 1970.

Waley. P. P. "Combined Operations in Sicily: AD 1060–1078." *Papers of the British School in Rome* 22 (1954): 118–25.

White, Lynn T., Jr. *Latin Monasticism in Norman Sicily*. Cambridge, MA: Harvard University Press, 1938.

Wickham, Chris. *Early Medieval Italy: Central Power and Local Society, 400–1000*. Ann Arbor: University of Michigan Press, 1981.

Index